The Modernism Handbook

Literature and Culture Handbooks

General Editors: Philip Tew and Steven Barfield

Literature and Culture Handbooks are an innovative series of guides to major periods, topics and authors in British and American literature and culture. Designed to provide a comprehensive, one-stop resource for literature students, each handbook provides the essential information and guidance needed from the beginning of a course through to developing more advanced knowledge and skills.

The Eighteenth-Century Literature Handbook
Edited by Gary Day and Bridge Keegan

The Medieval British Literature Handbook
Edited by Daniel T. Kline

The Post-war British Literature Handbook
Edited by Katharine Cockin and Jago Morrison

The Renaissance Literature Handbook
Edited by Susan Bruce and Rebecca Steinberger

The Seventeenth-Century Literature Handbook
Edited by Robert C. Evans and Eric J. Sterling

The Shakespeare Handbook
Edited by Andrew Hiscock and Stephen Longstaffe

The Victorian Literature Handbook
Edited by Alexandra Warwick and Martin Willis

The Modernism Handbook

Edited by

Philip Tew
and
Alex Murray

continuum

Continuum
The Tower Building   80 Maiden Lane, Suite 704
11 York Road   New York
London SE1 7NX   NY 10038

www.continuumbooks.com

© Philip Tew, Alex Murray and contributors 2009

British Library Cataloguing-in-Publication Data
A catalogue record for this book is available from the British Library.

ISBN: 978-0-8264-8842-8 (Hardback)
     978-0-8264-8843-5 (Paperback)

Library of Congress Cataloging-in-Publication Data
A catalog record for this book is available from the Library of Congress.

Typeset by RefineCatch Limited, Bungay, Suffolk
Printed and bound in Great Britain by MPG Books Ltd, Bodmin, Cornwall

Contents

Contents

Detailed Table of Contents

Acknowledgements

Acknowledgements are due to all the staff at Continuum in the London offices, in particular Anna Fleming (formerly Sandeman) and Colleen Coalter for efforts over and above what might be expected. Thanks also to: all of the contributors; the librarians in Humanities Two at the British Library; the organizers of the J.G. Ballard conference at UEA which proved to be such an important meeting point; librarians and colleagues at Brunel and Exeter Universities; and, Steve Barfield for his energy, enthusiasm, and good company.

Thanks are also due to A. P. Watt Ltd for kindly granting permission to reproduce *The Second Coming* by W.B. Yeats on behalf of Gráinne Yeats.

List of Illustrations

General Editors' Introduction

The Continuum *Literature and Culture Handbooks* series aims to support both students new to an area of study and those at a more advanced stage, offering guidance with regard to the major periods, topics and authors relevant to the study of various aspects of British and American literature and culture. The series is designed with an international audience in mind, based on research into today's students in a global educational setting. Each volume is concerned with either a particular historical phase or an even more specific context such as a major author study. All of the chosen areas represent established subject matter for literary study in schools, colleges and universities, all are both widely taught and the subject of ongoing research and scholarship. Each handbook provides a comprehensive, one-stop resource for literature students, offering essential information and guidance needed at the beginning of a course through to more advanced knowledge and skills for the student more familiar with the particular topic. These volumes reflect current academic research and scholarship, teaching methods and strategies and also provide an outline of essential historical contexts. Written in clear language by leading internationally acknowledged academics, each book provides the following:

- Introduction to authors, texts, historical and cultural contexts.
- Guides to key critics, concepts and topics.
- Introduction to critical approaches, changes in the canon and new conceptual and theoretical issues such as gender and ethnicity.
- Case studies in reading literary and theoretical and critical texts.
- Annotated bibliography (including selected websites), timeline and a glossary of useful critical terms.

This student-friendly series as a whole has drawn its inspiration and structure largely from the latest principles of text book design employed in other disciplines and subjects, creating an unusual and distinctive approach for the undergraduate arts and humanities field. This structure is designed to be user-friendly and it is intended that the layout can be easily navigated, with various points of cross-reference. Such clarity and straightforward approach should help students understand the material and in doing so guide them through the increasing academic difficulty of complex critical and theoretical approaches to Literary Studies. These handbooks serve as gateways to the particular field that is explored.

All volumes make use of a 'progressive learning strategy', rather than the traditional chronological approach to the subject under discussion so that they might relate more closely to the learning process of the student. This means that the particular volume offers material that will aid the student to approach the period or topic confidently in the classroom for the very first time (for example glossaries, historical context, key topics and critics), as well as material that helps the student develop more advanced skills (learning how to respond actively to selected primary texts and analyse and engage with modern critical arguments in relation to such texts). Each volume includes a specially commissioned new critical essay by a leading authority in the field discussing current debates and contexts. The progression in the contents mirrors the progress of the undergraduate student from beginner to a more advanced level. Each volume is aimed primarily at undergraduate students, intending to offer itself as both a guide and a reference text that will reflect the advances in academic studies in its subject matter, useful to both students and staff (the latter may find the appendix on pedagogy particularly helpful).

We realize that students in the twenty-first century are faced with numerous challenges and demands; it is our intention that the Handbook series should empower its readers to become effective and efficient in their studies.

Philip Tew and Steven Barfield

1 Introduction: Beginning with Modernism

Philip Tew and Alex Murray

With the plethora of existing handbooks and guides, it is worth considering the question of 'why another handbook on modernism?' First, this volume represents not just 'another' introductory guide but instead a new style of handbook for a new generation in the new academic environment. Gone are the days when students were simply required to know only a very few critical terms and some general background information when they turned to primary texts and spontaneously produced a competent close-reading. More and more the undergraduate, as well as the non-specialist graduate and academic, are expected to have a complex understanding of the field of 'modernist studies' with a sense of the relevant critical and intellectual debates. Where once the density of Joyce's *Ulysses* was the most intimidating prospect in undertaking a course on Modernism, these days it is arguably more difficult to situate and understand the complexities of a field of study that has changed and developed dramatically over the past 30 years. Even the nature and make-up of the primary texts generally studied have been revised radically, although there are a few that remain as recognizable cornerstones of the field.

It is in the context of such demands that this handbook seeks to provide an introduction to studying Modernism at university level. Instead of simply proceeding through thematic issues or central figures as a whole it is designed to help those beginning their study of Modernism. This book also provides a general introduction to Modernism – the extensive glossary, comprehensive encyclopaedia style entries on key critical concepts, as well as literary and cultural contexts, along with essays on key historical contexts, all work together to provide a wealth of information for the neophyte, that is the beginner. Yet the key feature of this handbook is that in addition to introducing Modernism it simultaneously works to orient its reader in the methodological and critical concerns of Modernist studies. While there are a range of Modernist critics who offer a 'survey' of the field, this is often done in a way which is inaccessible to the novice. The pieces included here demonstrate an awareness of these difficulties and provide rigorous yet accessible introductions to issues such as approaching canonicity, reading primary texts, evaluating critical trends, comprehending secondary criticisms, as well as an extended introduction to recent relevant gender studies, all contributing in helping the reader to situate Modernism in a complex academic environment. In this volume, the separate pieces work together to reiterate key points, allowing the reader to undertake a more critical engagement, to start piecing together, from different approaches to key concerns, an image of Modernism and Modernist studies.

The rest of this introduction, following this theme, provides some reflections on the idea of considering Modernism as a new beginning, almost a cultural and aesthetic revolution. Modernism is continually attempting to assert its own beginnings, to mark itself as rupture, whether aesthetic, social, political, sexual or cultural. Perhaps the most famous attempt to do so is Woolf's much quoted statement in 'Character in Fiction' (which statement also appears in the essay 'Mr Bennett and Mrs Brown') in which she asserts: 'that on or about December, 1910, human character changed' (421). Rather than being swayed simply by critical interpretation, it is sometimes wise as a reader or scholar to return to the original text. Woolf, in the far less frequently quoted paragraph that follows, goes onto qualify this statement:

> The change was not sudden and definite like that. But a change there was, nevertheless; and, since one must be arbitrary, let us date it about the year 1910. The first signs of it are recorded in the books of Samuel Butler, in *The Way of All Flesh* in particular; the plays of Bernard Shaw continue to record it. In life one can see the change, if I may use a homely illustration, in the character of one's cook. The Victorian cook lived like a leviathan in the lower depths, formidable, silent, obscure, inscrutable; the Georgian cook is a creature of sunshine and fresh air; in and out of the drawing-room, now to borrow the *Daily Herald*, now to ask advice about a hat. Do you ask for more solemn instances of the power of the human race to change? (421–22)

Periodization is always difficult and liable to be contested, but certain cultural and historical shifts clearly become evident over a period of time. The arbitrary nature of the shift identified by Woolf is important as it underpins the difficulty of stating with any certainty when the ruptures that herald the arrival of Modernism take place. Simultaneously the idiosyncratic and upper-middle class nature of Woolf's 'evidence' symbolizes the often elitist nature of the Modernist project. However others regarded the shift in social relations and the disintegration of hierarchical values in a more hostile fashion, but nevertheless are inscribing similar notions of transformation. Rudolf Eucken, a Professor of Philosophy at the University of Jena, in his study *Main Currents of Modern Thought: A Study of the Spiritual and Intellectual Movements of the Present Day* (1912), describes a state of 'confusion and uncertainty' in relation to ideas of the self, a change that he identified in particular with literature, but also associated both with the arts generally and broader social behaviour. He notes regarding individual behaviour and attitudes:

> The subject begins to regard itself and its condition as the most important factors in the situation; there grows up a tendency to throw off all outward restraint, to make individual feelings the only criterion. . . . It is, however, far too devoid of real content to be capable of overcoming opposition or of satisfying the human soul. All its appeals to individual forces cannot produce a connected inner life or a common truth, and in the end it leads back to the very vacuity from which it wished to fee us. (45)

Between Eucken and Woolf we can see that such radically different responses to modernity function on a continuum between approval and outward hostility. Yet both might agree about the profound nature of the social, aesthetic and changes matched by those of the contemporary consciousness more generally. In the following, we will provide a conceptual map of this space, detailing the ways in which Modernism marks a rupture with the past. Yet so as to offer a balanced view of critical viewpoints, we also want to call into question this sense of rupture, of asking if we can really take Modernism at its own word and regard it as a radical break with the past in all senses. Here we will introduce the relationship between Modernism and modernity, a key critical question that can perturb those encountering it for the first time, especially as the two terms are so alike. As we will see they are inflected with quite different meanings. In so doing, we ask about whether or not Modernism is so radical as regards what came before, and that analysis involves to some degree undermining the idea of historical ruptures and new beginnings, thereby both interrogating Modernism's own problematic announcement of its birth, as well as recollecting that those studying this period may be so overwhelmed by the radicalism of Modernism in this initial encounter that they too easily accept its differences and revolutionary qualities at face value.

All Change

A change in culture seemed to be heralded when the shocking precision of photography had rivalled traditional aesthetic methods of representation. In the last years of the nineteenth and the beginning of the twentieth century, the visual arts formally depicted a radical shift, suddenly seeming so different, with a thorough-going impressionism displacing the representational, mimetic accuracy apparently abandoned. In myriad fields, Modernism heralds its own arrival providing endless images of a changing cultural landscape, a world in which war, technology, early feminism (in particular the Suffragettes), radical aesthetic innovation, shifts in the idea of the bourgeois family, class hostility, the growth of urbanism, the rise of the mass print media and increasing literacy had all contributed to creating a world markedly different from that of their Victorian forebears. This excess of imagery has provided Modernist studies with a set of irresistible textual set-pieces with which to elucidate and illustrate these images of change and division. This first section of the introduction will provide a number of representative examples, from both Modernist practice and Modernist studies criticism, to orient readers who may be new to the rhetoric of change that typifies Modernism.

Technology, Transport, Communication

There is perhaps no more representative image of Modernism than that of the railway. Many classic texts of Modernism allude to the train or the tram as the locus of innovation, speed, changing social relations. As Nicholas Daly reflects in *Literature, Technology, and Modernity, 1860–2000* (2004): 'modernity [was] represented synecdochically by the train' (1–2). He goes onto argue that 'the railway transformed the nation, dramatically reshaping the landscape, blurring the lines between rural and urban, facilitating the growth of the major cities, sweeping away local times, and introducing its own standard time – in effect, "annihilating" an older perception of time and space' (20). In Modernist texts, a similar sense of reverence is given to the train as altering the very notion of time and space. Take Woolf's *The Waves* in which the train is a unifying metaphor for all six central 'characters' as they leave school and face the uncertainty of their future. As Louis states: 'Now I hang suspended without attachments. We are nowhere. We are passing through England in a train. England slips by the window, always changing from hill to wood, from rivers and willows to towns again. And I have no firm ground to which I go' (65). For these youthful characters, the train becomes both the vehicle of, and symbol for, their movement through both time and space with the two categories marked as increasingly fluid and dynamic.

Yet the exhilaration and excitement of the railway was also marked by a fundamental ambivalence, seeing modern transport as a microcosm of an alienated modernity. Franz Kafka's fragment 'The Passenger' is a classic example:

> I am standing on the platform of the tram and am entirely uncertain as to my place in this world, this town, in my family. Not even approximately could I state what claims I might justifiably advance in any direction. I am quite unable to defend the fact that I am standing on this platform, holding onto this strap, letting myself be carried along by this tram, and that people are getting out of tram's way or walking along quietly or pausing in front of the shop windows. – Not that anyone asks me to, but that is immaterial. (27)

The sense of the only community being one of collective dislocation is a powerful one, and marks the perceived negativity and gloominess (to use Auerbach's term) of many Modernist works. As suggested earlier, the space between Lewis and the narrator of Kafka's fragment is the space of Modernism, never singular and locatable, always multiple and ambivalent.

If the train was a symbol of technological development, then the rise of communication was no less potent in marking the 'newness' of the modern. The development of the cinematograph, the increasing prevalence of the telephone, the emergence and subsequent ubiquity of the gramophone and the wireless all featured as representative of an entry into the modern. The responses to these shifts in communicative technologies were varied. For T.S. Eliot, the gramophone famously became in *The Waste Land* the symbol for a mechanized humanity:

> She turns and looks a moment in the glass
> Hardly aware of her departed lover;
> Her brain allows one half-formed thought to pass:
> 'Well now that's done: and I'm glad it's over.'
> When lovely woman stoops to folly and
> Paces about her room again, alone,
> She smoothes her hair with automatic hand,
> And puts a record on the gramophone. (50)

The concordance between technology and self marks the later, and also more contemporary responses to a 'mass media', seeing in the increasing homogeneity of cultural production provided by technology an increasingly homogenized and importantly apathetic society. A certain antipathy on the part of so-called high or classical British Modernists towards technology has been implied or articulated by many critics of this period, but Sara Danius in *The Senses of Modernism* (2002) argues that the challenge to conventional perception and therefore thinking lies at the heart of this aesthetic overturning and 'that classical Modernism represents a shift from idealist theories of aesthetic experience to materialist ones, or, which ultimately amounts to the same thing, that the emergence of Modernist aesthetic signifies the increasing internalization of technological matrices of perception' (2). Darius specifically identifies phonography, cinematography, radiography, telephony, electricity, and techniques of speed as particularly important, all part of the expanding forms and technologies of variously communication, selfhood and leisure thus capable of engaging the subject with further manifestations of a radical sense of the self.

Yet for other writers, technology marked instead the possibility of dramatic social change and political revolt. While as indicated earlier, the photograph changed the Victorian notion of 'realism' and of art as mimesis, the moving image was the Modernist period's great aesthetic development. All art seemingly had to see itself in relation to this new technology that was rapidly changing the notion of the self, and in particular of the body. The German cultural theorist, Walter Benjamin was to regard it as producing a new image of the body and therefore a new humanity. As he stated, reflecting on slow-motion in his famous essay 'The Work of Art in the Age of Mechanical Reproduction', 'Evidently a different nature opens itself to the camera than opens to the naked eye – if only because an unconsciously penetrated space is substituted for a space consciously explored by man' (238–39). This shift in space from the conscious to the unconscious reveals not only Benjamin's debt to Surrealism, but also his sense of a radical political potential provided by new technologies. This was also apparent in many Modernist fictional texts in which the cinematograph was treated with a certain ambivalence, its innovation, like technology itself, seeming inexorable in its voracious and eruptive nature. As Bergmann, the director in Christopher Isherwood's novel *Prater Violet* states: 'The film is an infernal machine. Once it is ignited and set in motion, it revolves with an enormous dynamism. It cannot pause. It cannot apologize. It cannot refract anything. It cannot wait for you to understand it. It cannot explain itself. It simply ripens to its inevitable explosion. This explosion we have to prepare, like anarchists, with the upmost ingenuity and malice' (23). This sense of cinema's ambivalent malice captures the lure of technology for various Modernist writers and thinkers. If a new world – potentially both redemptive and destructive – was possibly, even inevitable, then it was technology that was to usher it in. As if to emphasize this quality, the next day Isherwood repeats over breakfast to his mother: 'You see, the film is really like a sort of infernal machine——' (25).

The First World War

While technology significantly changed any number of social and cultural relations, it was the First World War that brought the dynamic nature of modern life to a terrifying and dramatic head. The unprecedented loss of life and the utilization of technological innovation for destructive ends called into question notions of progress and civilization with writers such as Woolf, Eliot, Evelyn Waugh, Wilfred Owen, and Siegfried Sassoon all responding to the Great War with an air of despair and hostility. Tim Armstrong in *Modernism, Technology, and the Body: A Cultural Study* (1998) focuses on science and technology and conveys a sense of such a fascination being specifically concerned with the body and medical interventions (2), which one can conclude is not simply a product of technological advance but that the very emphasis upon such procedures may have come about as a result of the individual and cultural traumatological impact of the Great War. As Armstrong says, 'Modernist texts have a particular fascination with the limits of the body, either in terms of its mechanical functioning, its energy levels, or its abilities as a perceptual system' (4–5). Additionally, as Armstrong makes evident any interventionism was a strong impulse (6), but cannot simply be regarded as altruistic, since it extends to 'Eugenics [which] sought to govern reproductive potential' (2). This movement was supported widely including certain key Modernist

Figure 1: The Hampstead home of Sigmund Freud. © Philip Tew 2008

figures and which gained credibility as a result of the poor physical condition of many lower class recruits to the forces during the war years.

While the First World-War marked a new concern with the body, it also heralded an atmosphere of mourning, a deep melancholy that infuses Modernism. This inscription of mourning and loss has become a focus for Modernist studies as it, following a broader development of trauma studies in the humanities, attempts to plot fiction as a space in which highly complex forms of collective and individual trauma can be played out. For instance, Ariela Freedman in *Death, Men, and Modernism: Trauma and Narrative in British Fiction from Hardy to Woolf* (2003) regards 'the quintessentially modern figure of the young dead man' (3) and 'the modernist death plot' (4) as intrinsic to the aesthetic of Modernist fiction. Freedman positions this death plot among the 'ruins of masculinity' (5) 20 years prior to the First World War, responding to the a sense of crisis inherent in the changing age symbolized by the successive deaths of Queen Victoria and Edward VII, but reinforced by Modernism's response to the traumatic cultural experience of crisis and loss of the First World War. For Freedman '[Woolf's] *Mrs. Dalloway* and [Mansfield's] "The Garden Party" are stories of innocence carefully and deliberately regained over a male dead body' (4). Referring to H.D.'s *Tribute to Freud*, Freedman concludes that not only does H.D. explicitly claim her brother's death in the First World War as causing her own trauma but implicitly positions her mourning for Freud as the quintessential subject of her own memoir. Thus for Freedman H.D. privileges male death, and in effect Freud sustains such new narratives of mourning. For Freedman crucial to and emphatic in the Modernist self-consciousness are the uncanny, repetitive structures of traumatic loss, Freud exploring such traumatic repetition in *Beyond the Pleasure Principle*, in which he extends his observations on traumatic repetition in shell-shock victims to a wider account of an economy of human existence, where the movement of the subject is always towards death, anticipating trauma (6–7). For Freedman 'Freud's theories are crucial to the Modernist reconceptualization of death [. . .]' (10). So Freud helps Modernism to understand death not as an end-point. The deaths on the battlefield of the First World War were not simply the end of one age (the Victorian) and the arrival of the new, but evidence of the intrinsic element of a human orientation towards *thanatos*, a self-disintegration.

One of the dangers of discussing the war from the perspectives of themes and developments is that we tend to lose the very real ways in which individual Modernist writers engaged with and responded to the war. For the war marked, in many ways, an experience which was able to both challenge and uphold ideas of collective identity based upon an idea of collective experience. The struggle to make sense of one's experience of the war can be seen through a brief examination of Virginia Woolf's diaries. Woolf suffered her second phase of madness in February 1915 two months after starting a diary, published later in *The Diary of Virginia Woolf Volume 1: 1915–1919* (1977), in which in her first entry on 1st January she reflects on the sinking of the battleship *Formidable* in the channel (4), on 3rd January she concludes 'I think patriotism is a base emotion' (5), on 5th January she reflects on an article in the *Times* that suggests 'war has taught us a sense of proportion with respect to human life' (7). On the 3rd February, she reports the nervousness about Zeppelin attacks (32), and on 14th February she speculates on the prospects of her friends in the army (34). After her long breakdown she resumes a diary and on 6th August 1917, a Bank Holiday, she reports hearing at Lewes on the Sussex Downs the sound of guns at intervals (40) and seeing German prisoners on 11th August cutting wheat (41). The impact of the conflict was profound and one can see that its effects were both very precise and literal, yet as suggested in Woolf's later responses, by the war's end nevertheless it was a context that had become both quotidian and familiar.

Another indicative response was William Butler Yeat's delayed and complex attempt to symbolize the apocalyptic vision that the violence of the War had conjured up. Yeats' oblique response to the war came retrospectively in 'The Second Coming' a poem first printed in *The Dial* (November 1920) and characterized by its religious symbolism, a partly apocalyptic vision. In a work that has since become celebrated, the poet opines the apparent decline of the European ruling class, and expresses an occult belief that Western civilization (possibly the entire world) was nearing a terminal point of its 2000-year historical cycle. In part, echoing Shelley's 'Prometheus Unbound' Yeats writes about the dissolution of a world steeped in conflict and suffering from a loss of moral confidence:

> Turning and turning in the widening gyre
> The falcon cannot hear the falconer;
> Things fall apart; the centre cannot hold;
> Mere anarchy is loosed upon the world,
> The blood-dimmed tide is loosed, and everywhere
> The ceremony of innocence is drowned;
> The best lack all conviction, while the worst
> Are full of passionate intensity.
> Surely some revelation is at hand;
> Surely the Second Coming is at hand.
> The Second Coming! Hardly are those words out
> When a vast image out of Spiritus Mundi
> Troubles my sight: somewhere in sands of the desert
> A shape with lion body and the head of a man,
> A gaze blank and pitiless as the sun . . .

Is moving its slow thighs, while all about it
Reel shadows of the indignant desert birds.
The darkness drops again; but now I know
That twenty centuries of stony sleep
Were vexed to nightmare by a rocking cradle,
And what rough beast, its hour come round at last,
Slouches towards Bethlehem to be born? (184)

The poem also signifies an aesthetic theme subtending much Modernist thought, since the occult according to Leon Surette in *The Birth of Modernism: Ezra Pound, T.S. Eliot, and W.B. Yeats* (1993) is central to Yeats's influence on certain younger Modernists, Pound in particular despite the American's later

Figure 2: A contemporary view of Woburn Walk (previously Woburn Buildings).
© Philip Tew 2008

'reticence' (231) because of his more sceptical disposition (232). However, one judges Yeats's occult inclinations, and although interpretations of his poem are varied, certainly it provides a most striking representation of a dramatic rupture and break with the past. The notion of a second coming, a change of biblical, perhaps apocalyptic proportions captures Modernism's conviction that it was bearing witness to dramatic change. Yet for a revelation to be one of unspeakable evil captures the nihilistic and apocalyptic tendencies that continually emerge in Modernist literature.

Modernity and Modernism

One of the most significant challenges facing both students and teachers of Modernism is differentiating it from the terms 'modern' and 'modernity'. A consideration of Modernism in relation to the idea of modernity can work to call into question Modernism's own contention that it was a dramatic shift or rupture by looking at the idea of a modern epistemology (or theory of knowledge) that stretches from renaissance and the enlightenment through to the contemporary. From this perspective Modernism becomes a response to the Enlightenment discourses of rationality and reason that further defined the impulses of the Renaissance, one that can be seen as a continuation of previous social and literary critiques rather than a wholly new and dramatic rejection of these values. In doing so, we will also be able to establish the relationship between European Modernisms and theories of the modern, providing an important context for English and American Modernism whose critical reception has lead to an impression of it as an isolated and dramatic 'movement'.

The Enlightenment is marked by the development of discourses of rationality and reason, a rejection of previous ways of organizing thought and the development of an autonomous subject. The one unifying feature of any account of the Enlightenment is the disagreement over when it began and what constituted it. For some it began with the renaissance; for others Columbus discovering the new world; the industrial revolution; the French Revolution; the establishment of organized scientific bodies such as the Royal Society or the publication of Descartes *Meditations*. In his essay 'What is Enlightenment', Immanuel Kant provided the following definition:

> Enlightenment is man's release from his self-incurred tutelage. Tutelage is man's inability to make use of his understanding without direction from another. Self-incurred is this tutelage when its cause lies not in lack of reason but in lack of resolution and courage to use it without direction from another. *Sapere aude!* (Horace, Dare to know!). 'Have courage to use your own reason!' – that is the motto of the enlightenment.

The tutelage Kant refers to here is often regarded as the ways in which religion and the monarchy determined world views: people believed that natural phenomena was controlled by a higher power – a storm was the wrath of god – or that subjection under forms of social hierarchy was 'natural' (the notion of the great chain of being). For Kant, this tutelage was 'self-incurred' as it was actively agreed to. Therefore, it took the development of rational reflection and courage to use that in order to free mankind from subservience.

Modernity is the name most often given to mark this period of human history, the point at which man was able to reject other forms of control and asserts self-determination. It is also characterized by rationality driving history forward. Modernity is then a 'teleological' process, a movement forward with an unflinching belief in progress and that the contemporary represents the most advanced state of human endeavour only to be superseded by the future. The most dramatic event of modernity is arguably the French Revolution, the point at which collective human will sought to overturn tyrannical monarchical power and establish the sovereignty of the people. For the French social theorist Alain Touraine, it marks a decisive point in the development of the modern and a move towards an idea of human freedom, but a freedom that is found in, not opposed to, rationality. As he states in his important study *Critique of Modernity* (1995):

> In its most ambitious form, the idea of modernity was the assertion that men and women are what they do, and that there must therefore be an increasingly close connection between production, which is made more efficient by science, technology or administration, the organization of a society governed by law, and a personal life governed by both self-interest and the will to be free of constraints. What could provide a basis for this correspondence between a scientific culture, an ordered society and free individuals, if not the triumph of reason? Reason alone could establish a correspondence between human action and the order of the world. Religious thought had indeed tried to do so, but was paralysed by the finalism characteristic of monotheistic religions based upon a revelation. Reason inspires science and its applications; it also requires the adaptation of social life to individual or collective needs. Reason replaces the reign of arbitrary power and violence with the legal state and the market. By acting in accordance with the laws of reason, humanity was advancing towards affluence, freedom and happiness. (1–2)

This notion of human freedom and happiness as constituted through reason is called into question by Modernism which often fails to share such a strong faith in ideas of progress. While figures such as Franco Marinetti or Wyndham Lewis had an irrational faith in the transformative effect of technology and progress, many Modernist writers expressed doubts in such a faith by highlighting the dangers of such a conviction and the need to develop other systems of knowledge and determination, often aesthetic. Modernism can then be seen as a response to modernity and the idea of the modern. If we are to see Modernism as responsive to these discourses of reason it allows us to both object to the assumption that first Modernism was such a radical break with the past, and second the notion that it is somehow so different to our own age that is often given the title of 'postmodern'. In looking at modernity as a project to which Modernism responded, often aggressively, we can see it in relation to such aesthetic movements as Romanticism and Classicism, as well as its relation to our own critical concerns. How one might move beyond the modern is very much open to question, and if Modernism is a dialogue with these forms of reason then it is very much a part of enlightenment discourse. Michel Foucault, writing shortly before his death in the 1980s underlines in 'What is Enlightenment?' (2000) the fact that those in the contemporary age are not opposed to the Enlightenment, but very much part of it since 'it must be conceived as an attitude, an ethos, a philosophical life in which the critique of what we are is at one and the same time the historical analysis of the limits imposed on us and an experiment with the limits of going beyond them' (319). Seeing Modernism as part of a response to these limits can broaden our idea of Modernism and in particular its own problematic relation to previous literary traditions.

Perhaps initiated or accelerated by the renaissance and Protestant Reformation, the central radical shift of modernity has long been recognized in the capitalist economy that fundamentally alters social relations, shaping new identities or subjectivities. An acute sense of individualism and such subjects' self-account is highly developed in modernity. This is shared by Modernism, and although there is resistance to convention, first it is often highly individualistic, and second a more radical interrelation of Modernism to modernity can be read in the fact that modernist cultural and aesthetic resistance to particular elements of a capitalist economy and culture become themselves rapidly absorbed and assimilated by that larger culture. John Xiros Cooper in *Modernism and the Culture of Market Society* (2004) claims that Modernism exhibits a complex relationship with capitalist culture, and there is a certain irony in creating new lifestyles that later are adapted into further examples of commodification, that is they become products of the very system many modernists viewed with apparent disdain. Modernism's legacy continued as the space between the avant-garde and so-called conventional society appeared to narrow throughout the Twentieth Century (1). Initially the very difference of the modernist subject from the masses was encoded by literary and cultural producers and critics. Cooper suggests a new reading of Modernism is possible, since 'The modernist bohemias were the social spaces where an unrestrained market society first began to reveal itself in its most concrete social forms, including offering a social space in which the gender and sexual emancipation that characterizes fully developed market societies could begin' (4). Clearly, many of the challenges to Victorian conventions undertaken by the modernists from the simple acts of disturbing Victorian codes of social behaviour, using colourful fabrics for clothing, whitewashing walls, drinking coffee when tea was traditionally consumed, engaging in a freer, looser sexual relationships and so forth have permeated society more widely. What Cooper indicates is that capitalist society is capable of absorbing and commodifying (essentially the turning of anything into a product) almost any protest, resistance or dissent, especially those rooted either in aesthetics or new codes of cultural behaviour that can be reflected by fashion. The radical zeitgeist can spawn a whole range of new forms of product that will inevitably be re-incorporated into the marketplace.

There is perhaps a further, more complex relation to modernity that should be considered. Paradoxically, Modernism has a complex relationship to the underlying dynamics of modernity that relate to the latter's compulsion for order and structure, given that modernity's primary medium apart from mathematics and science in its account of a universal, rational order is language, which it regards as logical and rational. As the social theorist, Zygmunt Bauman notes in *Modernity and Ambivalence* (1991) there is a central contradiction in trying to account for things rationally through language, in what he identifies as one of the conflicts underlying modernity, one that later Modernism as an aesthetic and cultural movement of Modernism seeks to foreground, to examine and question. According to Bauman, in modernity 'Through its naming/classifying function, language posits itself between a solidly founded, orderly world fit for human habitation, and a contingent world of randomness, in which human survival weapons – memory, the capacity for learning – would be useless, if not downright suicidal. Language strives to sustain the order and to deny or suppress randomness and contingency', (1). It is something that remains particularly relevant to fiction since as a form and genre all such narratives represent themselves and engage with the world through writing (language) and yet in the Modernist ambition to access the impressionistic, the disordered and chaotic must attempt to subvert the very innate emphasis of that medium, constrained by the innate qualities of language in its naming/classifying function. In some ways, as many argue, this appears to create a paradoxical impasse. However, first by defying convention and expectations, Modernists do suggest a sense of fluidity and unexpectedness in their writing, and second in so doing Modernist writers in particular manage to convey something of the other key aspect that Bauman defines as a central characteristic of modernity which is its 'ambivalence' and inner conflict. Both inform the nature of modernity, and both stem from the modern age's almost obsessive requirement that the modern subject account for their presence by establishing order and control within the world. As Bauman says, 'Ambivalence is a side-product of the labour of classification; and it calls for yet more classifying effort. Though born of the naming/classifying urge, ambivalence may be fought only with a naming that is yet more exact . . .' (3). Nothing is ever sufficiently defined in this view, so that the very engagement with the world becomes centrifugal, or ever more dispersed and elusive. The attempt results in a plethora of increasing inexactitudes that spawn yet others. Exactly the attempt to name and classify (as in narration and language) results in the thing you wish to define escaping from you, subsumed in or replaced by the logic of the naming process and as Bauman indicates concerning our relation both to the name (the word) and the object: 'Order and chaos are *modern* twins' (4). Modernist fiction, in particular, can be difficult to situate and account for, precisely because in a general sense it often seeks either explicitly or implicitly to absorb and reflect the logic and presence of modernity's contradictions. However, it cannot finally perhaps either reconcile or supersede them since it seeks a similar account of things through an economy or logic of the subjective, remaining largely focused on the individual perspective, expressed in language or following its logic. Using Bauman's terms formally, such narrative rejects the 'naming/classifying urge' but is rooted in a language that because it follows precisely that logic of naming cannot ultimately access the 'contingent world of randomness.' Finally, many of the articulations of Modernism then perhaps remain radically rooted in and yet restrained by the very contradictions of modernity.

These contradictions ought not to be avoided and rejected in the study of Modernism, but instead embraced. To that end, the reader will notice that at various points throughout this book we will provide parenthetical notes suggesting where readers might want to look for further information within this book. We do this as we envisage the book working as a series of interlinked chapters that, while they may be read individually and out of sequence, are designed to form a whole. These links then work to help the reader make connections, but also to provide a structure that encourages an independent engagement in which readers can begin with contradictions and questions, rather than with formulaic narratives.

2 Timeline 1890–1941

Nicola Allen

Year	Literary	Historical	Cultural
1890	James George Frazer, *The Golden Bough* Oscar Wilde first publishes *Picture of Dorian Gray* in *Lippincott's Magazine* William Morris *News from Nowhere*		William Morris founds Kelmscott Press
1891	George Gissing, *New Grub Street* Thomas Hardy, *Tess of the D'Urbervilles* George Bernard Shaw, *The Quintessence of Ibsenism* Oscar Wilde, *Picture of Dorian Gray*		
1892	Shaw, *Mrs Warren's Profession* George and Weedon Grossmith's *Diary of a Nobody* first appears in book form	Tennyson dies Whitman dies	
1893	Francis Herbert Bradley, *Appearance and Reality* Gissing, *The Old Woman* Henry James, *The Private Life* W.B. Yeats, *Celtic Twilight*		
1894	Gissing, *In the Year of the Jubilee*	Gladstone resigns	Walter Pater dies
1895	Joseph Conrad, *Alamayer's Folly* Morris, translation of *Beowolf* Hardy, *Jude the Obscure* W.B. Yeats, *Poems*	Oscar Wilde Trial London School of Economics and Political Science founded Friedrich Engels dies	First performance of Wilde's *Importance of Being Earnest*

1896	A.E. Housman, *A Shropshire Lad* James, *The Other House*	William Morris dies X-ray machine first exhibited and used	*Daily Mail* launched First modern Olympic Games in Athens
1897	Joseph Conrad, *Nigger of the Narcissus* Hardy, *The Well Beloved* James, *What Massie Knew* Bram Stoker *Dracula*	Queen Victoria's Diamond Jubilee J.J. Thompson discovers the electron Goldfields discovered in the Klondike	
1898	Gissing, *Human Odds and Ends* H.G. Wells, *War of the Worlds* Wilde, *Ballard of Reading Gaol* Leo Tolstoy, *What is Art?*	Gladstone dies Curries discover radium Bismarck dies Spanish-American War	Stéphane Mallarmé dies Lewis Carroll dies
1899	Joseph Conrad's *Heart of Darkness* published in *Blackwood's* Kate Chopin *The Awakening* Gissing, *Crown of Life*	Boer War begins Dreyfus pardoned	
1900	Conrad, *Lord Jim* Sigmund Freud *Interpretation of Dreams*	Ruskin dies Wilde dies Nietzsche dies Relief of Mafeking after 7 month siege	The British Labour Party is founded Paris World Exhiobition
1901	James, *The Sacred Fount* Rudyard Kipling, *Kim* Wells, *First Men in the Moon*	Queen Victoria dies Edward VII succeeds throne Theodore Roosevelt becomes United States President	First wireless communication between United States and Europe Electric vacuum cleaner patented Sully Prudhomme awarded first Nobel Prize for literature
1902	Arnold Bennett, *Anna of the Five Towns* James, *The Wings of the Dove* Kipling, *Just So Stories* Yeats, *Cathleen Ni Houlihan*	Boer War ends	Nobel Prize for literature is awarded to T. Mommsen

Year	Literary	Historical	Cultural
1903	James, *The Ambassadors, The Better Sort* G.E. Moore *Principia Ethica* Samuel Butler *The Way of All Flesh*	Gissing dies Spencer dies Whistler dies First flight by the Wright Brothers	*Daily Mirror* launched Nobel Prize for literature is awarded to Bjørnson
1904	J.M. Barrie, *Peter Pan* Conrad, *Nostromo* Walter de la Mare, *Henry Brocken* Hardy, *The Dynasts I* James, *The Golden Bowl* Wells, *The Food of the Gods*	Entente Cordiale between Britain and France Anton Chekov dies	Nobel Prize for literature is awarded to Mistral
1905	E.M. Forster, *Where Angels Fear to Tread* Shaw, *Major Barbara* J.M. Synge, *The Shadow of the Glen* • *Riders to the Sea* • *The Well of the Saints* Wells, *A Modern Utopia, Kipps* Edith Wharton, *The House of Mirth* Wilde, *De Profundis*	Liberal cabinet formed in Britain Sinn Fein founded in Dublin Albert Einstein publishes special theory of relativity	Nobel Prize for literature is awarded to H. Sienkiewicz Fauvism movement founded
1906	Conrad, *Mirror of the Sea* Kipling, *Puck of Pook's Hill* Upton Sinclair *The Jungle*	General strike in Russia Ibsen dies	Movement for Women's Suffrage becomes active First ever feature film released Nobel Prize for literature is awarded to Carducci
1907	Conrad, *The Secret Agent* E.M. Forster, *The Longest Journey* James Joyce, *Chamber Music* Shaw, *John Bull's Other Island* Synge, *Playboy of the Western World*	Edvard Grieg dies Joris-Karl Huysmans dies	Nobel Prize for literature is awarded to Rudyard Kipling
1908	Forster, *A Room With a View* Wells, *The War in the Air*	Asquith becomes Prime Minister of Great Britain Old Age Pension introduced in Great Britain	F.M. Huffer founds *English Review* Nobel Prize for literature is awarded to R.C. Eucken

1909	Ezra Pound, *Personae and Exultations* Gertrude Stein *Three Lives* H.G. Wells *Tono Bungay*	Synge dies Swinburne dies Meredith dies Bleriot flies across English Channel	Nobel Prize for literature is awarded to Langerlöf Ford produces first Model-T car
1910	Bennett, *Clayhanger* Forster, *Howards End* James, *The Finer Grain* Wells, *The History of Mr Polly*	George V succeeds throne Mexican revolution	London's first postimpressionist exhibition Nobel Prize for literature is awarded to Paul Heyse Cabaret begins in Berlin
1911	Conrad, *Under Western Eyes* James, *The Outcry* D.H. Lawrence, *The White Peacock* Shaw, *The Doctor's Dilemma* • *Getting Married* • *The Shewing-up of Blanco Posnet*	Parliament Act Rutherford's discovers structure of atom Amundsen reaches South Pole	Nobel Prize for literature is awarded to Maeterlink
1912	Conrad, *Twixt Land and Sea* Walter de la Mare, *The Listeners and Other Poems* D.H. Lawrence, *The Trespasser* Pound, *Ripostes* Wells, *Marriage*	Sinking of the *Titanic*	Futurist exhibition in Paris Futurist manifesto in Russian Nobel Prize for literature is awarded to Hauptmann Harold Monro publishes *Poetry Review*
1913	de la Mare, *Peacock Pie* D.H. Lawrence, *Sons and Lovers* • *Love Poems* Gertrude Stein, *Portrait of Mabel Dodge at Villa Caronio* Gorky, *My Childhood* George Bernard Shaw *Pygmalion*	Woodrow Wilson becomes president of the United States of America Einstein general theory of relativity Bohr's discovery of the atom structure	John Middleton Murry and Katharine Mansfield publish the *Blue Review* magazine
1914	Conrad, *Chance* Joyce, *Dubliners* Robert Frost, *North of Boston* D.H. Lawrence, *The Prussian Officer* • *The Widowing of Mrs Holroyd*	First World War begins Ford Motor Company announces 8 hours day and minimum wage	Wyndham Lewis founds Vorticist Movement Lewis publishes *BLAST* until 1915

Year	Literary	Historical	Cultural
	Pound, (ed.) *Des Imagistes* Shaw, *Misalliance* • *Fanny's First Play* • *The Dark Lady of the Sonnets*		
1915	Conrad, *Victory* D.H. Lawrence, *The Rainbow* Pound, *Cathay* Edith Sitwell, *The Mother* Virginia Woolf, *The Voyage Out*	Lusitania sinks	Nobel Prize for literature is awarded to R. Rolland Premier D.W. Griffith's *Birth of a Nation*
1916	Robert Graves, *Over the Brazier* Joyce, *Portrait of the Artist as a Young Man* D.H. Lawrence, *Amores, Twilight in Italy* Pound, *Lustra* Shaw, *Androcles and the Lion* • *Overruled* • *Pygmalion* Wells, *Mr Britling Sees it Through* Yeats, *Reveries Over Childhood and Youth*	Henry James dies Albert Einstein's *General Theory of Relativity* published	Dada launched in Zurich with Cabaret Voltaire Nobel Prize for literature is awarded to Heidenstein
1917	Norman Douglas, *South Wind* T.S. Eliot, *Prufrock* Graves, *Fairies and Fusiliers* D.H. Lawrence, *Look! We Have Come Through* Yeats, 'The Wild Swans at Coole'	T.E. Hulme dies Edward Thomas dies United States America enters WWI Bolshevik revolution	Virginia and Leonard Woolf start Hogarth Press at Hogarth House in Richmond, Surrey Nobel Prize for literature is awarded to Gjellerup and Pontoppidan
1918	D.H. Lawrence, *New Poems* Wyndham Lewis *Tarr* Joyce, *Exits* Lytton Strachey *Eminent Victorians*	Rutherford splits the atom Britain occupies Palestine Wilfred Owen dies World War One Ends First case of Spanish flu in March which becomes a pandemic	

1919	J.M. Keynes, *The Economic Consequences of the Peace* Shaw, *Heartbreak House* • *Great Catherine* Wells, *Outline of History* Woolf, *Night and Day* Yeats, *The Cutting of an Agate* • *Two Plays for Dancers*	First Trans-Atlantic flight Treaty of Versailles Break up of Austro-Hungarian Empire First flight across Atlantic	Nobel Prize for literature is awarded to Spitteler Hogarth Press publishes Woolf's *Kew Gardens*
1920	D.H. Lawrence, *Women in Love* T.S. Eliot, *The Sacred Wood* Robert Graves, *Country Sentiment* D.H. Lawrence, *The Lost Girl* • *Touch and Go* Wilfred Owen, *Poems* Pound, *Umbra* • *Hugh Selwyn Mauberley* Yeats, *Michael Robartes and the Dancer*	Prohibition begins in the United States of America First meeting of League of Nations Oxford University admits women students	Paris Dada festival Cologne Dada exhibition shut down by police Nobel Prize for literature is awarded to Knut Hamsun
1921	Aldous Huxley, *Crome Yellow* Shaw, *Back to Methuselah* Woolf, *Monday or Tuesday* Yeats, *Four Plays for Dancers* H. Rider Haggard *She*	Irish independence Hitler becomes leader of Nazi party Einstein awarded Nobel prize for Physics	Nobel Prize for literature is awarded to Anatole France
1922	T.S. Eliot, *The Waste Land* John Galsworthy, *The Forsyte Saga* (as a complete work) Joyce, *Ulysses* (published in France) D.H. Lawrence, *Aaron's Rod* Woolf, *Jacob's Room* Yeats, *Later Poems*	Proust dies Mussolini marches on Rome	Nobel Prize for literature is awarded to Benavente Y Martinez
1923	Conrad, *The Rover* E.M. Forster *Pharoes and Pharillon* Aldous Huxley, *Antic Hay* D.H. Lawrence, *Birds, Beasts and Flowers* • *Kangaroo* • *Studies in Classic American Literature*	German inflationary crisis Union of Soviet Socialist Republics (U.S.S.R.) established	Nobel Prize for literature is awarded to W.B. Yeats John Middleton Murry publishes *The Adelphi* (succeeded by *The New Adelphi*, 1927–1930)

Year	Literary	Historical	Cultural
1924	E.M. Forster, *A Passage to India* Ernest Hemingway, *In Our Time* D.H. Lawrence, *England, My England* Shaw, *St Joan*	First labour government under Macdonald Joseph Conrad dies Stabilization of German mark Kafka dies	Nobel Prize for literature is awarded to W. Reymont
1925	Emily Dickinson, *Complete Poems* T.S. Eliot, *Poems 1905–1925* F. Scott Fitzgerald, *The Great Gatsby* Hardy, *Collected Poems* Adolf Hitler, *Mein Kampf* Woolf, *The Common Reader* • *Mrs Dalloway*	Mussolini announces dictatorial powers	Nobel Prize for literature is awarded to George Bernard Shaw New Yorker publishes first issue
1926	Conrad, *Last Essays* William Faulkner, *Soldier's Pay* Fitzgerald, *All the Sad Young Men* Hemingway, *The Sun Also Rises* D.H. Lawrence, *The Plumed Serpent* T.E. Lawrence, *Seven Pillars of Wisdom* Pound, *Personae* Wells, *The World of William Clissold*	General strike in Britain	Nobel Prize for literature is awarded to Delandda John Logie Baird demonstrates first mechanical television system Fritz Lang *Metropolis*
1927	E.M. Forster, *Aspects of the Novel* Hemingway, *Men Without Women* Joyce, *Poems Pennyeach* D.H. Lawrence, *Mornings in Mexico* Woolf, *To the Lighthouse* Yeats, *October Blast*	Lindbergh completes first solo Atlantic flight First Transatlantic telephone call	Nobel Prize for literature is awarded to Bergson Wyndham Lewis publishes *The Enemy* magazine until 1929
1928	T.S. Eliot, *For Lancelot Andrews* E.M. Forster, *The Eternal Movement* Huxley, *Point Counter Point* Joyce, *Anna Livia Plurabelle* D.H. Lawrence, *Lady Chatterley's Lover* Woolf, *Orlando* Yeats, *The Tower* Evelyn Waugh *Decline and Fall*	Women in Britain are granted the right to vote Penicillin discovered Thomas Hardy dies	Nobel Prize for literature is awarded to Undset

1929	Ivy Compton-Burnett, *Brothers and Sisters* T.S. Eliot, *Dante* Faulkner, *The Sound and the Fury* Graves, *Goodbye to All That* Hemingway, *A Farewell to Arms* D.H. Lawrence, *Pansies* T. Woolfe, *Look Homeward, Angel* Woolf, *A Room of One's Own* Yeats, *The Winding Stair*	Wall Street Crash	Nobel Prize for literature is awarded to T. Mann
1930	W.H. Auden, *Poems* T.S. Eliot, *Ash Wednesday* William Empson, *Seven Types of Ambiguity* Faulkner, *As I Lay Dying* D.H. Lawrence, *The Virgin and the Gypsy* Lewis, *The Apes of God* Shaw, *The Apple Cart*	D.H. Lawrence dies Amy Johnson becomes first woman to fly solo from England to Australia	Nobel Prize for literature is awarded to Sinclair Lewis
1931	Neil M. Gunn *Morning Tide* Virginia Woolf *The Waves* Samuel Beckett *Proust*	Bhagat Singh dies Arnold Bennett dies Thomas Edison dies	*The Persistence of Memory* is put on display for the first time in Paris at the Galerie Pierre Colle Nobel Prize for literature is awarded to Erik Axel Karlfeldt
1932	Stella Gibbons, *Cold Comfort Farm* Aldous Huxley *Brave New World*	British Union of Fascists founded by Oswald Mosley Gandhi arrested Ernest Cockcroft and J.D. Walton first split atom in Cambridge	George V makes first royal Christmas Day broadcast Nobel Prize for literature is awarded to John Galsworthy
1933	George Orwell, *Down and Out in Paris and London* Antonia White *Frost in May* Stein, *Autobiography of Alice B. Toklas*	Hitler appointed Chancellor of Germany Reichstag fire	Geoffrey Grigson publishes *New Verse* magazine until 1939 Nobel Prize for literature is awarded to Ivan Bunin

Year	Literary	Historical	Cultural
1934	Robert Graves *I, Claudius* Beckett *More Pricks Than Kicks* Scott Fitzgerald *Tender is the Night* Henry Miller *Tropic of Cancer* Evelyn Waugh *A Handful of Dust*	British Union of Fascists holds rallies in Birmingham and London Roger Fry dies	Nobel Prize for literature is awarded to Luigi Pirandello
1935	Christopher Isherwood *Mr Norris Changes Trains* Eliot *Murder in the Cathedral* Orwell *Burmese Days*	Stanley Baldwin becomes Prime Minister Sectarian rioting in Belfast	Penguin founded by Allen Lane Nobel Prize for literature is not awarded
1936	Dylan Thomas *Twenty-five Poems* Michael Roberts (ed.) *The Faber book of Modern verse* Louis-Ferninand Céline *Death on the Installment Plan* William Faulkner, *Absalom, Absalom!*	George V dies Edward VIII becomes King only to abdicate Spanish Civil War begins	Manifesto fir Surrealism [Surrealist Group in England] *Declaration on Spain* published The Left Book Club issues its first book Nobel Prize for literature is awarded to Eugene O'Neill
1937	George Orwell *Road to Wigan Pier* Virginia Woolf *The Years* J.R.R. Tolkien *The Hobbit*	George VI's coronation Bombing of Guernica	Nobel Prize for literature is awarded to Roger Martin du Gard John Middleton Murry *The Necessity of Pacifism*
1938	Graham Greene *Brighton Rock* Samuel Beckett *Murphy* John Dos Passos *United States of America* trilogy Woolf *Three Guineas* Evelyn Waugh *Scoop* Orwell *Homage to Catalonia*	British Empire Exhibition Munich Conference Germany occupies Austria	Nobel Prize for literature is awarded to Pearl S. Buck

1939	Christopher Isherwood *Goodbye to Berlin* James Joyce *Finnegans Wake* Louis MacNeice *Autumn Journal* John Steinbeck *The Grapes of Wrath* Bertolt Brecht *Mother Courage and Her Children*	I.R.A. bomb kills five people in Coventry World War II begins	Nobel Prize for literature is awarded to Frans Eemil Sillanpää
1940	Graham Greene *The Power and the Glory* W.H. Auden *Another Time* Carson McCullers *The Heart is a Lonely Hunter*	Chamberlain resigns as Prime Minister Churchill succeeds as PM Blitz begins 1000 killed in bombing of Coventry	Nobel Prize for literature is not awarded Cyril Connolly founds *Horizon* magazine J.F. Hendry (ed.) *The New Apocalypse* anthology announces New Apocalypse poets
1941	Woolf, *Between the Acts* [published posthumously]	Woolf commits suicide Joyce dies Germany invades Russia Pearl Harbor attack by Japan Lend-Lease Act becomes law Henri Bergson dies Plutonium first synthesized	Orson Welles *Citizen Kane*

Historical Context of Modernist Literature

Leigh Wilson

Chapter Overview

The following considers the period from the last decades of the nineteenth century through to the beginning of the Second World War via a selection of events, developments and discourses which were both generally significant and important in terms of literary Modernism.

The First World War and Its Aftermath

War had been a feature of the nineteenth century, from the Napoleonic Wars at its opening to the Anglo-Boer Wars at its close. Such wars did have an impact on the civilian population, but their effects pale into insignificance beside those of the First World War (1914–1918), which was fought by the Allied powers – Great Britain, France, Russia, until 1917, and, after 1917, the United States – against Germany, the Austro-Hungarian Empire and the Ottoman (Turkish) Empire. Italy began the war on the side of Germany, but changed its allegiance to the Allied side in 1915.

Much of the action of The Great War, as it was known at the time, was concentrated around the western front – the line of trenches running through Flanders in Belgium and north-eastern France – and a much larger and more mobile eastern front bounded by the Baltic, Moscow, St Petersburg and the

Black Sea. This concentration was not dissimilar to the practices of war in the nineteenth century, where the action was contained within relatively small locales, and on the whole did not involve large numbers of civilians. However, certain differences of scale made the 4 years of warfare, and their aftermath, one of the most traumatic experiences of the twentieth century. Technological innovation meant that military armoury was far more powerful and effective than ever before; the use of machine guns, tanks, armoured cars, aircraft, shells and chemical weapons had devastating consequences in terms of numbers of casualties. The war led to 9 million deaths among the combative nations, of which approximately 750,000 were British (Winter 2003: 75). It led to the destruction of three empires – the Ottoman, the Austro-Hungarian and the Russian – and the collapse of the German monarchy, and was at its close the bloodiest war in history. After the war, almost everyone would have had direct experience of loss and bereavement, of a family member, lover, neighbour or work colleague. In families and in public spaces during the interwar years the presence of men shattered by the experience of war, physically or mentally, acted as a terrible reminder not just of the war's cost and waste, but, as in Virginia's Woolf's novel *Mrs Dalloway* (1925), of the beliefs, class hierarchies and conventional moralities that made it possible (for Woolf, see also Baxter, Murray, Paddy, Randall and Stinson).

Indeed, remembering the war was given a visible presence almost as soon as hostilities ended, remembrance of a new kind. War memorials were built in almost every town and village in Britain and France in the decade following the war. The Cenotaph in Whitehall in London, designed by Modernist architect Sir Edwin Lutyens, was originally built as a temporary site of remembrance in 1919, but became permanent in 1920. The understatement of the design, the absence from it of any symbols of triumph, glory or patriotism, and its immense popularity from the beginning, are testament to the very deep sense that the war, despite the victory of the Allies, had been a terrible mistake, and that conventional forms of remembrance were no longer appropriate (Winter 1998: 102–5). Similarly, the creation of the tomb of the Unknown Soldier in Westminster Abbey in 1920 became a site for collective memory in a way that statues of victorious generals or representations of heroic deeds no longer could.

As suggested above, civilian casualties were not huge. As Chris Wrigley details in 'The Impact of the First World War' deaths caused directly by the war – aside from explosions at munitions factories and so on, or the deaths of civilians near the front – numbered around 1,400 people killed during air raids in Britain. Around 3,400 were wounded during the raids, and a smaller number were killed when German battleships shelled the north-east coast of Britain in December 1914 (505). However, in other ways the impact on the civilian population could hardly have been greater. The enormous loss of life among combatants obviously had a great effect on those at home, but also everyday life altered for many, and not just in negative ways. The war effort, and its enormous and unprecedented demands in terms of raw materials and labour power, led the British government to intervene in the economy and in the private lives of its citizens in ways that would have been unthinkable before, for either of the two main political parties, Liberals or Tories. Food rationing, conscription into the armed services (begun in 1916), the Defence of the Realm Act (1914) and the systematic use of propaganda interfered with the supposed freedoms of the British as never before. The government took control of the coal mines and railway network, previously in the hands of private business, directed labour from one sector of the economy to another, and fixed levels of rent. There is some evidence that significant sections of the population, in particular the urban poor, experienced improvements in living standards during the war such as improved nutrition and a decrease in infant mortality (Winter 2003). Another offshoot was the rising importance of psychiatry, or the 'talking cure,' used to rehabilitate shell-shocked soldiers rather than court-martial them.

However, despite these gains for some of the civilian population, the overwhelming legacy of the war was one of trauma and loss. Not only millions of young men had been lost throughout Europe, but also a whole belief system, a whole view of the world, had been shaken to its core. The faiths of nineteenth-century Europe – in progress, in science and technology, in civilisation and in the belief that the European tradition represented the best of these things – was shattered by the bloody destruction. While many, of course, maintained such faith despite the challenges, for those who produced the most significant cultural representations after the war, a shocked pessimism dominates.

After the war, though, the rhetoric of governments, and the hopes of many, suggested that the war would be 'the war to end all wars' and that its horror would act as a deterrent. The Treaty of Versailles was signed in 1919 by all the major powers involved in the war, and its aim was indeed to prevent such a war happening again. It declared Germany responsible for the war, required Germany to pay enormous reparations and to be subject to arms control, and it awarded territories to the victors; measures which some at the time saw as dangerous, and which many since have seen as major causes of the Second World War.

Politics and Economics

The attempt to organize relations between nations differently after the First World War was consolidated by the establishment of the League of Nations in 1920, with goals of disarmament, collective security and the use of diplomacy to settle disputes. However, very quickly, it became clear that the organisation was not going to be the solution to international conflict that some hoped. Its failure to act over France's invasion of the Ruhr Valley in 1923 was an early indication of this. Added to this, the punitive economic aspects of the Treaty of Versailles had dire consequences for Germany throughout the 1920s, bringing massive inflation, widespread suffering, and consequent political instability. The British economist John Maynard Keynes warned against the potential catastrophic consequences of this in his study, *The Economic Consequences of The Peace* (1919), and his predictions were borne out (see also Stinson).

It was not just Germany that suffered economically after the First World War, however. All the European powers involved in the war had used up huge amounts of their national wealth in fighting such a long and costly war. As Wrigley indicates in Britain, for example, by the end of the war the government was drawing 50 per cent of national income, compared to 8–9 per cent before the war (505). Although there was a brief post-war boom in Britain, the economy was weakened throughout the 1920s.

In order to pay for its war effort, Britain had borrowed heavily from the US. Following the war, although Europe remained the most powerful bloc politically and economically, this masked an increasing American power. This rise was due not so much to the war, although the war certainly accelerated the process, but more that, as the US rapidly industrialized (along with Japan), it no longer needed British goods, and rather became a competitor. In particular, while in Britain the products of nineteenth century industrial processes continued to dominate, in the US the rapid growth area was in new consumer goods, such as the motor car.

The economic instability of the period – a consequence in the 1920s of the First World War and in the 1930s of the Depression caused by the Wall Street Crash of October 1929 – had serious political consequences. The historian Eric Hobsbawm has argued that, because of the combined effects of these two disasters, the period became one of 'international ideological civil war' (Hobsbawm 1994: 144). This 'war' saw the rise of numerous right-wing parties in Europe in the 1920s, most notably the rise to power of Benito Mussolini's fascists in Italy in 1922, and the increased activities of left-wing groups organized around union activity and the labour movement. In Britain in the 1920s there was increasing unrest among labour groups, culminating in the General Strike in 1926. The strike lasted 9 days, and involved around 1.75 million workers. In terms of its later consequences, however, the most significant event in the developing 'ideological war' was the election victory of the National Socialists in Germany in 1933, and Adolf Hitler becoming Chancellor. There were many in Europe who saw this as positive for Germany – the election of a strong leader and party who could bring some stability after the chaos of the 1920s – and that the repression carried out by the regime was a necessary part of restabilizing Germany. Certainly in Britain, the Nazis drew enthusiastic support from many on the right. Britain's own major fascist group, Oswald Moseley's British Union of Fascists, while never achieving a mass following, were also seen by many, particularly in those in establishment with a desire to maintain traditional class hierarchies, as a positive force (Pugh 2002b: 232).

The attraction of fascism during the period was inextricably linked with the fear of communism since the Bolshevik Revolution in Russia in 1917. Joseph Stalin had risen to power in the Soviet Union through the 1920s, becoming General Secretary of the Communist Party in 1922, and de facto leader from the late 1920s. Through the 1930s his power was consolidated, and his vision for the USSR implemented, through the use of mass exile and mass murder. The murderousness of Stalin's regime was known about throughout the 1930s. However, despite this, the extreme economic conditions led many to see communism as the most obvious response. In Britain, membership of the Communist Party rose significantly through the 1930s – from 2,500 in 1930 to 18,000 in 1938.

The most resonant setting for the conflict between left and right during the 1930s was the Spanish Civil War (1936–1939). In 1936 the Spanish election was won by the Popular Front (a party made up of various centre and left groups), and they formed a government. A military coup to topple this government was staged by forces on the right in Spain, led by army generals. The coup was not wholly successful, but the resulting instability developed into a full-blown civil war. Both sides looked for support from outside Spain – the generals looked to Nazi Germany and fascist Italy, the government to the USSR and the democratic countries of Europe. Britain, France and the USSR decided on a public position of non-intervention, although the USSR did give support to the government of Spain. This flouting of its supposed policy of non-intervention did improve the standing of the USSR in the eyes of many Europeans, though. While other European governments maintained their detachment from events in Spain, thousands of ordinary European people were horrified at the attack on the legitimate government, and many joined international brigades in order to fight on the government side, or give support in other ways, such as driving ambulances. Over the course of the war 40,000 people from over 50 nations joined the international brigades, including many writers and artists. As is made clear in *Homage to Catalonia* (1938), George Orwell's account of his time in Spain fighting on the government side, despite this support, the infighting between various factions and the lack of support from other governments meant that in the end the right won, beginning the dictatorship of General Franco which lasted until the mid-1970s.

The Spanish Civil War attained a status in Europe in the late 1930s far beyond its local origins and ramifications. The war was seen as a microcosm of the wider conflict which was increasingly dominating the continent. The international brigades were peopled with those who believed that a victory for the right in Spain would lead to a Europe dominated by fascism. When the Spanish Civil War ended, the Allied Powers, including Britain under Neville Chamberlain, had already begun their policy of appeasing Hitler and a belligerent Germany. Britain, France and Italy signed the Munich Agreement with Germany in September 1938, effectively acceding to German demands for part of Czechoslovakia. The declaration of war with Germany a year later, following the German invasion of Poland, engaged the Allies (Britain, France and the USSR) against a common enemy, and the experience of the war undermined any claims by fascism to political legitimacy for the majority of Europeans.

The Position of the 'Other'

Towards the end of the nineteenth century the demands of three groups began to challenge the hegemony of imperial, patriarchal culture. While there is no sense in which working-class men, the colonized or women necessarily acknowledged common ground, very often far from it, it is possible to see the combination of their demands as radically unsettling.

Trades unions had finally achieved a reasonably secure legal basis in Britain in the 1870s, and unions acted as pressure groups in the last decades of the century. However, the goal was direct access to parliament through political representation. By the 1890s the extent of union membership made them powerful enough to establish a new political party. The Independent Labour Party was formed in 1893, and in 1900 it affiliated to the Labour Representation Committee, the political arm of the trade union movement, which started to field candidates in by-elections completely independently of the Liberals. In the election of 1906, 29 candidates supported by the LRC won seats, and became the Labour Party.

At this time the party had no explicit policies beside support for unionism and a desire to elect working-class men to parliament, but the First World War greatly accelerated its political evolution, and after the election in 1918 – which followed the extension of the franchise in the Representation of the People Act of that year – for the first time working-class men made up the majority of the electorate. Although the party did not perform that well in this election, it did become the largest opposition group. The party became the official opposition in 1922 and formed its first government (albeit a minority one) under Ramsay MacDonald in January 1924, to the horror of much of the political establishment and of many ordinary citizens. Ramsay

MacDonald's government only existed through Liberal support and was made cautious by its desire to show it could govern. The government lasted only 9 months, brought down by a vote of no confidence over alleged revolutionary sympathies. That such accusations could be so powerful demonstrates the extent to which for many seeing the representatives of the working class at home at the centre of national power was an unsettling and frightening experience.

British industrial development and growth had dominated the nineteenth century. By the 1870s Britain was the richest, most powerful nation in Europe, and via its empire, its culture was spread throughout the world. However, in the last decades of the century, a number of other countries began to industrialize rapidly. This competition caused significant anxiety in Britain, and fuelled the country's search for new markets and raw materials. In the 1880s Britain, Germany, France and Belgium all took part in what became known as the 'Scramble for Africa', when the continent was rapidly divided up between the major European powers. Rather than stemming anxiety, however, this process involved Britain in numerous skirmishes with rival nations, indigenous peoples, and settler groups, and more significantly the expansion of British imperial interests into Africa came to complicate and seriously undermine the country's sense of its imperial mission.

This effect of the division of Africa did not become apparent for some time, however. The colonial matter dominating this period was much closer to home. Irish resentment at absentee Protestant landlords, discriminatory legislation and British negligence during the famines in the middle of the century produced a republican movement which had instigated a violent campaign against British rule. The final decades of the century were dominated, though, by an Irish Parliamentary Party led by Charles Stewart Parnell which worked within the Westminster system to attempt to secure Home Rule for Ireland. His Irish MPs at Westminster enjoyed a reasonably powerful position due to the closely balanced parliaments during these years, and William Gladstone – Liberal Prime Minster four times between 1868 and 1894 – announced his support for Home Rule in 1885. The question of Home Rule was contested right up to the First World War. A Home Rule bill was passed in September 1914, but suspended until after the war. By the end of the war, the situation in Ireland had changed beyond recognition.

Opposition to English rule was not only expressed through Westminster politics. There was also an important cultural movement which attempted to recover and disseminate a specifically Irish culture as a resistance to English dominance. Of particular importance was a focus on Gaelic, and on the myths and folklore of Ireland's past. The Celtic Revival, as this movement came to be known, inspired many of the younger writers of the time, including the poet W.B. Yeats and the playwright J.M. Synge. In 1904 Yeats was involved in opening the Abbey Theatre in Dublin, with, among others, his patron Lady Gregory, who published several volumes of Irish myths and legends (for Yeats: see also Baxter, Paddy, Randall, Stinson and Thacker). The theatre mounted performances of many important plays which spoke to Irish audiences directly about their inheritance, their subjection to British rule, and the possibilities for change.

It was such cultural attention to a revivified sense of Irishness that inspired the small group who, during Easter 1916, hoping to take advantage of British involvement in the First World War, seized the main post office and a few other sites in Dublin and declared an independent Irish republic. The British crushed the Rising after 6 days. Fifteen of the leaders were court-martialled and executed, and many who had had nothing to do with the Rising were interned. The speed of the executions, the internment of so many and the destruction of the centre of Dublin galvanized Irish public opinion. In 1917 a new political movement was formed under the already existing banner of Sinn Féin. In the general election of December 1918, Sinn Féin won a landslide victory. Its elected MPs refused to sit in the British Parliament, and at the beginning of 1919 formed the Dáil Éireann, a new Irish parliament, and declared independence. This led to the Irish war of independence, which ended with the signing of the Anglo-Irish Treaty in 1921, and the formation of the Irish Free State (excluding the six counties of the north) in 1922.

The Easter Rising and its effects in Ireland acted as an important model for independence movements in other parts of the empire, especially India and Egypt. In India, Britain's largest and in many ways most significant colony, 1916 also marked a turning point. Agitation led to the Montagu-Chelmsford Report of August 1918, which set out a step-by-step approach to dominion-hood. In April 1919 a massacre in Amritsar in the Punjab turned many in India finally against British rule. The violence of the British response – the army opened fire on an unarmed crowd – undid the colonizer's claims to civilisation and honourable intentions. The rest of the interwar period saw increasing violence against the Raj in India, tension between various factions in India and always too-slow moves to reform on the British part. Indian independence was finally achieved at the end of 1947, but the inability to resolve sectarian differences led to partition, and an unprecedented level of sectarian violence.

The campaign to secure the vote for women had begun in the run up to the Second Reform Act of 1867. The National Society for Women's Suffrage (NSWS) was formed in 1872, and the National Union of Women's Suffrage Societies (NUWSS) in 1897. Campaigning continued without much success until the early years of the twentieth century. In 1903 the Women's Social and Political Union (WSPU), led by Emmeline Pankhurst, was formed, and after a couple of years, frustrated at the lack of progress through campaigning within the Westminster framework, the WSPU instigated a militant campaign, involving civil disobedience, destruction of public property, such as post boxes, the smashing of shop windows and other acts of targeted vandalism and arson. The militant campaign led to large numbers of middle and upper class women being arrested and spending time in prison, an unprecedented situation which challenged fundamental assumptions about women's capacities, their treatment and the basis of the relation between men and women. Although the WSPU was in many ways very conservative, and limited its challenge to society to the claim for the vote, the militant's campaign exposed the constricting effects of patriarchal notions of chivalry beyond the suffrage. From 1909 suffragettes in prison went on hunger strike to protest at conditions and to back up their demands to be treated as political prisoners. Force feeding, where a tube was inserted through a women's mouth into her stomach against her will, was introduced in September of that year, and the practice threw into stark relief questions of women's ownership of their bodies.

The militant campaign organized around the WSPU certainly attracted most of the public's attention, but it was not the whole of the campaign for the vote, even less did it represent demands for changes beyond the narrow confines of the suffrage. The NUWSS continued to campaign peacefully for the vote and in 1907 organized a march which culminated in the largest open air demonstration. Campaigns around other areas of concern for women had been in place since the mid-nineteenth century, including campaigns for reform in the divorce laws, around women's rights to keep their own property and wealth after marriage, and around their rights to the custody of their children. These all focused on improving women's position within bourgeois marriage, but by the end of the century, many middle and upper class women began to demand access to those things that would make a life outside of marriage possible, most particularly access to higher education. The first women's colleges at Oxford and Cambridge were set up during the late 1860s and 1870s, although women were not fully members of the university, and could not be awarded full degrees until 1920 at Oxford and 1947 at Cambridge. This struggle is reflected famously in Woolf's essay published in book form, *A Room of One's Own* (1929), where she contrasts the privilege of male colleges as opposed to the marginality of female provision at Cambridge.

More generally, middle and upper class women began to see that other kinds of political, cultural and aesthetic challenges to the conventions of patriarchal capitalism – innovations in artistic practice, the rejection of Christian morality, Marxist economic beliefs, and so on – were linked to their own sense of oppression and their own desire for change. A number of writers in particular began to make these links explicit, for example in the journal *The Freewoman* and *The New Freewoman*, published between 1911 and 1914, where women's economic and political status were linked to her psychological state, and women's freedom as an individual – sexually, morally, psychologically – was seen as more important than achieving the vote. *The New Freewoman* began to publish new and innovative literary works by, among others, Ezra Pound (for Pound see also Murray, Paddy, Randall, Stinson and Thacker) and H.D., and in 1914 it changed its name to *The Egoist*, becoming the most influential British small magazine in the publishing and promotion of Modernist writing.

Much has been made by some critics and historians of the crucial role of the First World War in changing the role and status of women in Britain (Marwick 1991; Gilbert and Gubar 1988). Many working-class women were moved from domestic service into work previously the preserve of men, and for many middle and upper class women the experience of war work, either at home or as nurses and ambulance drivers near the battlefields, offered employment beyond the home which would have rarely been previously sanctioned. However, according to Wrigley, female employment overall rose by only a quarter between 1914 and 1918 (508), and some have challenged the idea that the war made such a straightforward radical impact on women's lives (Braybon 1981; Braybon and Summerfield 1987; Ouditt 1994). Such employment patterns were reversed after the war, especially for working-class women, and women's pay was still significantly behind that of men.

The Representation of the People Act (1918) extended the vote to women over 30, and 10 years later the Equal Franchise Act (1928) gave men and women the vote on equal terms. The extent to which the campaigns of the suffragettes achieved this has been questioned (Pugh 2002a), but the 1928 Act meant that for the first time, women made up the majority of the electorate.

Culture

The period from the 1880s to the beginning of the Second World War saw the emergence and domination in America and Europe of a mass culture. In Britain, changes in technologies and industrial practices at the end of the nineteenth century, together with the gradual extension of education following the Education Act in 1870, saw the transformation of publishing, leisure and entertainment.

While the compulsory elementary education established by the 1870 Act was far from a recipe for extensive social mobility, it did raise literacy levels in Britain (Keating 1991: 400, 501n). At the same time, more reading material – in the form of newspapers, periodicals and books – was available than ever before. It is difficult to establish exactly the relation between these things, but it is the case that editors and publishers constructed new reading material that would be attractive to the 'new' reading classes, that is, working-class people who could read, but whose education was limited. In 1896 the first daily tabloid newspaper, Alfred Harmsworth's *The Daily Mail*, began publication, designed explicitly to appeal to the largest number of people through its accessibility, its entertaining features and its low price. *The Daily Mail* was just one of the most successful new publications in a market that exploded at the end of the nineteenth century. Very low cover prices were made possible by the new practice of raising income by the selling of advertising space. Of course, this did not just fund the publications; it was a significant determinant in their editorial makeup and tone. This explicit interrelation of the commercial and the cultural was one of the central characteristics of the developing mass culture, and it was this aspect in particular that provoked the anxiety and opprobrium of critics and 'serious' writers. For them, 'culture' was not so much expanding as degrading, as the products of the mass market were dictated by the tastes of the partially educated. This anxiety about the degradation of culture was a strong feature of the whole period, and was shared, although with different explanations and effects, by both establishment figures and younger experimental writers such as Ezra Pound and Virginia Woolf.

The change in book publishing during the period also provoked such responses, for it too expanded massively. Cheaper books and an increase in the publication of books for the purposes of entertainment established for the first time the possibility of reading as a leisure activity for a large number of people, and not just from the working class. The term 'bestseller' was first used in the 1890s, and during this decade too for the first time lists of 'bestsellers' were published in periodicals and journals. The term was not just a description of quantity, but very quickly came to denote a certain quality (or lack of it) too (Keating 1991: 440). As far as novels were concerned, bestsellers were neither serious literature, nor the cheapest form of popular fiction, but rather occupied the broad middle ground, and appealed to a mass of readers, educated, but not highly, looking for entertainment, gripping plots, understandable characters and a widely shared view of the world confidently affirmed. In this, bestseller novels of the period were the polar opposite of the work being produced by Modernist writers, and indeed numerous critics have argued that the experiments of the latter were conducted in explicit response to those books which dominated the mass market (Trotter 2001).

Anxiety about the rise of mass culture, and the increasingly polar split perceived between the culture of the masses and those of the highly educated took a significant form at the end of the First World War. The British government believed that one of the reasons that an Allied victory had looked unlikely for so long was the superior education and skill of the German troops. After the war the government decided that British educational standards needed to be raised, not just to keep up with the recent enemy, but also to allay fears of a dissatisfied and mutinous working class. Where mid-nineteenth century consensus was that the working class could be kept from revolt by being kept illiterate, the early twentieth century came to believe that they could be kept docile by reading the 'right' books. The government set up royal commissions to investigate the teaching of a number of subjects in schools. The resulting report of the commission which investigated the teaching of English – known as the Newbolt Report – was published in 1921and become something of a bestseller itself (compared to other government reports, at least). The commission argued that the teaching of English literature – as that which represented the best of the shared language of the nation – was vital in instilling in the population shared beliefs and values which could act as a kind of glue, mitigating the threat of class animosity and division. This vision of English literature as a set of values which could restore harmony to society was shared by those establishing English literature as a university subject at the time, in particular I.A. Richards and F.R. Leavis at Cambridge.

For such cultural critics, the attractions of 'good' writing were in competition, not just with the 'bestsellers', but also with new forms of entertainment produced through technological developments – the gramophone, the cinema and the radio. The gramophone, and the records played on them, became commercially available at the very end of the nineteenth century, and brought recorded music into the home. The 'cinematograph' developed by the Lumière brothers was first demonstrated in Paris in 1895 and London in 1896. Early films, just a few minutes in length, were shown in music halls, at circuses and fairgrounds, and their content either mimicked these older forms of entertainment – people doing music hall 'turns' or circus acts – showed popular sporting occasions such as the Derby or boxing matches, or recorded everyday events. Very quickly, though, film technology made it possible to extend the running time of films. Longer narrative films, shown in cinemas, were established as the norm of the medium by the outbreak of the First World War. At this time there were already 4,000 film theatres in the country, and around 7–8 million people attended the cinema each week. By 1920 this had risen to 20 million (Armes 1978: 32). By the end of the war, a major film industry had been established in most industrialized countries, and the US film industry was already the seventh most important industry in the country (Armes 1978: 15). Charlie Chaplin's first films appeared in 1914, and very quickly Chaplin and other Hollywood actors were known and loved throughout the world, becoming very rich and influential and creating the concept of 'celebrity'.

On the whole the intellectual middle and upper classes were deeply suspicious of the cinema. Its early associations with music hall and fairgrounds marked it out as popular culture, and its status as technology and reliance on machines separated it from a traditional culture valued by critics such as Leavis. The association quickly established between cinema and American culture also made it suspect. More particularly, the actual experience of viewing film was problematic. Particularly once the seductions of narrative came to dominate the medium, films were seen as inducing passivity in their audiences. Even more dangerously, they excited emotions in their (mainly working class) audiences which, it was assumed, such audiences did not how to use in an appropriate way. The coming of 'talkie' movies in the late 1920s deepened this anxiety.

In the interwar period, the leisure of millions was dominated by cinema-going. However, in the home the radio was king. Radio technology had been developed in the early twentieth century, most significantly by Marconi. In 1922 the British Broadcasting Company was founded by a number of telecommunications companies, including Marconi's, to broadcast experimental radio services. In 1927 the company became a publicly owned corporation, the BBC. The power of the radio was enormous, and the BBC's remit to educate and inform as well as entertain led to an output – split between three programmes, the 'Light', 'Home' and 'Third' – which enacted contemporary assumptions about class, education, in social mobility and social cohesion.

Science and Technology

The biological sciences had dominated the nineteenth century. Their rapid, extraordinary discoveries and parallel establishment as a delineated, professionalized area of science, with their own practices, conventions and methodologies, made them the leading sciences of the period. This of course had significant consequences for medicine through the century, and it moved from a rather barbaric, hit and miss affair at the beginning of the century, to a professional practice at the end which we can recognize as modern medicine. The widespread use of anaesthetics from the 1840s allowed for massive developments in surgical techniques. Louis Pasteur's germ theory and Joseph Lister's development of antiseptic treatment of wounds revolutionized preventative medicine and patient care.

At the heart of the intellectual domination of the biological sciences was Darwin's theory of natural selection. The publication of *The Origin of Species* (1859) and *The Descent of Man* (1871), and the dissemination of Darwin's ideas throughout the rest of the century (see also Baxter and Wilson), in particular by the biologist T.H. Huxley, fundamentally undermined the idea that human beings were somehow separate from the rest of the natural world, and not subject to its laws. The age of the earth implied by evolutionary theory, the suggestion that human beings shared common ancestors with apes, and the assertion that evolutionary change was due to impersonal accidents of chance rather than the benevolent choices of 'Providence' or 'God' all challenged the idea that human concerns were special, that human life spans were significant and that human beings were primarily rational and civilized.

These new ideas produced new ways of understanding human beings. For example, Freud's development of psychoanalysis in the 1890s seemed to suggest that under the attributes of a supposedly civilized person were the greedy instincts and destructive urges of animals (for Freud see also Baxter, Paddy, Stinson and Thacker). Much fin de siècle writing responded to these ideas by abandoning the secure world vision of realism and creating fantasy worlds which could more usefully contain and examine the new human being. In R.L. Stevenson's *The Strange Case of Dr Jekyll and Mr Hyde* (1886), the urbane and civilized Dr Jekyll is no match for the violent urges of his alter ego Mr Hyde. In the end, the civilized man can only destroy the dark, animal-like desires underneath by destroying himself.

By the end of the century, the ramifications of developments in the biological sciences were felt strongly throughout European culture, with both positive and unsettling effects. Important new developments did happen in the biological sciences in the early twentieth century, such as in genetics, but the wider consequences of these were not really felt till the second half of the century and physics began to usurp its position as pre-eminent science.

In the mid-nineteenth century, some leading physicists had begun to suggest that all the great problems in physics were solved; the rest was just the tidying up of loose ends. However, throughout the century, a number of leading physicists had worked to understand the nature and properties of the electromagnetic spectrum, and this was to lead to the radical discoveries around the turn of the century.

Experimentation in the area of electricity led to the discovery of X-rays by Wilhelm Röntgen in the late 1890s and the discovery of radioactivity by Henri Becquerel in 1896. Both these, and the discoveries which followed from them, profoundly affected ideas of vision, hierarchies of surface and depth, and the substantiality of the human body, and the nature of the material world. More radical still, Max Planck's quantum theory of 1900 was a fundamental challenge to classical physics. It established a new system of physics and suggested a worldview which, contrary to Newtonian physics, seemed to deny the possibility of a complete understanding of reality. For physics, then, the central problem at this time was to demonstrate how Newton's mechanical laws, the bedrock of classical physics, could accommodate the new equations of electromagnetics.

By the turn of the century, it was clear that light was a form of electric and magnetic interaction, but the problem was establishing how it moved from place to place. Newton's mechanical laws demanded a substance through which it could move. Physicists called this notional substance ether, but no experimental work could establish the presence of ether, its properties, or its effects. It was the investigation of this conundrum that led to the publication in 1905 of Albert Einstein's work known in English as the 'Special Theory of Relativity' (for Einstein see also Paddy and Stinson). Einstein had been influenced by the work of Max Planck in his challenge to Newtonian physics. Einstein's theories became popularly known as relativity (not a term he favoured), but actually his discovery was based on the idea that the speed of light is absolute. However, he argued, if the speed of light is absolute then space and time, those two absolutes of the Newtonian universe, could not be. If space and time are not absolutes, then 'ether' is not required to explain either the transport or movement of light (Panek 2005).

Einstein's theories were reported in the press and popularized to an unprecedented degree, especially after work of the astronomer Arthur Eddington in 1919 established the theories set out in Einstein's General Theory (1915) as correct. Einstein himself participated in the popular dissemination of his work in his *Relativity: The Special and the General Theory* (1920). In 1921 Einstein was awarded the Nobel Prize, and became the most famous scientist in the world.

Einstein's challenge was followed by an onslaught against classical Newtonian physics. In 1911 the English physicist Ernest Rutherford discovered the make up of the atom, the behaviour of which undid the expectations of the mechanical worldview. In 1913 the physicist Niels Bohr furthered Rutherford's discoveries about the make up of atoms. What all this work suggested was that, contrary to the view of classical physics, where physical process are continuous and smooth, 'quantum thinking' was characterized by discreteness and discontinuous jumps. In 1927 the German theorist Werner Heisenberg formulated his uncertainty principle, arguing that it is impossible to have perfect knowledge of both the position of something and its momentum simultaneously. In the new world revealed by quantum physics, half knowledge was the best that could be hoped for.

These rapid and radical changes in scientific theories around the turn of the century were matched by huge changes in the area where most people experience scientific discoveries – in their practical application in technology. Crucially, the extent to which technological change began to impact on people's lives at a most intimate and quotidian level provoked enormous pride that human beings could exert such control over their environment, but at the same time enormous anxiety that technology was changing the nature of what it meant to be human, if not threatening to make human beings redundant.

The first cars were produced in the late nineteenth century, but mass production did not arrive until 1908 with the introduction of the Model-T by the American car manufacturer Henry Ford, which by 1914 had sold more than all other car makes combined. Immediately the car became a privileged status symbol denoting not only wealth, but also modernity. However, there was much anxiety about the potential damage to drivers, passengers and unsuspecting pedestrians, and regulation of the roads was soon necessary with, for example, the first traffic light going into operation in 1914.

While such regulation was seen as necessary to protect people, it was the increase in regulation per se as a consequence of technological change that exerted a more fundamental challenge. In order to supply cars at the pace demanded, Henry Ford developed the first assembly line in 1913, creating a model of mass production which seemed to relegate the role of the human being to a mere part of a larger, more powerful machine. The assembly line model changed the nature of work in that the worker, rather than controlling processes, and following a manufacturing process through from beginning to end, instead repeated the same tiny element of a process over and over, their actions and practices determined by the demands and needs of machines. The development of motor cars changed not only an understanding of the nature and capacities of the individual human body, but changed to relations between human bodies.

The motor cut the time it took to transport things – people, goods, information – from one place to another. The period also saw significant changes in other kinds of communication, and in each case an increased speed of connection between people, countries and continents reshaped human experience of self and world (Kern 2003). The telephone had been invented by Alexander Graham Bell in the late 1870s, and by the turn of the century it was widely commercially available. In 1901 the first successful transatlantic radio signal was sent, and in 1903 for the first time a radio message circumnavigated the world. The ability to communicate almost instantaneously with those on the other side of the world meant that differences in time needed to be regularized. There were a number of conferences held in the last decades of the nineteenth century and the early twentieth century to bring this about. In 1911 Greenwich Mean Time was adopted as the universal standard. Again, technological change necessitated other changes which worked to standardize and flatten out differences between places and people. As with the motor car, changes in communication meant that individual's identification and desire could shift from their immediate locales to anywhere on the globe.

By the early twentieth century, the scientific worldview had become the most authoritative one for the Western world, undoing the previous authority of religion. Although, as suggested above, early twentieth century science was itself questioning at a most fundamental level the conventional view of the world and the certainty with which it could be known, for most scientific truth became synonymous with truth itself. However, what can also be seen during the period is an emergence of interest in areas able to speak of those aspects of human life and experience beyond the remit of science. Interest in psychology, philosophy, spiritualism and the occult is a notable feature of the period, and figures prominent in one of these areas often looked to the others too for methods, practices and theories that may unlock the 'unseen' elements of human beings and the natural world for human exploration (Owen 2004).

Literary and Cultural Contexts: Major Figures, Institutions, Topics, Events

Emmett Stinson

Figures

Wystan Hugh ('W.H.') Auden (1907–1973)

Although Auden is a generation younger than the most famous Modernist poets, his poetry nonetheless remains an essential contribution to British Modernism. Raised in Birmingham, England, Auden received a scholarship to Oxford, where he became the central figure of the Oxford Group of poets, which also included Stephen Spender and Louis MacNiece. Auden's relationship to Modernism is clearest in his first collection, *Poems* (1930), which features an aesthetic sensibility heavily indebted to the work of **T.S. Eliot** (for Eliot see also Baxter, Murray, Paddy and Randall). His collections of the 1930s show him moving further and further away from the intellectual, allusive difficulty of Modernist poetics towards a poetry that was more clearly emotional and accessible, appropriating a variety of traditional and populist forms, including ballads and songs. His most famous works include 'Musee des Beaux Arts', 'Funeral Blues' and 'September 1st, 1939'. In 1939, Auden left England for America, where he resided for the rest of his life, and, in the following year, he reconverted to Anglicanism. Religious experience would become of major importance in his later verse, though his religious views were idiosyncratic rather than doctrinaire. Auden switched styles throughout the remaining decades of his life, with his varying approaches receiving mixed reviews, often drawing criticism from his British contemporaries, while influencing later generations of American poets.

Samuel Beckett (1906–1989)

One of the most intriguing Modernist writers, Samuel Beckett also provides an important bridge from Modernism to postmodernism. Born outside of Dublin, Beckett attended Trinity from 1923 to 1927, and briefly taught there, resigning in frustration with the academic lifestyle. Perhaps the most significant aesthetic event in Beckett's life occurred when he befriended James Joyce in 1929. Beckett's early fiction, such as his first novel, *Dreams of Fair to Middling Women* (1932, published posthumously), *More Pricks Than Kicks* (1934) and *Murphy* (1938), bear the influence of Joyce. Beckett later moved to France and began composing in French, with the desire to simplify the structure and vocabulary of his prose, which he decided would not be drawn from a Joycean academicism, but entirely from his own internal world. The work that resulted demonstrates his trademark mixture of pessimism and absurdist humour written in spare prose. Beckett's first significant publication in French was the play, *En Attendant Godot*, or *Waiting for Godot* (1952), which remains his most famous work. Beckett gained renown for subsequent plays, such as *Endgame* (1957), *Krapp's Last Tape* (1958) and *Happy Days* (1960). He also produced an influential trilogy of novels, *Molloy* (1951), *Malone Dies* (1951), and *The Unnamable* (1953), during this period. Beckett's work remains enigmatic, blending philosophical speculation with absurdist gallows humour. Beckett's work also explores the human need to continue on even in the face of insurmountable obstacles, perhaps best exemplified in *Worstword Ho*: 'Ever tried. Ever failed. No matter. Try again. Fail again. Fail better' (1983, p. 7). In this sense, Beckett's work is not entirely defeatist. His experimentation with language, surreal conceits and skepticism of systematic philosophies and grand unifying theories have made him a major influence for subsequent postmodern authors such as Donald Barthelme and Harold Pinter.

Joseph Conrad (1857–1924)

Born in Poland and not achieving fluency in English until the age of 20, Joseph Conrad nonetheless became perhaps the most influential novelist of early Modernism (for Conrad see also Baxter, Murray, Paddy and Randall). In his impressionistic descriptions and use of unreliable narrators, Conrad employed fictional techniques that would become hallmarks of literary Modernism. Until the age of thirty-six, Conrad spent most of his adult life travelling around the world as a mariner, and most of his fiction draws on this experience at sea. Like other Modernists, Conrad was pessimistic about the effects of modernity on the world; his work graphically depicts the devastating repercussions of colonialism and imperialism. Although he wrote many novels, Conrad is perhaps best remembered for a long novella, *Heart of*

Darkness (1899), which narrates Marlowe's journey up the Congo in search of Kurtz, an ivory-trader who has gone mad. The text employs a frame story, being related by an unnamed narrator who hears Kurtz's narrative, and in so doing creates wilful ambiguity about the authority of the tale. This technique directly influenced F. Scott Fitzgerald, who intentionally modelled Nick Carraway, the narrator of *The Great Gatsby* (1925), on Conrad's unnamed observer in *Heart of Darkness*. The apocalyptic mood of the book also directly influenced *T.S. Eliot*, who originally used an excerpt from *Heart of Darkness* as an epigraph to his masterwork, *The Waste Land* (1922), before removing it at the suggestion of *Ezra Pound* (for Pound see also Murray, Paddy, Randall, Thacker and Wilson); nonetheless, a reference to Kurtz does appear in Eliot's later poem, 'The Hollow Men' (1925).

Thomas Stearns ('T.S.') Eliot (1888–1965)

Along with **James Joyce's Ulysses**, T.S. Eliot's long, allusive poem, *The Waste Land* (see Baxter), remains one of the two most iconic texts of English Modernism, but Eliot produced many other significant works, including influential literary criticism and plays. Born in St Louis, Missouri, Eliot attended Harvard where he researched a doctoral dissertation in Indian philosophy (its formal award not taking place in the Great War because of hostilities at sea), aspects of which would appear in the last section of *The Waste Land*. Afterwards, Eliot moved to England where he met other early Modernist writers, including **Wyndham Lewis** and **Ezra Pound**, and began publishing his poems in **Modernist journals**, including the **Vorticist** publication *BLAST*. Like these authors, Eliot produced an experimental poetry that, although learned and steeped in the history of literature, simultaneously sought to expand the tradition by refraining from excessive emotion in favour of a learned impersonality, employing obscure allusion and including subject matter that was considered inappropriate for polite society of the time. Eliot came to notoriety with the publication of his poem 'The Love Song of J. Alfred Prufrock' (1915), both for the poem's unusual style and references to sexuality, but with the publication of *The Waste Land* in 1922, Eliot became an overnight celebrity. *The Waste Land* was heavily edited by Pound, who also acted as a de facto agent for the poem, convincing several editors of its significance and creating a bidding war between magazines, leading to the poem's near-simultaneous publication in three places in America and England. The publicity campaign worked, as newspapers across both countries ran editorials debating the poem's merit. In 1922, Eliot took over editorship of the journal, *Criterion*, and began publishing essays in literary criticism that influenced the creation of the New Criticism, with essays like his 'Tradition and the Individual Talent' (1919), which is critical of the Romantic conception of poetry. Also influential was his idea of the 'objective correlative,' in which the poetic expression of emotion must always be grounded in actual objects or events. After *The Waste Land*, Eliot's poetic output became less prolific, but subsequent to his 1927 conversion to Anglicanism and his assumption of British citizenship, he published *The Four Quartets* (1936–1942), a series of poetic meditations on time and religion. Most of Eliot's later output was directed towards dramatic works, but his plays have held less continuing interest than his early poetry. More recently, Eliot has become known for his difficult first marriage with Vivienne Haigh-Wood, dramatized in the film *Tom and Viv* (1994). Like Lewis and Pound, Eliot's right-wing politics have caused continuing difficulties for his critical reception and led to questioning of apparent anti-Semitic sentiments in his poetry.

William Faulkner (1897–1952)

Born in the unlikely location of New Albany, Missisippi, Faulkner remains an unusual case in Modernism, in that his expression of Modernist aesthetics was mixed in with a literary regionalism; virtually all of Faulkner's fiction is set in the American deep south. The majority of Faulkner's novels take place in the fictional county of Yoknapatawhpha, Mississippi. His fiction deals with the crumbling of the Southern aristocracy and social order in the wake of losing the American Civil War, and criticizes the South's backwardness on issues of race, sexuality and gender. Many (though not all) of Faulkner's novels partake of a radically Modernist style, especially in their deployment of the stream-of-consciousness technique. *The Sound and the Fury* (1929), arguably his masterpiece, offers three first-person narratives of the Compson brothers, all of whom are obsessed with their absent sister Caddy. *As I Lay Dying* (1930), allegedly written in 46 days, uses 15 separate narrators to describe the process of burying the coffin of the recently deceased Addie Bundren. *Absalom, Absalom!* (1936), perhaps Faulkner's most difficult work, compares Thomas Sutpen's attempt to rebuild his family's legacy after the civil war to the biblical story of David and Absalom. *Absalom, Absalom!* again uses multiple narrators, many of whom report stories that they have heard second and even third-hand, creating a web of palimpsests that leaves even the basic order of events in a haze of obscurity. Faulkner was awarded the Nobel Prize in 1949, and, while influential in the United States, has also had a significant impact in France and Latin America, with writers as diverse as Toni Morrison, Claude Simon and Gabriel Garcia-Marquez among those indebted to his *oeuvre*.

Sigmund Freud (1856–1939)

Although his earliest writings antedate Modernism, Freudian psychoanalysis was one of the most important intellectual inheritances for the Modernist vision. Freud sought to create a scientific, non-theological understanding of the self, and created the modern conception of psychiatric counselling, or the 'talking cure' (for Freud see also Baxter, Paddy, Thacker and Wilson). Of particular note was Freud's conceptualization of the unconscious mind, which is the more 'primitive' area of the mind that contains our instinctive needs; Freud termed this side of the self the 'id.' The ego on the other hand is the individual's rational consciousness. In order to function in civilization, the ego represses the id's desires, but this repression can result in the manifestation of neurosis, hysteria and other psychological disorders. The unconscious mind also expresses itself in other ways, not only in the creative arts and poetry, but also in dreams, which Freud saw as revealing important aspects of the self. Freud also saw sexual desire as one (if not the) basic motivation for human action, redefining sexuality as a developmental process whereby the child seeks various outlets for its desire. The stages include oral and anal, fixations before successful socialization turns desire towards an appropriate object of desire. The Oedipal Complex (based upon Sophocles' play *Oedipus Rex*, emerges when the child develops desire for the mother in the stages of sexual development and begins to fear castration of the father. This, according to Freud, results in a repressed wish to cause the father harm which becomes manifest in a number of symptoms. After World War I, Freud's thought turned more decisively toward collective human forms of desire, centred in his later *Beyond the Pleasure Principle* (1920), around the oppositional relationship between *Eros* (the principle of a positive, pleasurable erotic life) and *Thanatos* (or the death-drive). Freud's ideas were exceptionally important to Modernist authors, as they were both published and extremely controversial during the advent of Modernism, itself. Alongside Einstein's influence, Freud's ideas influenced writers who employed the stream-of-consciousness technique, since psychoanalysis allowed for greater verisimilitude concerning mental processes. The idea of the unconscious and the importance of dreams influenced **Surrealism**, which tried to express the unconscious through visual and literary means. A number of important Modernist authors adopted Freud's insights and developed them in their narratives, such as D.H. Lawrence, whose novel *Sons and Lovers* is often regarded as a Freudian text, exemplifying the Oedipus Complex, despite Lawrence's declared antipathy towards Freud. Although Freud's work has attracted criticism, especially from the perspective of feminism, his work on the self and the mind remains among the most important theories to appear in the twentieth century.

James Joyce (1882–1941)

Despite publishing only three novels, one book of short stores, a play and two books of poetry, James Joyce remains perhaps the single most important figure of Modernism. Born to a devoutly Catholic family in Dublin, Joyce attended University College Dublin before moving to Paris. In his first book of stories, *Dubliners* (1914), Joyce attempted to depict the political, emotional and cultural paralysis of the Dublin of his youth; these stories, mostly 'realist' in execution, anticipated the minimalist fiction of later twentieth century authors, such as Ernest Hemingway and Raymond Carver. *Dubliners* also introduced Joyce's conception of the epiphany – the internal insight that provides an emotional, rather than plot-based, conclusion to a story. **Ezra Pound** admired *Dubliners* and, by his intercession, Joyce had his first novel, *Portrait of the Artist as a Young Man*, serialized in the **Modernist journal**, *The Egoist*, from 1914 to 1915. A semi-autobiogrpahical work, *Portrait* is perhaps the single most important *kunstlerroman* (story of an artist's development) written in the twentieth century. Using experimental prose techniques that reflect the psychological development of the novel's protagonist, Stephen Daedelus, Joyce depicts Stephen's growth from a young boy in Dublin to his decision, as a young man, to leave for the continent and become a writer. Joyce pushed his experimental techniques even further in *Ulysses* (1922), often considered a key work in the development of the novel (for *Ulysses* see also Day). Taking place on a single day in 1904, Joyce compares the seemingly insignificant actions of Leopold Bloom to the epic journey of Odysseus. Employing stream-of-consciousness, dense intellectual allusion, and a variety of other rhetorical strategies over nearly a thousand pages, *Ulysses* was hailed as a masterwork upon its publication. Due to its depictions of bodily functions and female sexuality, however, it was banned as 'obscene' in the United States until 1933 and in England until 1936. Joyce spent the rest of his life on another large, dense text provisionally entitled *Work in Progress*, but published as *Finnegans Wake* (1939). Critically divisive at the time of its publication, *Finnegans Wake* pushes linguistic experiment to its uppermost limit. Written in a style that Joyce termed 'nightlanguage' due to its dreamlike qualities, *Finnegans Wake* includes neologisms and multi-level puns drawn from multiple languages, and contains little in the way of readily clear plot or characters. Nonetheless, the work had a seminal influence on later fiction, and some critics have seen *Finnegans Wake* as the first postmodern novel.

David Herbert Richards ('D.H.') Lawrence (1885–1930)

Although one of the most popular Modernist authors and once considered quite radical, D.H. Lawrence's fiction now seems considerably less experimental than the work of his contemporaries. In many senses, his work represents continuity between the nineteenth century novel and his brand of Modernism, especially in his didactic critiques of social relations and explorations of spirituality. Lawrence's views on spirituality were intricately linked to his particular form of Nietzschean vitalism. Lawrence believed that modernity had suppressed an innate form of human sexuality and expression that allowed us a greater commune with nature. In his work heterosexual relations beyond the bounds of bourgeois domesticity are often celebrated as a potentially redemptive form. While his exploration of sexual themes, such as in *Lady Chatterley's Lover* (1928), subjected him to the same charges of obscenity that plagued Joyce's *Ulysses* (1922), and emphasized Lawrence's break with Victorian values his work is often considered to be less formally experimental than his contemporaries. While some of his novels, such as *Women in Love* (1920), use impressionistic description and engage with Modernist themes of alienation and loss, other works of his are more explicitly 'realist.' *Sons and Lovers* (1913) is largely autobiographical with parallels between Paul Morel's relationship to his mother and Lawrence's own, and similarly drawn from life is the novel's oedipal theme which expresses Freudian concepts and will recur throughout his fiction. Lawrence was also an important poet, who briefly associated with **Imagism**. Raised in a working-class family, Lawrence's fiction often discussed class-based issues, although some critics have accused him of harbouring fascist sympathies and anti-Semitic beliefs. While an undoubtedly important novelist, Lawrence's precise relationship to Modernism remains a subject of critical debate.

Wyndham Lewis (1882–1957)

Although he never achieved the fame and recognition of many of his contemporaries, as a painter, novelist, critic, essayist and avant-garde propagandist, Wyndham Lewis remains a significant and dynamic force behind English Modernism. Born to an American father and British mother in a boat off the coast of Nova Scotia, Lewis was raised primarily in England, attending art school at the Slade. He toured the European continent for several years afterwards, living a Bohemian lifestyle, and returned to England in 1908, where he published essays about Brittany in Ford Madox Ford's journal, *The English Review*, in 1909. Through Ford, Lewis met other avant-garde writers and artists, such as **T.S. Eliot, Ezra Pound** and T.E. Hulme, who shared both his aesthetic radicalism and right-wing politics. Both Picasso's **Cubism** and Marinetti's **Futurism** deeply influenced Lewis's painting at the time, but he rejected both movements as insufficient responses to industrialized society. After an argument with Roger Fry caused him to leave the **Omega Workshops**, Lewis decided to create his own, distinctly English, avant-garde movement known as **Vorticism**, along with Pound, Henri Gaudier-Brzeska, Jacob Epstein and others, resulting in the publication of the journal, *BLAST: The Review of the Great English Vortex*, in 1914 with a second issue in 1915. Lewis was then called to serve in the First World War and published his first novel, *Tarr* (1918). Upon his return, he embarked on a prolific writing schedule that resulted in the publication of numerous works including the political tract *The Art of Being Ruled* (1926), art and literary criticism in *Time and Western Man* (1927) and *The Lion and the Fox: The Role of the Hero in the Plays of Shakespeare* (1927), and fiction with *The Childermass* (1928) and *The Apes of God* (1930), a blistering satire of the **Bloomsbury Group**. Lewis's reputation took a turn for the worse in the 1930s, due to the publication of his work *Hitler* (1931), which offered tentative praise of the future fascist leader. Despite his later rejection of German fascism in *The Hitler Cult* (1939).

Hugh MacDiarmid (1892–1978)

A significant Scottish poet, Macdiarmid remains less well-known than many of his contemporaries due to his frequent poetic usage of the Scots dialect, unfamiliar to his English peers. He also published frequently and in a great variety of styles throughout six decades, making his work difficult to categorize. MacDiarmid spent most of his life in rural Scotland distant from England's urban cultural centres, and his books were often released by local Scottish publishers in low volumes with limited distribution. Nonetheless, his poetry shares much in common with other Modernists, both in its bleak depiction of the effects of modernity on human life, and in his foregrounding of the experimental possibilities in language. Indeed, by writing books in the Scots dialect, MacDiarmid drew on national myths and traditions, while emphasizing the strangeness of his poetic language. MacDiarmid's poetry reveals a deep interest in scientific developments and observation on the one hand, but also revels in obscurity and oblique allusion on the other. His later poetry, written mostly in standard English, is actually, in many cases, every bit as difficult and evasive as the early lyrics in Scots. While MacDiarmid shared the political radicalism of contemporary Modernist writers, such as **T.S. Eliot**, **Wyndham Lewis**, and **Ezra Pound**, MacDiarmid's politics were leftist, offering an idiosyncratic blend of Marxism, C.H. Douglas's Social Credit Economics, and Scottish Nationalism. Since his death, MacDiarmid's stature has grown and he is now regarded as an important, if unusual, Modernist poet.

Friedrich Nietzsche (1844–1900)

The work of German philosopher Friedrich Nietzsche remains essential for an understanding of Modernism, dramatically influencing literature, visual art and politics (for Nietzsche see also Murray and Paddy). Nietzsche wrote in an intentionally aphoristic and aestheticized style that blurred the boundaries between philosophy and literature. Providing a cohesive overview of Nietzsche's philosophy remains problematic largely because of his intentionally anti-systematic method of proceeding by aphorism. Nonetheless, his theorization of modernity as a moment in which traditional social values and institutions had eroded remains a clear and important insight. Nietzsche's famous statement that 'God is dead,' reflected the understanding that, in secularized modernity, religion no longer provided a viable authoritative grounding for ethical, social and aesthetic values. This collapse of an absolute authority enabled the possibility of relativism and nihilism, leading to the modern sense of alienation. Nietzsche, however, was not an entirely pessimistic or nihilistic thinker, and sought new ways to create a sense of purpose and meaning in life. Some of the ideas Nietzsche employed to combat nihilism included his theorization of the *Ubërmensch*, or 'overman,' a new type of being who would be able to surmount the challenges of modern life, and the 'will to power,' a vitalist force that could overcome relativism. He also created the conception of 'eternal return', theorizing that one should undertake decisions with the idea that each action would be repeated over and over again forever; Nietzsche suggested that this theory could serve as the basis of a new ethics for modernity. Importantly for many Modernists, Nietzsche's investigation of Classic Greek tragedy split art into two opposing spheres, the Apollonian and the Dionysian. The Apollonian was centred around the importance of control and form in art, whereas the Dionysian was characterized by an intoxication and compulsion towards destruction. Nietzsche's philosophy was popularized in England by Alfred Orage's *Nietzsche in Outline and Aphorism* (1907), and influenced such writers as **T.S. Eliot, D.H. Lawrence, Wyndham Lewis, Ezra Pound**, and **W.B. Yeats**. Nietzsche's critique of modernity and call for new systems of values resonated with artists seeking to create a radical new aesthetics for modernity. Nietzsche's energetic, often humorous writing style resembles many avant-garde **manifestoes**. Lastly, Nietzsche's philosophy greatly influenced the political doctrine of fascism in both Italy and Germany, although many scholars argue that fascist thinkers intentionally misapplied Nietzsche's ideas.

Figure 3: Plaque commemorating the London home of W.B. Yeats in rooms in Woburn Walk, Bloomsbury. © Philip Tew 2008

Ezra Pound (1885–1972)

Born in Hailey, Idaho, Ezra Pound became one of the most significant poets of the twentieth century, co-founding both **Imagism** and **Vorticism**, and issuing the Modernist directive to 'Make it new'. Both his shorter lyrics and his epic poem, *The Cantos*, written over a period of 50 years, exerted an enormous influence over both such contemporary and later poets as H.D. (Hilda Doolittle), Richard Aldington, **William Carlos Williams**, Louis Zukofsky, Charles Olsen and Robert Lowell. Despite his own literary output, Pound is perhaps best-known as the editor of T.S. Eliot's poem *The Waste Land* (1922), which is dedicated to Pound as 'il miglior fabbro' ('the better craftsman'). Pound also worked tirelessly to promote the work of his friends, playing a significant role in aiding not only Eliot, but also **James Joyce** and **William Butler Yeats** (for Yeats: see also Baxter, Paddy, Randall, Thacker and Wilson), to whom he served as a secretary. His role in shaping English Modernism has lead the critic Hugh Kenner to describe this period as the 'Pound Era' (1971). Pound also became interested in politics and economics, specifically C.H. Douglas's theory of Social Credit Economics, which he encountered while working under Alfred Orage for the journal, *The New Age*. Pound moved to Rapallo, Italy, in the 1920s, and, under the belief that Italian leader Benito Mussolini would implement Douglasite economic reforms, supported Italian fascism. Remaining in Italy during World War II, Pound repeatedly broadcasted on Rome Radio, issuing statements critical of United States involvement in the war. As a result, he was arrested during the Allied liberation of Italy in 1945. During his internment in Italy, he wrote *The Pisan Cantos*, which won the Library of Congress's Bollingen Prize in 1949, while he was being tried for treason in the United States. Pound pleaded insanity to escape the charges, and was institutionalized at St Elizabeth's mental hospital in Washington, DC, for 12 years. After his pardon and release in 1958, Pound returned to Italy, where he died in 1972. Although both his fascist associations and anti-Semitism have made Pound a controversial figure, he remains a seminal force in the creation of Modernist aesthetics.

Marcel Proust (1871–1922)

Proust, a French novelist who is mostly known for his sprawling, multi-volume work *A la Recherche du Temps Perdu* (1909–1921), initially trans-lated as *Remembrance of Things Past*, but now usually known as *In Search of Lost Time*; generally held to be a key French novel of the twentieth century. While not a memoir *per se*, the work is autobiographical in basis, and, like Joyce's *Portrait of the Artist as a Young Man*, it is a *kunstlerroman*, detailing the growth and vocation of a young artist. Renown for its beautiful prose, *In Search of Lost Time* offers an elegant exploration of memory and the personal experience of time, as well as offering an incisive and often satirical portrait of the aristocratic French society that Proust was born into. In its intimate and detailed investigation of social values and customs, Proust's work shares certain characteristics with the nineteenth century realist novel. Indeed, Proust is not conventionally Modernist in terms of using experimental prose techniques, but in its philosophical investigations, massive scope and emphasis on style over dramatic action, his work engages with Modernist aesthetic concerns. Despite its enormous length, Proust's work has influenced writers internationally, serving as a point of departure for Austrian novelist Robert Musil's *The Man without Qualities* [*Der Mann ohne Eigenschaften*] (1921–1942), although unfinished is highly important in comprehending Modernist aesthetics with its unreliable narration and complex moral ambiguities.

Gertrude Stein (1874–1946)

One of the most unusual and experimental Modernist writers, Stein's fiction and poetry not only made her notorious during her lifetime, but anticipated many later developments among postmodern writers. Raised in Pennsylvania, Stein studied with William James at Radcliffe University before moving to Paris with her brother Leo in 1903. The Steins amassed an impressive collection of contemporary art, including works by Matisse, Cézanne and Picasso, and Stein befriended the latter. She also befriended writers such as **Ezra Pound**, Ernest Hemingway and Sherwood Anderson. Stein is perhaps best known for her prose, which, although written in a surprisingly simple language, is characterized by an almost aleatory sense of repetition. Consider her essay 'Composition as Explanation': 'And after that what changes what changes after that, after that what changes and what changes after that and after that and what changes and after that and what changes after that' (1926, 410). Here, Stein reveals that her interest in how repetition with subtle changes focuses attention on language and reveals patterns within it. Her work generally examines language, itself, rather than plot, exposition or character development. In *Tender Buttons* (1914), a series of prose poems, Stein applies her unusual method of description to everyday objects, estranging them from reality in a manner analogous to the techniques of **Cubism**. In *The Making of Americans* (1925), Stein uses repetition in an attempt to represent American history in over 1,000 pages. One notable exception in Stein's *oeuvre* is *The Autobiography of Alice B. Toklas* (1933); although putatively written by Stein's lifelong partner, the book is actually Stein's own autobiography written in the voice of Alice. Although much misunderstood and sometimes maligned by contemporaries, such as in **Wyndham Lewis's** *Time and Western Man*, many critics have seen in Stein's repetition an anticipatory postmodernism since her language reacts to itself, rather than seeking, in any form, to adhere to the world as it exists.

William Carlos Williams (1883–1963)

While he retained close ties to the early English avant-gardes, William Carlos Williams's poetry is marked by a desire to adapt Modernism to a local, American context that retains the spirit of formal invention without relying on dense literary allusion and intellectual difficulty, which characterized works like **Joyce's** *Ulysses* or **T.S. Eliot's** *The Waste Land*. Williams studied medicine at the University of Pennsylvania where he met **Ezra Pound** and Hilda Doolittle. Afterwards, Williams's experience as a local doctor in New

Jersey provided material for his poetry and prose, reflecting his dictum 'No ideas but in things.' Williams also spent extensive amounts of time in New York, meeting with important American avant-garde authors and artists, such as Alfred Steiglitz, Georgia O'Keefe, Jean Toomer, Marriane Moore and Wallace Stevens. His earlier lyrics, written in simple language about material things, retain the imprint of **Imagism**. The most important aesthetic event in Williams's life was the publication of Eliot's *The Waste Land* in 1922, which Williams saw as mired in academicism and pessimism. He responded with *Spring and All* (1923), a reference to the first line of *The Waste Land*, which emphasizes the regenerative powers of the imagination and contains his most famous poem 'The Red Wheelbarrow'. Equally important, however, is his long poem, *Paterson* (1946–1958), which attempts to adapt the epic form to tell the story of the local American town of Paterson, New Jersey.

Virginia Woolf (1882–1941)

One of the most important novelists of the twentieth century, Virginia Woolf was also a significant essayist, making essential contributions to feminist thought and practice. Born Virginia Stephen, the daughter of the famous Victorian biographer, co-editor of the National Dictionary of Biography, Sir Leslie Stephen, Woolf was raised in an eminent and wealthy family with ties to the earlier Clapham Sect, with famous friends like George Eliot and Henry James, and family contacts with the Chamberlain family of Birmingham, and social ones to Winston Churchill. Along with E.M. Forster, John Maynard Keynes, Lytton Strachey, Clive Bell, Roger Fry and Leonard Woolf, she was a member of the coterie of loosely affiliated intellectuals known as the **Bloomsbury Group**. Virginia married Leonard Woolf in 1912, but subsequent critics have speculated that the Woolfs' marriage was not intimate, and Virginia Woolf took on other lovers, often women. Woolf is, perhaps, most famous for using the stream-of-consciousness technique, partially influenced by **Freudian** psychoanalysis, in which a novel or story is narrated as if the reader is inside the consciousness of the protagonist, employed in her three major novels: *Mrs Dalloway* (1925) (see Baxter), *To The Lighthouse* (1927) and *The Waves* (1931). As Malcolm Bradbury and James McFarlane have noted, these 'are novels of pattern rather than plot' in which 'the representation of the flow of a sensitive human mind . . . constitute[s] a total universe' (1976, 408–9). *Orlando* (1928) explores the life of a young Elizabethan man, who metamorphoses into a woman. This plotline, which explores social mores surrounding gender and sexuality, also reflects Woolf's belief in the necessity of androgyny: 'It is fatal to be a man or woman pure and simple; one must be woman-manly or man womanly' (1929, p. 136). While Woolf does argue for writers to aim at androgyny in her seminal feminist work, *A Room*

Figure 4: 51, Gordon Square, the home from 1919 of Lytton Strachey, author of *Eminent Victorians*. © Philip Tew 2008

of One's Own (1929), she also argues powerfully for the need for a more equal relationship between men and women, noting from her own experience that women need the possibility of financial security and personal independence in order to achieve equality. Throughout her life, Woolf was troubled by depression and nervous breakdowns, which tragically culminated in her suicide by drowning in 1941 (For Woolf: see also Baxter, Parsons and Wilson).

William Butler Yeats (1865–1939)

Born a generation before writers like **T.S. Eliot** and **Ezra Pound**, Yeats's poetry was a major influence on Modernism, if not always paradigmatically Modernist, itself. Born in Dublin County, Yeats moved to London in 1887, where he founded the Rhymers Club. His poetry partook of contemporary European aestheticism and symbolism (see Day), employing visionary descriptions of landscape and figures from mythology. Yeats, himself, took a deep interest in mysticism, both Irish and Hindu, and was heavily involved with the Theosophical society and other contemporary hermetic groups. Yeats's reaction to modernity is characteristically negative, and poems, such as the 'Lake Isle of Innisfree,' from his collection *The Rose* (1893), suggest a desire to leave contemporary urban modernity and return to a more spiritual, rural existence. In 1913, Yeats encountered Ezra Pound, who acted as his secretary for the winter, and had several of Yeats's poems published in **Poetry**. Yeats became a signal influence for Pound, Eliot and others, although Yeats's own work still revealed nineteenth century influences, especially in his frequent employment of rhyme, metre and other conventional rules of versification. Like other important authors of his generation, such as **Joseph Conrad**, Ford Maddox Ford and Henrik Ibsen, Yeats's work presages the advent of Modernism, while still retaining ties to Victorian aesthetics. Nonetheless, some of his poetry, such as the famous 'The Second Coming', originally published in *Michael Robartes and the Dancer* (1921), exemplifies the often apocalyptic and negative modes of Modernism, with its famous line, 'the centre cannot hold'(184). Regardless of his own ambiguous relationship with Modernism, Yeats won the Nobel Prize in 1923, and remains the premier Irish poet of the twentieth century (for Yeats: see also Baxter, Paddy, Randall, Thacker and Wilson).

Genres, Movements and Contexts

Bloomsbury Group

Comprised of writers, intellectuals and artists drawn from the professional classes of English society, the Bloomsbury Group or set was one of the most important cultural networks within British Modernism (for Bloomsbury, see also Day, Murray and Paddy) emerging from the regular meetings of a group of friends, notably Virginia Woolf, Vanessa Bell, E.M. Forster and Lytton Strachey, at 46 Gordon Square, Bloomsbury. Unlike other avant-garde movements, such as **Dadaism**, Bloomsbury lacked either a defining philosophy or a coherent radical aesthetic. Its organization was loose, based on social relations and various overlapping projects, rather than a specific collaborative program. Nonetheless, participants shared common interests, particularly the philosophy of Bertrand Russell and in particular G.E. Moore's *Principia Ethica* (1903) which stated that the most valuable things in life were the pleasures of company and the enjoyment of beautiful things. Their political beliefs were generally left-wing and liberal, and although adherence to specific ideologies varied, all the members believed in the necessity of social reform and liberation from restrictive Victorian values. Important members include the novelists **Virginia Woolf** (for Woolf, see also Baxter, Murray, Paddy, Randall and Wilson) and E.M. Forster, the economist John Maynard Keynes (see also Wilson), cultural critics Lytton Strachey and Clive Bell, and such artists as Duncan Grant, Roger Fry and Vanessa Bell. Most of the members of the circle became friends prior to their fame, and the group first attained notoriety due to Roger Fry's controversial **Post-impressionist Exhibition of 1910**. By the 1920s, however, Bloomsbury had become a dominant force in British Culture; most of its members had ascended to the highest ranks of their various fields. Due to the group's involvement in written media and a variety of different art forms, the Bloomsbury perspective influenced aesthetic, political, economic and social discourses. Not all responses to Bloomsbury were positive, however; in particular, **Wyndham Lewis's** satiric novel, *The Apes of God* (1930), presents a blistering portrait of the Bloomsbury Group as wealthy socialites and artistic dilettantes. By the late 1930s and into the Second World War, Bloomsbury's cultural influence waned, partially due to the premature deaths of many of its founders, most notably Virginia Woolf's suicide in March 1941.

Cubism

First developed by Pablo Picasso and George Braques in the first decade of the twentieth century, Cubism derived from their mutual interest in African art and the paintings of Paul Cézanne. Cézanne's late landscape paintings sought to break the image into the play of planes and angles underneath, and cubist works extended this tendency to even more abstract levels. The early works of Picasso and Braques form the basis of what is known as analytic cubism. In analytic cubism, an image from real life is painted from multiple angles, resulting in conflicting perspectives and angular lines that make the painting look as if it is composed of cubes, cylinders, spheres and other geometric features. This inclusion of multiple relative perspectives has induced some critics to see a parallel with **Einstein's Theory of Relativity** (for Einstein see Paddy and Wilson). Synthetic cubism was the second wave of this development, in which elements of collage were introduced. Materials beyond paint (e.g. pieces of cloth, writing) were added to the canvas both to create a flattening of perspective and to introduce a tactile element to the painting. In both cases, however, Cubism rarely moved into pure abstractionism, its forms (although unusual) were still representative of everyday objects or scenes. In this sense, 'Cubist pictures give a metaphorical account ... of what the pursuit of likeness [in painting] now looks like, in a situation where all versions of such a pursuit have proved impossible to sustain' (Clark 1999, p. 221). Like other Modernist ventures, Cubism's experimentalism strove to find new forms of representation since older forms seemed inadequate to modern life, but also self-reflexively drew attention to the painter's mimetic processes. Cubism was one of the most significant avant-gardes of the early twentieth century, and influenced later movements, such as **Vorticism** and **Dada**.

Dada

Dadaism was an avant-garde movement comprised of poetry, prose, visual art and performance that began in Zurich in 1915 at a small bar named the Cabaret Voltaire; its four initial founders were Hugo Ball, Richard Huelsenbeck, Marcel Janco and Tristan Tzara. The meaning of term 'dada' itself, is intentionally obscure, with the phrase mimicking the verbalized nonsense of infants; as Tristan Tzara said in *The Dada Manifesto: 1918* (1918), 'DADA DOES NOT MEAN ANYTHING' (4) Although Dadaists associated with the **Futurists** and **Cubists**, it was a distinct movement derived from left-wing anarchist principles. Dadaism was an intentionally irrational movement that sought to attack conventional logic and bourgeois values, and as Tzara asks rhetorically: 'Do people really think that, by the meticulous subtlety of logic, they have demonstrated the truth and established the accuracy of their opinions?' (9). Though most of its proponents have now been canonized into their respective artistic traditions, they did not see themselves as artists, and Dadaist art traditionally serves not an autotelic (having an end or purpose in itself) function, but rather as a critique of the communal values used in determining what 'art' is. Although irrational, it was still humanist; the Dadaists saw a possible liberation of humanity through smashing the unnecessary restrictions of bourgeois society. Dadaism eventually became international, with Hans Arp and Max Ernst in Cologne, and another group in New York, comprised of Marcel Duchamp, Francis Picabia and Man Ray, although the relation of this latter group to continental Dada is disputed. Several French Dadaists, including Andre Breton, Louis Aragon, Philippe Soupault and Paul Eleuard went on to found **Surrealism**, a related movement that Tzara later joined.

Einstein's Special Theory of Relativity

Einstein's Special Theory of Relativity first appeared in a 1905 paper entitled 'On the Electrodynamics of Moving Bodies,' although he himself did not use the term 'relativity theory' until 1911 (Whitworth 2003, p. 213) (for Einstein see Paddy and Wilson). Nor was Einstein relativity's sole creator; Henri Poincaré also noted the possibility of a principle of relativity in electrodynamics in 1904, although he did not reach Einstein's conclusions. Einstein's theory contradicted Newtonian physics suggesting that both distance and time were based on the viewpoint of the observer, which were both later experimentally confirmed. However, in special relativity, the speed of light is always constant, regardless of the observer's perspective. Einstein's theory undermined principles that had been previously perceived to be fundamental and absolute, and this overturning of perceived certainties resonated with Modernism's interest in time, such as in **Proust's** *Remembrance of Things Past*, **Cubism** and the stream-of-consciousness technique, in which time and reality are mediated by the perspective of an individual consciousness. Many important Modernists were aware of Einstein's theory, including **T.S. Eliot**, **Ezra Pound**, **W.B Yeats** and **Virginia Woolf**.

Futurism

Futurism was born when the Italian poet Filippo Tommas Marinetti published 'The Founding and the Manifesto of Futurism' in the newspaper, *Le Figaro*, in 1909. Marinetti adapted the methods and delivery of radical politics to his aesthetic cause, which was to exalt 'the beauty of speed,' (41) and celebrate the mechanical aspects of industrial culture, since 'a roaring car that seems to ride on grapeshot – is more beautiful than the *Victory of Samothrace*' (41). Aside from the glorification of a machine aesthetic, Futurism also prized aggression and endorsed politically conservative tendencies, for as Marinetti writes: 'We intend to glorify war – the only hygiene of the world – militarism, patriotism, the destructive gesture of emancipators, beautiful ideas worth dying for, and contempt of woman' (4). The Futurists' aestheticization of political language and ideas attracted the attention in 1917 of a former Socialist named Benito Mussolini, who used Marinetti's ideas and aesthetics in formulating his own doctrine of fascism. The fascist inheritance of Futurism continues to be an issue for its critical reception, but, although the movement produced few significant literary works, it was hugely influential at the time, due largely to Marinetti's propagandist tactics and charismatic speaking style. Later movements, including **Vorticism**, **Surrealism** and Situationism, have borrowed elements of Futurism's agit-prop rhetoric (on Futurism see also Day).

Imagism

Often spelled 'Imagisme', this movement was inspired by T.E. Hulme, who wrote the first Imagist-style poems. In 1909, Hulme and F.S. Flint met the American, **Ezra Pound**, who had similar poetic affinities. Ezra Pound, after reading and editing a poem by his ex-fiance, Hilda Doolittle, signed it 'H.D. Imagiste' giving both a name to a movement and a pen-name to Doolittle. Imagism's three central tenets were listed by Pound in an article by Flint, and in marginally modified form published in 'A Retrospect:'

1. Direct treatment of 'the thing', whether subjective or objective.
2. To use absolutely no word that does not contribute to the presentation.
3. As regarding rhythm: to compose in the sequence of the musical phrase, not in sequence of a metronome' ([1954] 1911, 3).

The general emphasis of Imagism, then, was to create a direct line between the world and the word, without relying on artificial Victorian poetic traditions, such as prescribed rhyme and metre. In this sense, the free verse of the French Symbolist poets was an important precursor, although East Asian poetry and the work of European troubadours also played an important role. Imagist verse was spare and direct, free of intellectualization or excessive emotion. Although Imagism was avant-garde in certain ways, it was also neo-classical since it emphasized precision and treatment of the 'thing' over florid language and emotional affect, which the Imagists associated with Romanticism. Internal disputes caused Pound to leave the group and found **Vorticism**, but the Imagists continued producing anthologies under the direction of Amy Lowell. Many important authors took part in the movement, including Pound, Richard Aldington, H.D., **William Carlos Williams**, **James Joyce**, **D.H. Lawrence**, Marriane Moore and Ford Maddox Ford.

Manifestoes

Perhaps the literary genre par excellence of the European avant-garde, the manifesto adapted the rhetorical techniques and revolutionary energy of political propaganda in order to promote new aesthetic principles. Although some critics have accused such manifestoes of a naïve conflation of radical aesthetics with radical politics, they provided an exciting moment in which artists and writers could reflect on their own relation to tradition. Some of the most notable examples of the genre include Filippo Marinetti's *Futurist Manifesto* (1909), **Wyndham Lewis's** *Vorticist Manifesto* (1914), Tristan Tzara's *Dada Manifesto: 1918* (1918) and Andre Breton's *Surrealist Manifesto* (1924). Despite their tendency toward hyperbole and the language of urgency, avant-garde manifestoes typically also display a verbal ingenuity and keen sense of humour.

Modernist Journals

Modernist literary journals, often referred to as 'little magazines', played an important role in the dissemination and creation of the Modernist aesthetic in both England and the continent (see also Thacker on Modernist journals). Much of the literature and art produced by avant-gardists and early Modernists was considered too radical for the mainstream (indeed, it was often intentionally so) and little magazines provided the only outlet for their publication. Often little magazines were created in order to popularize a specific movement, as was the case with *BLAST* and **Vorticism**, and helped bring together a group of like-minded individuals. Important journals of the time included *Poetry Magazine*, which first published T.S. Eliot's 'Love Song of J. Alfred Prufrock,' Dora Marsden's *The New Freewoman* and *The Egoist*, which serialized Joyce's *Portrait of the Artist as a Young Man*, T.S. Eliot's *Criterion*, Ford Maddox Ford's *The English Review*, Alfred Orage's *The New Age*, Wyndham Lewis's *BLAST* and the American journals, *The Dial* and *The Little Review*, among many others. For critics, little magazines have become an important scholarly resource for placing Modernist works within the cultural debates and contexts of their time.

Omega Workshops

The Omega Workshops were a design company created by Roger Fry in 1913, and generally employed painters and visual artists associated with the **Bloomsbury Group**. All pieces produced by the workshop were shown anonymously, indicating their attribution only to the company by the display of an omega. Famously, **Wyndham Lewis** left the company after a dispute with Fry, which lead directly to the foundation of **Vorticism**, and the creation of the publication *BLAST*. While disbanded in 1919, the design employed by the Omega Workshops remained influential for decades.

Post-Impressionist Exhibition of 1910

Organized by Roger Fry, founder of the **Omega Workshops**, the exhibition 'Manet and the Post-impressionists,' opened on 5 November 1910. As the first public viewing in England of paintings by such artists as Picasso, Gauguin, Van Gogh, Matisse and Cézanne, it created an enormous stir in the media and the public imagination. The post-impressionists' work suggested a radical break with traditional modes of visual representation, and the subject matter, which contained hints of eroticism, seemed pornographic and morally degenerate to Victorian sensibilities. The post-impressionists represented a new development in artistic representation, shifting away from depicting the world as it is, towards an aesthetic that privileged unique, individual vision and personal expression. The show deeply affected many British writers and painters, who were influenced by the post-impressionists formal experimentation and emphasis on painterly idiosyncrasy, rather than verisimilitude. Notably, Fry coined the term 'post-impressionist' for this exhibition, and it still remains in critical circulation in terms of art specifically and culture generally today.

Suffragettes

In 1832, women were formally denied the right to vote in England, and, while prior activists attempted to implement universal suffrage, the movement began to build significant force with the founding of several umbrella organizations: the National Society for Women's Suffrage (NSWS) in 1872, the National Union of Women's Suffrage Societies (NUWSS) in 1897 and subsequently the Women's Social and Political Union (WSPU) in 1903. The latter, which employed more radical and militant methods and tactics, became the foundation of the suffragettes since unlike other many women's groups advocated universal suffrage, the suffragettes chose to employ methods of direct action(see also Wilson). Responding to the hunger strikes in prison, the British government responded with the so-called 'Cat and Mouse Act' of 1913 which although theoretically provided for the release of prisoners who were weak from hunger (previously the government had engaged in force-feeding recalcitrant suffragettes), actually enabled the government to acquit itself of any harm done to those jailed. Although full suffrage was achieved in England in 1928, the suffragette movement remains important to any history of Modernism. In the suffragettes' rejection of traditional Victorian roles for women, they engaged in a characteristically Modernist strategy – overturning tradition. Furthermore, such actions remain exceptionally important in the creation of twentieth century feminism.

Surrealism

Emerging from the anti-rationalist elements of **Dadaism** (for **Dada** see Day) Surrealism was officially founded in 1924, with the publication of Andre Breton's *Surrealist Manifesto*. Along with other artists and writers, such as Louis Arragon, Paul Éluard, Philippe Soupault, René Crevel and, later, Salvidor Dali, Surrealism advocated the exploration of the unconscious in art, using techniques such as automatic writing, collaborative drawings and structures based on random chance. While the work of **Sigmund Freud**, especially his analyses of dreams were of importance for the surrealists, their goal was to explore the unconscious artistically, rather than to understand and control it through rational, scientific measures. In the unconscious, the Surrealists detected the possibility of unifying concepts that were diametrically opposed according to the dictates of logic, and, for this reason, Surrealist work often presents itself as wilfully self-contradictory, affronting attempts at rational analysis. Like the Dadaists, the Surrealists were politically motivated, but whereas Dada tended towards anarchic principles, most of the Surrealists were Marxists. Nonetheless, Surrealism's refusal of rational thought also lead them to a rejection of traditional social values. Surrealist paintings often openly depicted erotic themes, along with other content that would have been considered unacceptable for public consumption in the nineteenth century. In order to achieve social change, the Surrealists advocated the concept of perpetual revolution in line with the utopian strain of Marxist politics (for Marx see Paddy). While Surrealism as a cohesive movement disintegrated by the 1940s, its influence can be seen in an enormous amount of later writing and visual art in the twentieth century.

Vorticism

Co-founded by **Wyndham Lewis**, **Ezra Pound**, Henri Gaudier-Brzeska and others, Vorticism was created as an English response to contemporary continental avant-gardes. The movement found its expression in the journal, *BLAST: The Review of the Great English Vortex*, edited by Lewis, which was originally advertised as containing 'Discussion of Cubism, Futurism, Imagisme'; it is these three prior movements that most influenced Vorticism (Kenner 1971, p. 238). With its bright pink cover and bold-faced type, *BLAST 1* (1914) appropriated the propagandist style of **Futurism**, while also importing the jagged geometry and multi-perspectival approach of **Cubism**. Much of the journal was composed of various **manifestoes** written in an aphoristic style that moves between aesthetic criticism, agit-prop and wry humour. The image of the vortex was central to the movement, since a vortex whirls around its edges but remains still at the centre; the Vorticists saw their art as created by this contradictory mixture of rapid movement (emphasized in Futurism) and removed observation (imported from **Cubism** and **Imagism**). In this manner, the Vorticists attempted to adopt the machine aesthetic of the industrial age, while still leaving a space for both the individual observer and artistic tradition. In **Freudian** terms, Vorticism was, in this sense, an overdetermined movement, precipitated by contradictory traditions, but it remains perhaps the only authentic avant-garde of English Modernism. The second and final issue of the journal, *BLAST 2: The War Number* was published in 1915, but the movement faltered with the onset of WWI, and the deaths of important Vorticist fellow-travellers Gaudier-Brzeska and T.E. Hulme. *BLAST* published work by many important authors and artists, including Ford Maddox Ford, Rebecca West, **T.S. Eliot**, Lewis and Pound.

5 Case Studies in Reading 1: Key Primary Literary Texts

Jeannette Baxter

Chapter Overview

Who's Afraid of Reading Modernism?

In the introduction to *Modernism: An Anthology* (2005), Lawrence Rainey foregrounds the dilemma which any first time reader of Modernist literature faces: 'Modernism is preceded by its reputation, or even by several reputations: it is endowed with authority so monumental that a reader is tempted to overlook the very experience of encountering Modernist works' (xix). This chapter is a modest response to the 'dilemma' of reading Modernism. By offering short yet engaged readings of five key Modernist texts – *The Waste Land* (1922), 'Easter 1916' (1921), *Heart of Darkness* (1899), *The Life and Death of Harriett Frean* (1922) and *Mrs Dalloway* (1925) – I hope to demonstrate that it is precisely through close textual encounters that the reader can begin to negotiate his or her way through the various aesthetic and intellectual complexities of literary Modernism.

My first reading is an analysis of the formal and contextual complexities of T.S. Eliot's *The Waste Land*. By placing the issue of 'difficulty' at the forefront of this discussion, I attempt to turn a readerly problem into a critical tool: while it is tempting to dismiss Eliot's overt intellectualism as an elitist Modernist gesture, a more useful way of thinking about the 'difficulty' of *The Waste Land*, I suggest, is to see it less as an obstacle to reading and more as a necessary starting point for interrogating the obscurities and obfuscations of this intimidating poem (for Eliot see also Murray, Paddy, Randall and Stinson). From here, I move on to a discussion of W.B. Yeats's 'Easter 1916'. Yeats is something of a transitional literary figure: although his major work is published contemporaneously with Eliot's, his poetry spans the late Victorian and Early Modern period (for Yeats: see also Paddy, Randall, Stinson, Thacker and Wilson). My reading of 'Easter 1916' foregrounds the personal, poetical and political tensions which arise out of Yeat's ambiguous Modernism. Focussing, in particular, on the linguistic manifestations of Yeats's equivocal nationalist politics in 'Easter 1916', I ask whether we should read this poem as a monument to, or a critique of, one of the most brutal chapters in modern British colonial history? My reading of Joseph Conrad's *Heart of Darkness* shifts the focus from colonial relations at home to imperialist politics abroad (for Conrad see also Murray, Paddy, Randall and Stinson). Specifically, I limit myself to a discussion of the 'racism row' in which the Nigerian novelist Chinua Achebe attacked *Heart of Darkness* as a racist denigration of Africa and its peoples. By introducing Homi Bhabha's postcolonial writings on racial identity and subjectivity into the critical debate, I argue that the linguistic textures of Conrad's Modernist narrative are far more ambivalent and anti-imperialist than Achebe's unflinching diatribe would suggest. The fourth reading in this chapter focuses on May Sinclair' imaginative engagement with Freudian and Jungian psychoanalytical paradigms in *The Life and Death of Harriett Frean*. Another Modernist figure in transition (she was 61 when *Harriett Frean* was published), and the first writer to apply the term 'stream of consciousness' to literature (she coined the phrase in a review of Dorothy Richardson's novel *Pilgrimage*), Sinclair develops a minimalist Modernist aesthetic, I suggest, in order to hold Victorian patriarchal ideology up to interrogation. Finally, I read Virginia Woolf's *Mrs Dalloway* as a psychogeographical exercise in feminist critique (for Woolf, see also Murray, Paddy, Randall Stinson and Wilson). Focussing on Clarissa Dalloway's psychological peregrinations across London, I suggest that Woolf constructs a vertiginous narrative labyrinth in which official, male-authored versions of post-war history and culture are placed on trial.

T.S. Eliot, The Waste Land (1922)

Of all of the works of high Modernism, *The Waste Land* (1922) has acquired the reputation for being the most difficult. Composed of five non-narrative sections ('The Burial of the Dead', 'A Game of Chess', 'The Fire Sermon', 'Death by Water', 'What the Thunder Said') which flaunt a profusion of disparate utterances, dense allusions, obscure mythological references and multi-lingual citations, *The Waste Land* challenges the reader to fashion patterns of meaning out of its radically disorientating forms and diverse intellectual contents. Even Eliot's authorial notations are something of a source of anxiety for the reader, tending to obfuscate rather than elucidate as they deposit yet more enigmatic fragments into the textual body. Given its complex range of aesthetic innovations and its overwhelming encyclopaedism, it is hardly surprising that a culture of anxiety has arisen around the act of reading *The Waste Land*: how is one to tackle this formidable text?

Eliot foregrounds the question of 'difficulty' in 'The Metaphysical Poets' (1921; 1975), a critical essay written one year prior to the publication of *The Waste Land*:

> We can only say that it appears likely that poets in our civilisation, as it exists at present, must be *difficult*. Our civilisation comprehends great variety and complexity, and this variety and complexity, playing upon a refined sensibility, must produce various and complex results. The poet must become more and more comprehensive, more allusive, more indirect, in order to force, to dislocate if necessary, language into his meaning (65).

For Eliot, 'difficulty' is a necessary poetic response to the 'various' and 'complex' historical, cultural and philosophical contexts of the early twentieth century: the devastations of the First World War (1914–1918); the transformation of human subjectivity within an increasingly industrialized world; the post-Darwinian erosion of religious faith; the rewriting of conventional notions of time, space and reality by advancing science and technologies. Writing out of a decimated post-war Western civilization, the modern poet recognizes the need to replace traditional realist models of representation with an avant-garde Modernist poetics that will 'dislocate' language into meaning by an indirect process of association. Poetic reality will no longer be fixed and knowable in Eliot's terms, but allusive, multiple and estranging. For it is only out of 'difficult' texts, texts which disorientate and provoke, that the myriad fragmented realities of the modern world can be reconstructed in ways that might just be intelligible.

With specific reference to 'The Burial of the Dead', this reading will focus on Eliot's allusive poetics. As James Longenbach has pointed out, while the experience of reading *The Waste Land* is enriched by the process of identifying its multiple 'models and sources', it is perhaps more useful to engage with the nature of the poem's collaged allusiveness, for as Longenbach comments it may be necessary 'to ask not only *what is the source?* but *why does Eliot allude? and how do we experience the allusions?'* (176). Following this line of questioning, I want to explore the relationship between Eliot's allusive poetics and his historiographic practices: at the same time that *The Waste Land*'s exploded form speaks to the post-war contexts of its production, I suggest, it also performs Eliot's idiosyncratic vision of the role of the individual poet within literary history. Originally titled, 'He Do the Police in Different Voices' (a reference to Dickens's *Our Mutual Friend* (1864–1865) the polyphonic structure of *The Waste Land* enacts Eliot's 'Doctrine of Impersonality', a model of poetic subjectivity (first outlined in 'Tradition and the Individual Talent' [1919]) in which the modern poet continually surrenders himself to a collective tradition or 'ideal order'. By tracing a range of intertextual echoes in 'The Burial of the Dead', I interrogate the aesthetic, historical and political dimensions of Eliot's 'ideal' order: is the allusive modern poet appealing to a collective and democratic imaginative enterprise which will help to shore up the fragments of modernity against its ruins? Or is he laying down the terms for a system of literary value and authority which is politically and ideologically motivated?

Allusive Histories in 'The Burial of the Dead'

'The Burial of the Dead' is rich in allusions of every kind: literary, cultural, mythological, anthropological and religious. The title of this opening section is taken, for instance, from the burial service in the *Anglican Book of Common Prayer* in which a handful of dust (a recurring image in *The Waste Land*) is thrown onto the coffin of the deceased. This primary allusion introduces a key symbolic sequence into the poem, namely the cycle of life, death and rebirth. As Peter Childs has noted, the titles of the five sections of *The Waste Land* 'revolve around ideas of death, sex and sterility' with 'The Burial of the Dead' section intimating 'a future rebirth' (76). In his preface to *Notes on The Waste Land*, Eliot makes mention of two further intertextual sources that inform the regenerative contexts of his poem: Jessie Weston's study of the Grail legend, *From Ritual to Romance* (1921), and James George Frazer's meditation on myth, magic and religion, *The Golden Bough* (1890). Drawing on Weston's study of the mythology of the Fisher King, Eliot incorporates imagery from ancient vegetation and fertility rites into his modern narrative as a 'way of controlling, or ordering, of giving a shape and significance to the immense panorama of futility and anarchy which is contemporary history' (Eliot 1975, '*Ulysses,* Order and Myth; 177). Specifically, Eliot's allusive 'mythic method' functions in 'The Burial of the Dead' to regenerate the physical and psychological 'dead land' of post-war Europe. While images of growth and renewal counter the War's legacy of death and destruction, the physical force of Eliot's poetic language struggles to create a feeling of momentum. The repetition of present participles such as 'breeding', 'stirring' and 'mixing' work accumulatively, for instance, to convey the sense of a gradual transition from barrenness to fecundity, from death to life, as the spring flowers are encouraged out of the cold and confined earth by the light touch of spring rain.

Although these opening lines work hard to convey a sense of futurity, the reader is nevertheless disquieted by a number of tensions discernible in Eliot's poetic language. Most urgently, his negative description of the renewing activities of spring challenges the reader to stall the reading process momentarily in order to interrogate the inappropriate nature of this epithet: why is April the 'cruellest' month (41)? One possible answer emerges out of Eliot's modification of the textual source of this reference, the General Prologue to *The Canterbury Tales* by Geoffrey Chaucer. Although Eliot alludes to Chaucer's range of fecund images (Aprill/April, shoures/rain, roote/root, flour/lilac), he does so in order to parody them, and to dislocate, in turn, the medieval poet's vision of universal fertility into an unflinching account of the material and psychological complexities of the modern post-war condition. The 'cruelty' of Eliot's spring awakening can be read, therefore, as a complex metaphor for the pain of rehabilitation and the trauma of historical witnessing. At the same time that Eliot's poetic monument recognizes the need to remember the dead of the First World War, it is also alive to the survivor's complex desire to forget. Note how the alliterative weight of adjectives such as 'dead', 'dull' and 'dried' threaten to pull the emerging natural world back under the 'warm' cover of 'forgetful snow' (41).

As Eliot's allusive practices demonstrate, the dead not only haunt *The Waste Land* on a historical level, but they also haunt it aesthetically. Eliot develops this theory of poetic return in 'Tradition and the Individual Talent': 'No poet, no artist of any art, has his complete meaning alone [. . .] His significance, his appreciation is the appreciation of his relation to the dead poets' (38). According to Eliot in 'Tradition and the Individual Talent', poetic individuality is not to be found in works of art that strive to isolate or differentiate themselves from what has gone before, but in works of art in which the voices of their literary ancestors 'assert their immortality most vigorously' (38). The densely allusive style of *The Waste Land* enacts this critical doctrine as intertextual echoes proliferate throughout the poem in order to resurrect, and make audible, a past tradition of dead poets for a modern audience. As Goldman has pointed out, however, Eliot's reinvention of himself as a spokesperson for the dead advances a paradoxical model of poetic subjectivity: while the modern poet subordinates individuality to the power of the literary collective, the poet is, in a sense, 'reaffirmed by this cycle of extinction and resurrection' (98).

Under the guise of self-sacrifice, Eliot actually insinuates himself into a literary tradition which preserves and protects him:

> what happens when a new work of art is created is something that happens simultaneously to all works of art that preceded it. The existing monuments form an ideal order among themselves, which is modified by the introduction of the new (really new) work of art among them (38).

As Goldman, indicates the nature of Eliot's 'ideal order' has been the focus of much critical analysis (92–7). Resisting the temptation to associate Eliot with the 'defence of a traditional canon', Louis Menand interprets Eliot's 'ideal order' in philosophical rather than prescriptive terms: 'Our perception of the new work of art depends on our perception of the history of art, which takes a certain shape – is 'idealised' in our minds' (Goldman 93). Terry Eagleton, in contrast, rejects the possibility that the poet's 'ideal order' can be read in ahistorical terms precisely because its 'radical historical relativism' is 'endowed with the status of classic authority' (147). Eagleton is referring, of course, to the *kind* of company that Eliot keeps in *The Waste Land*: Homer, Ovid, Shakespeare, Milton, Baudelaire and Chaucer are just a few of the dead poets whom Eliot revives and reorganizes within his poetic monument. Eliot's 'ideal order' calls for the preservation of a particular kind of literary order, then, namely a Western European literary tradition which, far from being abstract and democratic (it is almost exclusively male) perpetuates an already established system of cultural value and authority.

Eagleton is correct, I think, to stress the political and ideological dimensions of *The Waste Land*. The interjection of a Lithuanian voice in 'The Burial of the Dead' – 'Bin gar keine Russin, stamm' aus Litauen, echt deutsch' [line 12] (41) – foregrounds the extent to which Eliot's poem is alive to, and nervous of, the cultural and geo-political mutations of post-war Europe. Notably, the adjective, 'echt', not only translates into English as 'real', but it also translates as 'pure'. Marie's defence of her pedigree (she is the illegitimate daughter of Ludwig Wilhelm, the heir to the throne of Bavaria) introduces the reader to complex narratives of national belonging, political displacement and, most urgently, racial difference. Indeed, her self-conscious assertion of racial purity can be read, in this context, as an implicit declaration of what she is *not*, namely a Russian Jew. Given the rising tide of fascism across 1920s Europe and Eliot's own anti-Semitic sympathies, this multivalent epithet is conspicuous and ideologically resonant in its various manifestations across *The Waste Land*. It surfaces again, for instance, towards the end of 'The Burial of the Dead' when Eliot describes post-war London as impure or 'Unreal' (42). Alluding to Charles Baudelaire's poem, 'The Seven Old Men' (1859), which describes a series of urban encounters with grotesque, self-replicating apparitions that resemble a three-legged 'jew,' *The Waste Land* enacts a narrative of political prejudice and paranoia: the wandering, cosmopolitan Jew haunts Eliot's poem as an impure intertextual presence, as an external threat to the integrity, homogeneity and purity of the 'ideal order' of Europe.

While Eliot's allusive practices work hard to preserve what he describes in 'Tradition and the Individual Talent' as 'the mind of Europe' (39) from *outsider* threats, they also function to protect it from adulterating forces from *within*, such as the supplanting of high literary culture by a newly emerging 'mass' or 'popular' culture, the erosion of religion by commercialism, the denigration of poetry to advertising, and the intellectual and political mobility of women and the working classes (Childs 63). Once again, in *The Waste Land* Eliot figures the threat of internal corruption in terms of 'impurity':

> Unreal City
> A crowd flowed over London Bridge, so many,
> I had not thought death had done so many (42–3)

Imbricating an allusion to Baudelaire's city of nightmarish encounters with a reference to Dante's Hell (the lines 'so many [. . .] so many appear' (43) are taken from *Inferno III*, lines 55–7), the modern poet re-imagines London as a place of material and cultural desolation. Note how Eliot employs the poetic device of assonance ('crowd flowed over' [43]) in order to articulate the undifferentiated nature of the urban collective. His use of anaphora ('so many, so many'), meanwhile, not only articulates the sheer physical scale of the Modernist city, but it also evokes the regimented, alienated and moribund psychology of urban life. Shuffling to the rhythm of the consumer-capitalist machine (the 'City' also refers to the financial district of London where Eliot worked as an underwriter for Lloyds bank from 1917 to 1925), these spectres of modernity are motivated by the promise of financial rather than cultural prosperity. The collective death which the observer alludes to is not merely physical, but emotional, spiritual and intellectual.

The allusive textures of *The Waste Land* boast a double-impulse: at the same time that they seek to replenish the vacuous nature of modern culture through intertextual dialogue, they simultaneously work to safeguard the cultural richness of the past against the cold intellectualism of the present. This paradoxical aspect of Eliot's avant-garde poetics opens up another way of thinking about the 'difficulty' of *The Waste Land*. As Eagleton has argued, the poem's obscurity is a crucial part of its meaning; its intellectual and ideological elitism maintains Eliot's 'ideal order' while it also prevents any threat to the 'closed, coherent, authoritative discourse of the mythologies that frame it' (150). The formal and intellectual complexities of *The Waste Land* operate as

Figure 5: Plaque marking the entrance in Thornhaugh Street to the offices of Faber and Faber and commemorating T.S. Eliot. © Philip Tew 2008

strategies of self-preservation for the paranoid modern poet. Writing himself into the 'ideal order' of the Western European literary tradition by means of a dense and overtly 'difficult' allusive poetic practice, Eliot succeeds in dislocating 'language into *his* meaning'.

W.B. Yeats, 'Easter 1916' (1921)

'Easter 1916' is a poetic response to one of the most violent chapters in modern Irish political history. On Easter Monday, 1916, a group of Irish nationalists launched a rebellion against British Imperialist rule by seizing a number of key Government locations in Dublin. A week of fierce clashes between the Irish dissidents and the British military ensued until the outnumbered rebels were eventually forced into submission. In his statement of surrender, the leader of the insurrectionists, Patrick Pearse, proclaimed that it would be in death, rather than in life, that the Irish revolutionaries would achieve a moral and political victory. His words were realized when he and 15 other fellow dissidents were court-martialled and executed in particularly brutal circumstances. One of the rebels, James Connolly, was so badly injured from the fighting that he could not stand before the firing squad – he was executed in a chair. As George Bernard Shaw later wrote in *John Bull's Other Island* (a play written at Yeat's request), 'Those who were executed accordingly became not only national heroes, but the martyrs whose blood was the seed of the Irish Free State. Nothing more blindly savage, stupid and terror-mad could have been devised by England's worst enemy' (Shaw, Preface).

Although 'Easter 1916' was written in the immediate aftermath of the failed rebellion, the poem was first published five years later in *Michael Robartes and the Dancer* (1921). This volume of poetry marks something of a formal and contextual shift in Yeats's creative output. While earlier works such as *The Rose* (1893) and *The Wild Swans at Coole* (1919) are characterized by a self-conscious Romantic lyricism which draws on dreams, folklore and Celtic mythology, the later, post-war writings engage with the precarious political and historical realities of modern Ireland in a poetic style which is at once more simple and accessible. As Childs has pointed out, however, the transformation of 'Yeats's 'the last Romantic' into 'Yeats the Modernist, nationalist and postcolonial poet' (83) is a process fraught with personal, poetical and political tensions. Oscillating between his two poetical personas, Michael Robartes (Yeat's private self – the occultist, mystic and idealist) and Owen Aherne (Yeats's public self – the political campaigner and activist), Yeats was also situated between historical and political extremes: he was as Childs explains simultaneously 'an Irish nationalist, an anti-communist, an anti-democratic aristocrat [. . .] member of the British Empire, a resident of southern England as much as Ireland' (84, 94). I want to examine 'Easter 1916' in the light of Yeats's political ambiguity. How should we read the dominant poetic 'I' in this poem? Is this a poetic strategy for political identification or political differentiation? And to what extent is 'Easter 1916' a commemoration or critique of the Irish nationalist project?

'A Terrible Beauty is Born': The Violence of Sacrifice

One of the most conspicuous features of 'Easter 1916' is the absence of any kind of account of the Rising itself. This can be explained, perhaps, by the fact that Yeats learned of the insurgency while in England, a country where he had lived and worked for most of his life. An architect of the Irish Literary Revival and founder of the Irish Literary Society (1891) and the Gaelic League (1893), Yeats had perhaps done more than any other literary figure to advance the cause of Irish nationalism. Following the horrific events of the Rising, in which her own husband (Major John MacBride) was executed, Maud Gonne makes explicit the link between Yeats's poetry and Ireland's politics, when she writes: 'Without Yeats there would have been no Literary Revival in Ireland. Without the inspiration of that Revival and the glorification of beauty and heroic virtue, I doubt there would have been an Easter Week' (27). At the same time that Yeats was instrumental in shaping the literary, philosophical and political landscapes of modern Ireland, however, he was, as Kiberd has pointed out, one of the first 'decolonising intellectuals to formulate a vision of their native country during a youthful sojourn in an imperial capital' (100). Yeats's role in reviving and rewriting colonial Irish culture and politics had, in other words, been played out at something of a distance.

Yeats's physical and political detachment from the events of the nationalist insurrection manifests itself in the ambivalent poetic 'I' which dominates 'Easter 1916'. At first glance, this substantial poetic self appears to speak to the Romantic heritage of a unified and transcendental poetic consciousness which allows the absent artist to speak on behalf of, and bear witness to, what Yeats later describes in a letter as his murdered 'friends and fellow workers' (1954, 614). As Rothenstein points out, however, Yeats's feelings of guilt and 'discomfort at being safe in England while his friends were risking their lives in Dublin' were also tinged with narcissistic envy; the poet also 'fretted somewhat that he had not been consulted, had been left in ignorance of what was afoot' (47). At the same time that the absent poet acknowledges a responsibility to commemorate the Irish nationalists and thus secure a place for them in literary and cultural history, he also writes himself into this re-imagined historical snapshot in order to reassert his own significance in the evolution of modern Ireland. What is even more striking about Yeats's revisionist manoeuvre is that the modern poet inscribes himself into 'Easter 1916' only to differentiate and distance himself once more from its political focus.

We see repeated evidence of this in the first two stanzas of Yeats's poem when the poetic subject draws on a variety of personal pronouns – 'they', 'them', 'this' and 'that' – in order to describe the Irish patriots whom he encounters on the streets of Dublin. That the poet and the nationalists meet each other at 'close of day' (176) is suggestive of the imminent and irrevocable political change which is about to befall Ireland. Standing out against the 'grey' stone of aristocratic 'Eighteenth-century houses', the rebels' 'vivid faces' radiate dissident energy and idealism (176). Yet, theirs is a political fervour which the aristocratic poet firstly admits indifference to – he exchanges 'polite' yet 'meaningless' words – and later mockery of, when he imagines how he might recall the details of these ostensibly idle political discussions in the refined atmosphere of the gentleman's 'club'.

As John Lucas has noted (120), Yeat's ambivalence towards the events of 1916 is also discernible in the structure and rhyming pattern of the poem. The regular, almost plodding rhythm which emerges outs of Yeats's predominant use of iambic tetrameter (a line consisting of four iambic feet) and iambic trimeter (a line consisting of three iambic feet) 'implies the trivia of a Dublin existence where all are thought to wear 'motley' (176). Only this is a nostalgic perception of a pre-revolutionary Ireland, a place of 'casual comedy' which is ruptured violently in the poem's powerful refrain:

All changed, changed utterly:
A terrible beauty is born (176)

Through the inappropriate marriage of the adjective 'terrible' with the abstract noun 'beauty', Yeats creates a new poetic rhythm and a new poetic reality in order to articulate the new political reality of modern Ireland. And as the poet's conspicuous use of the present tense 'is' suggests, this new political reality of violence, death and dissolution is one into which the Irish nation will be repeatedly reborn.

Yeats proceeds to construct a critique of the Easter Rising in the third stanza by setting up a series of oppositional tensions between metaphors of change and metaphors of stasis. The nationalists' unflinching commitment to advancing the political cause of Ireland is compared, for instance, to 'a stone', a lifeless and permanent object, whose stagnant presence in the natural land-scape disturbs the flow of the 'living stream' (177). In order to accentuate the unchanging nature of Irish nationalism, the poet draws on a selection of rhyming verbs of action – 'range', 'change', slide', 'plash', 'dive', 'call', 'live' – in order to create a landscape of dynamic activity and natural continuity. Furthermore, the repetition of lines with slight variation, such as 'Minute by minute they change [. . .] Changes minute by minute' (177), not only have an accumulative and energising effect, but they also foreground a tragic irony: in a world of constant flux, the Irish dissidents are as entrenched within their political and ideological objectives as the 'stone' which is embedded in the 'midst of it all' (177); and, as a consequence of their unyielding political intent, the young rebels have been thrust into a state of ultimate stasis – death.

As Cullingford notes in her study of Yeats's politics, Yeats 'distinguished carefully between martyrdom and victimage: the former not sought but accepted, the latter deliberately courted' (99). With 1916, she continues, 'something new and terrible had come in Ireland, the mood of the mystic victim', and although the responsible modern poet could not 'cease to praise the heroes' contribution to Irish freedom' out of a public and poetic duty, in 'Modern Ireland' cited in Cullingford he nevertheless questioned the ethic of sacrifice: 'It is not wholesome for a people to think much of exceptional acts of faith or sacrifice, least of all to make them the sole test of [a] man's worth' (100). Yeats introduces a tenor of scepticism into the final stanza of 'Easter 1916' when he dares to ask, among other things: 'Was it needless death after all?' (178) While gesturing to the historical possibility that England may have kept 'faith' and established Home Rule in Ireland after the end of World War I (Home Rule was eventually established in 1922), this rhetorical question also works to undermine the burgeoning post-revolutionary belief in Ireland that political progress could only be achieved through violence and bloodshed. Even though Yeats goes on, then, to inscribe the names of some of the rebels (Thomas McDonagh, Major John MacBride, James Connolly and Patrick Pearse) directly into his poem, reflecting in 'Easter 1916' this active process of (re)writing – 'I write it out in a verse' – (178) should not be read as a straightforward move towards memorialization. More ambiguous than that, Yeats's final gesture of poetic subjectivity creates a space in which the living poet can once again distance himself politically and poetically from the dead.

Joseph Conrad, Heart of Darkness (1899/1902)

> Joseph Conrad was a thoroughgoing racist . . . [*Heart of Darkness*] parades in the most vulgar fashion prejudices and insults from which a section of mankind has suffered untold agonies and atrocities in the past and continues to do so in many ways and many places today. I am talking about a story in which the very humanity of black people is called into question.
>
> Chinua Achebe (257–59)

Is *Heart of Darkness* a racist text? In 'An Image of Africa: Racism in Conrad's *Heart of Darkness*', Chinua Achebe launches an unflinching attack on the Eurocentricity of Conrad's novel, arguing that the author 'set Africa up as a foil to Europe, as a place of negations at once remote and vaguely familiar, in comparison with which Europe's own state of spiritual grace will be manifest'. *Heart of Darkness*, he continues, 'projects the image of Africa as "other world," the antithesis of Europe and therefore civilisation, a place where man's vaunted intelligence and refinement are finally mocked by triumphant bestiality' (251–52). While Achebe's indictment of *Heart of Darkness* is grounded partly in Conrad's reduction of 'Africa' to a vague and metaphorical setting (Africa is never identified in the narrative, but merely encoded as a new phrase, 'heart of darkness'), the decisive point at issue for the Nigerian critic is Conrad's seemingly relentless 'dehumanisation of Africa and Africans': how can a novel that diminishes an entire continent and its peoples to a 'metaphysical battleground devoid of all recognisable humanity' be called 'a great work of art'? (257).

As Kimborough indicates Achebe's accusatory remarks have influenced the trajectory of *Heart of Darkness* criticism significantly over the last three decades (ix). By focussing on a number of Achebe's key arguments, I suggest that his monochromatic response to the complex linguistic textures of *Heart of Darkness* fails to account for its equivocal representation of colonial subjectivity. Although my short reading contributes to a critical tradition which, since Achebe's diatribe, has striven to defend *Heart of Darkness* as an anti-imperialist critique (see, for instance, Cedric Watts's argument that Conrad's racist language is historically contingent), it sets out to advance this debate by drawing upon postcolonial theories of identity, subjectivity and language. Specifically, I explore Homi Bhabha's writings on the function of 'ambivalence', 'mimicry' and 'stereotype' within colonial discourse, and I suggest that the 'racist' textures of *Heart of Darkness* actually stage numerous ambiguous representations of racial otherness in order to challenge the limits of colonial authority and authenticity.

'The Horror, the Horror': Ambivalence in *Heart of Darkness*

Achebe begins his reading of *Heart of Darkness* by critiquing the stylistic aspects of Conrad's writing. Specifically, he suggests that the 'adjectival insistence upon inexpressible and incomprehensible mystery' (which F.R. Leavis discerned so early on in Conrad's work) should be seen less as a 'stylistic flaw' and more as a politically motivated narrative strategy. Conrad's tendency to incorporate a large number of adjectives into descriptions of the African landscape may pretend towards 'stylistic felicity', he suggests, but in reality, it is 'engaged in inducing hypnotic stupor in his readers through a bombardment of emotive words'. Achebe cites as an example of the author's 'underhand activity' (253) the following passage from Conrad:

> The earth seemed unearthly. We are accustomed to look upon the shackled form of a conquered monster, but there – there you could look at a thing monstrous and free. It was unearthly and the men were . . . No they were not inhuman. Well, you know that was the worst of it – this suspicion of their not being inhuman. It would come slowly to one. They howled and leaped and spun and made horrid faces, but what thrilled you was just the thought of their humanity – like yours – the thought of your remote kinship with this wild and passionate uproar. Ugly (37–8)

According to Achebe, Conrad's excessive use of repeating adjectives, such as 'unearthly', 'monstrous' and 'inhuman', functions as an insidious form of psychological imperialism. Colonial power relations which reduce complex interrelations between Europe and Africa to simple binary oppositions – European/African, humanity/inhumanity, coloniser/colonised, civilised/uncivilised – are embedded in Conrad's dense epithetical style, as Achebe insists, in order to perpetuate 'comforting myths' (253) of racial alterity and superiority in the Western reader.

Significantly, Achebe's reading of Conrad's artistic 'bad faith' does not even attempt to account for the ambiguity of the European visitor's response to his surroundings and its people. In a fleeting yet crucial moment of ontological blurring, for instance, according to Achebe Marlow is simultaneously 'thrilled' and threatened by the realization that he might just share a common humanity with the African people. While he is correct to suggest that it is not 'the differentness that worries Conrad but the lurking hint of kinship, of common ancestry' (252), Achebe fails, rather frustratingly, to develop the implications of his analysis beyond merely accusing Conrad of harbouring a fear of undifferentiation. How might we open this reading up? One possible line of enquiry is suggested by Homi Bhabha's theory of 'ambivalence' which posits that the relationship between the colonizer and the colonized is characterized by a complex mixture of attraction and repulsion. Never standing in simple or complete opposition to each other, the colonial subject and the colonized object are locked in a relationship of ambivalence. The colonial object or figure of 'otherness' which is at once an object of desire and derision', Bhabha suggests, is an 'articulation of difference contained within the fantasy of origin and identity' (67). In Conrad's narrative, 'ambivalence' manifests itself linguistically in the epithet 'Ugly', a conspicuously tight and collapsed linguistic space (for Conrad) which is occupied by the colonizers and the colonized simultaneously. The ideological resonance of the adjective, 'Ugly', should not, as Achebe suggests, be dismissed simply as yet another unequivocal instance of Conrad's racism. Rather, this ambivalent epithet functions precisely to disrupt prevailing assumptions about the ostensibly unambiguous nature of colonial domination and to question, in turn, what Bhabha calls the 'dogmatic and moralistic positions on the meaning of oppression and discrimination' (67).

Heart of Darkness, it seems to me, is replete with moments of ambivalence. Consider the following passage from *Heart of Darkness*:

> And between whiles I had to look after the savage who was fireman. He was an improved specimen; he could fire up a vertical boiler. He was there below me and, upon my word, to look at him was as edifying as seeing a dog in a parody of breeches and a feather hat walking on his hind legs. A few months of training had done for that really fine chap (38).

In 'The Colonialistic Bias of *Heart of Darkness*', Frances B. Singh stages an initial defence of Conrad's novel by alerting the reader to its ironic treatment of the ideology of colonialism. Focussing on the tone of Marlow's articulations (he refers to colonialism as a 'noble cause' and to the colonizers as 'jolly pioneers of progress'), Singh suggests that Marlow's characterization of the fireman as an 'improved specimen' works ironically to emphasize the 'immorality' of intention behind the European civilizing mission (269). While I agree with Singh, it is important to note that it is not only the tone of

Marlow's observations which is ironic. According to Bhabha's theory of 'mimicry', a process of colonial mimesis in which the colonized object is encouraged to assimilate the habits and values of colonial discourse, mimicry always represents in Bhabhais terms 'an ironic compromise' (86). He says that the colonized object, in other words, is a flawed copy of his colonial master, '*a subject of a difference that is almost the same, but not quite*' [Emphasis in original] (86). And it is within this flawed mimetic space that the potential for mockery or ironic imitation exists because according to Bhabha the 'conceptuality of colonial man as an object of regulatory power, as the subject of racial, cultural, national representation' (90) is held up to critique.

Interestingly, Marlow's response to the threat which the 'improved specimen [. . .] full of improving knowledge' poses is to shut down any potential for mockery by lapsing into stereotype. Drawing on an arrested and fixed form of representation, the civilized European recasts the savage in bestial terms. Although Achebe is correct to suggest that stereotype functions in this instance to put the colonized object back 'in his place' (Marlow is literally and figuratively looking down on the fireman), Conrad's use of stereotypical discourse is more ambivalent than he gives it credit for. As Bhabha argues, stereotype is a 'form of knowledge and identification that vacillates between what is always "in place", already known, and something that must be anxiously repeated' (66). This notion of anxious repetition is important in moving an analysis of the functions of stereotypes in *Heart of Darkness* beyond flat accusations of racism. For Conrad, according to Bhabha, stereotyping is not simply 'the setting up of a false image which becomes the scapegoat of discriminatory practices'. Rather it is a much more ambivalent strategy of projection and displacement which gestures self-consciously to the crisis at the heart of colonial subjectivity (81).

One finds further evidence of the ambivalent expression, and dynamic function, of stereotypes towards the end of *Heart of Darkness* when Conrad describes Kurtz's African mistress:

> She was savage and superb [. . .] She stood looking at us without a stir and like the wilderness itself, with an air of brooding over an inscrutable purpose (60).

Conrad's alliterative description of the 'savage and superb' African woman not only complicates strict dualistic notions of racial identity, but it also gestures to the simultaneous processes Bhabha describes of fear and fetishization at work in colonial stereotyping: 'the fetish or stereotype gives access to an identity which is predicated as much on [. . .] pleasure as it is on anxiety' (75). Achebe is a little hasty, therefore, in dismissing Conrad's 'considerably detailed' yet 'predictable' representation of the African woman as a structural component of the narrative, that for Conrad she represents according to Achebe 'a savage counterpart to the refined, European woman who will step forth to end the story' (255). Achebe's statement not only disregards the ambivalent textures of Conrad's stereotypical discourse – as Sarvan says the 'Amazon' is a 'gorgeous, proud, superb, magnificent, tragic, [and] fierce' (284) presence who threatens and transfixes the male European observers by returning their collective gaze – but it also grossly overestimates the individual agency of Kurtz's 'Intended'. Unlike her African 'counterpart', the European woman may speak at the end of the novel, yet her access to language does not accelerate her towards any semblance of power or knowledge. Indeed, having been denied a voice for so long – the Intended says toward the end of *Heart of Darkness* 'I have had no one – no-one-to-to · . . . I-I-have mourned . . . in silence-in silence' (74–5), and her voice is immediately silenced once more by Marlow's lie. Eurocentricity may be reasserted at the end of the *Heart of Darkness*, then, but it is not, as Achebe would have it, reasserted unambiguously. If Kurtz's 'Intended' is to be read as a symbolic representation of imperialist Europe, then her disempowered presence, coupled with her conspicuously anaemic complexion (she is deathly 'pale), gestures suggestively to the possibility that the imperialist centre is in crisis and just might not hold.

May Sinclair, The Life and Death of Harriett Frean (1922)

'At the present moment there is a reaction against all hushing up and stamping down. The younger generation is in revolt against even such a comparatively mild form of repression as Victorian Puritanism. And the New Psychology is with it. . . . Repression has had its chance in all conscience [. . .] You cannot attempt the destruction of the indestructible without some sinister results'. May Sinclair, review of Karl Jung's *Psychology of the Unconscious*, 1916 (qtd. Raitt, 2000, 254–55).

The Life and Death of Harriett Frean (1922) reads like a psychoanalytical case study of Victorian repression according to Suzanne Raitt (251). Set in the second half of the nineteenth century, it charts the stunted social and psychosexual growth of the eponymous Harriett, an only child and model daughter, who is instructed from an early age in the moral virtues of stoicism and self-sacrifice. Reviews of *Harriett Frean* were largely favourable and they focussed, for the most part, on Sinclair's fictional experimentation with certain elements of the 'New Psychology' (Sinclair became involved with the Medico-Psychological Clinic, the first clinic in Britain to practice psychoanalysis, in 1913). Writing in *Dial*, Raymond Mortimer responded to Sinclair's unflinching representation of arrested female development when he described the novel as 'a study of the psycho-pathology of Peter Pan'

(Mortimer quoted in Raitt 242). T.S. Eliot also placed importance on Sinclair's disquieting exploration of the human psyche, characterizing *Harriett Frean* as an examination of 'the soul of man under psychoanalysis' (Eliot qtd. in Raitt 246). This reading also foregrounds the psychoanalytical dimensions of *Harriett Frean*. In particular, I explore the ways in which Sinclair appropriates and modifies psychoanalytical theories of repression, sublimation, condensation and displacement in order to place strict Victorian paradigms of identity, sexuality and the family on trial. As Raitt has suggested, however, *Harriett Frean* cannot 'unproblematically' be labelled a work of Modernist literature (10). Formally and contextually, the novel stages a 'transition out of Victorianism into modernity' which is marked by nostalgia and ambivalence. At the same time that the novel enacts a critique of Victorian patriarchal values and attitudes, it also explores the 'sinister results' of one woman's submission to this repressive ideology.

'Pussycat, Pussycat': Repetition and Repression

On one level, *The Life and Death of Harriett Frean* explores what it is like to *not* be a part of history. This sense of ahistoricity is established in the opening scene of the novel when Harriett's parents perform their nightly recital of the same nursery rhyme – 'Pussycat, Pussycat, where have you been?' – before their dutiful daughter plays her part by asking 'the same question': 'Mamma, *did* Pussycat see the Queen?' [Emphasis in original] (6.). While the circular form of the nursery rhyme foregrounds the Freans' empty and repetitive mode of familial discourse, its story of a missed opportunity (the cat only ends up seeing the mouse rather than the Queen) foreshadows the trajectory of Harriett's uneventful life. Indeed, the suggestion that Harriett will not need, or even desire, to experience any aspect of life beyond the parameters of her familial and domestic identities is reinforced in the suggestively erotic encounter that takes place between father and daughter in the nursery. Following their ritualistic 'kiss-me-awake kiss' – a moment of physical arousal which is also 'their secret' – father and daughter partake in another form of role play: 'Papa was the Pussycat and she was the little mouse in her hole under the bedclothes' (7). As the patriarchal father insinuates himself into the dominant role of playful aggressor to his passive daughter, the Queen, the symbol of an active and public female history, is conspicuously absent; there is no room, it would appear, for female agency or autonomy in this disquieting oedipal drama.

Although the early years of Harriett's childhood are largely defined by passivity and acquiescence (she gives up her favourite doll to Connie Hancock; she misses out on the 'school-treat' out of fear of being seen to be greedy), Sinclair does weave moments of ambivalence and resistance into the young girl's narrative by employing the technique of free indirect discourse. On one occasion, for instance, Harriett questions the beauty and the omniscience of 'God and Jesus' only to revel in her mother's rebuke. She thinks to herself: 'Saying things like that made you feel good and at the same time naughty, which was more exciting than one or the other' (17). Openly defying her mother's instructions to not venture along 'Black's Lane,' Harriett then steps beyond the protective parameters of the 'orchard' garden in search of red campion. With its 'waste ground covered with old boots' and 'a little dirty brown house' about which the narrative specifies there was 'something queer [and] frightening' (18), 'Black's Lane' is what Raitt describes as the novel's 'version of a waste land', a 'modernist dystopia' (247) of sexual transgression (symbolized in the red, phallic blooms) and concealed knowledge (the narrative hints at an incident of paedophilia) which Harriett seeks to penetrate. In the novel the resultant conversation between the young girl and her father is informative and formative:

'Why did you do it, Hatty?'
  'Because – I wanted to see what it would feel like.'
  'You mustn't do it again. Do you hear, you mustn't do it?'
  'Why?'
  'Why? Because it makes your mother unhappy. That's enough why.'
  But there was something more. Mamma had been frightened. Something to do with the frightening man in the lane.
  'Why does it make her?'
  She knew; she knew; but she wanted to see what he would say . . .
  'Isn't there to be a punishment?'
  'No. People are punished to make them remember. We want you to forget.' His arm tightened, drawing her closer. And the kind, secret voice went on. 'Forget ugly things. Understand, Hatty, nothing is forbidden. We don't forbid, because we trust you to do what we wish. To behave beautifully . . .' (21–3)

Once more, repetition functions within Hilton Frean's patriarchal discourse as a means of deflecting any form of autonomous response. Harriett's spirited provocations are subsequently met with a series of stock imperatives which are designed to not only repress the unpalatable truths about Black's Lane, but also silence her into unquestioning acceptance.

    It is in Hilton Frean's move to aestheticise moral duty by 'asking' Harriett to 'behave beautifully', however, that the master-stroke of psychological manipulation and, indeed, punishment is dealt. The controlling he father's body-language, tone of voice (he uses his 'secret' voice) and the reiteration of the collective pronoun 'we' work insidiously to draw the daughter into the familial mindset. Hilton Frean's claim to liberalism (he eschews physical punishment) is, in effect, a disingenuous strategy for asserting a form of moral imperialism that shuts down any hint of ambivalence or resistance. In Sinclair's narrative very explicitly Harriett's internal response, therefore, is her parents' desired response: 'She would always have to do what they wanted; the unhappiness of not doing it was more than she could bear' (21). From this moment on, Harriett not only ceases to contest her family's repressive ideology, but, practising a false form of sublimation, she willingly submits to her parents' desires and thus internalizes their misplaced sense of moral superiority at the expense of her own progression towards an individuated self.

According to Jean Radford's 'Introduction' to the 1980 edition, *Harriett Frean* should be read as 'a vigorous indictment of a form of the family whose only issue is waste – a tumour, a dead baby' (NPag). Referring to the cancerous tumour which the infantilized Harriett (another kind of 'dead baby') inherits from her mother, Radford is correct to stress the abundance of aborted or unfulfilled relationships that litter the narrative landscape: Harriet's narcissistic renunciation of Prissie's fiancé, Robin (which engenders Prissie's subsequent neurosis and Robin's desperate unhappiness); her self-righteous attitude to Maggie's illegitimate pregnancy (this leads, of course, to the death of another 'dead baby'); her limited intellectual relationship with her father (she only takes an interest in the books which he reads: 'Darwin, and Huxley, and Herbert Spencer'); her obsessive yet empty identification with her mother, to name just a few (for Darwin see Paddy and Wilson). One way in which Sinclair develops her critique of Harriett's wasteful existence is in the representation of narrative time. In a letter to Sinclair Lewis, May Sinclair describes her novel as 'an experiment in compression. A story of a long life told in the shortest space possible' (qtd. in Raitt 244). Note how in Sinclair's narrative Harriett ages 7 years in only three sentences: 'Fifty-five. Sixty. In her sixty-second year Harriett had her first bad illness' (140). Practising a laconic form of writing, Sinclair's description of Harriett's advancing years is so concentrated that it almost reads like an imagist poem. Indeed, as Raitt argues, Sinclair saw imagism as 'the aesthetic correlative to psychoanalysis': imagist techniques of compression presented Sinclair with an appropriate 'minimalist aesthetic' for what Raitt regards as the kind of 'psychoanalytical re-mappings of culture and consciousness' (195) which Sinclair's fiction attempted.

This is most powerfully expressed towards the end of the novel when, preparing to go under anaesthetic for an operation for cancer, Harriett fears the return of the repressed:

Only one thing worried her. Something Connie had told her. Under the anaesthetic you said things. Shocking, indecent things. But there wasn't anything she could say. She didn't know anything . . . Yes. She did. There were Connie's stories. And Black's Lane. Behind the dirty blue palings in Black's Lane [. . .] There's a dead baby in the bed . . . Pussycat. Pussycat, what did you there? Pussy. Prissie. Prissiecat. Poor Prissie. (156)

In this passage, aesthetic form mirrors psychoanalytical content: Sinclair's compressed prose poetry explores the Freudian notion of 'condensation' which posits that multiple and latent unconscious thoughts are condensed into a single yet composite manifest idea or image (for Freud see also Paddy, Stinson, Thacker and Wilson). 'Black's Lane' emerges out of Harriett's ellipses, therefore, as a complex and resonant metaphor for 'unspeakable' stories of sexual and moral transgression. Furthermore, Harriet's hallucinatory vision of a 'dead baby' can be interpreted within Freudian psychoanalytical paradigms as a moment of 'displacement'; namely a moment of psychological transference in which the significance of one object is shifted to another object. Although the manifest image of 'the dead baby' recalls the death of Maggie's infant, the latent contents of the image speak to a larger narrative of abortive femininity. Harriett willingly accepts her cancer, for instance, as a final moment of identification with her mother and object of desire: 'With every stab, she would live again in her mother. She had what her mother had' (155). This sense of barren circularity manifests itself linguistically, of course, when, falling under the influence of the anaesthetic, Harriett attempts a final recital of her favourite nursery rhyme, 'Pussycat, Pussycat'. Lapsing into an example of what Freud called 'parapraxis', an error in speech (commonly known as the 'Freudian slip') which shows the potent powers of the unconscious at work, Harriet's confused mumblings reveal a life of experiential vacuity, psychosexual repression and guilt. Indeed, the portmanteau 'Prissiecat' exposes the destructive force of Harriett's moral aestheticism: the 'sinister results' of her 'beautiful behaviour' not only manifest themselves in the living death of Harriett Frean, but they also manifest themselves in the physically and psychologically unlived lives of others.

Virginia Woolf, *Mrs Dalloway* (1925)

He [The modern novelist] has to have the courage to say that what interests him is no longer 'this' but 'that:' out of 'that' alone must he construct his work [. . .] the emphasis is upon something hitherto ignored; at once a different outline of form becomes necessary, difficult for us to grasp, incomprehensible to our predecessors. (162)

Virginia Woolf, 'Modern Fiction' (1925)

Where is one to locate the female writer in Woolf's manifesto for Modernism?

One answer, perhaps, is to be found in the demonstrative pronoun 'that', in the 'hitherto ignored' aspects of a predominantly male literary history. While the male author is writ large across Woolf's essay in the form of the personal pronouns – 'He', 'him' and 'his' – the female author (her story, her history, her consciousness) remains unexplored and unrepresented. In this essay, I want to read *Mrs Dalloway* as an exercise in the recovery and revision of female stories, histories and consciousnesses. Specifically, I am interested in exploring Woolf's representations of 'that' which had been erased from patriarchal surface narratives of post-war history and culture: namely, female narratives of economic dispossession and political displacement; female stories of isolation and loss and the feminization of physical and psychological trauma in the shell-shocked soldier. In search of a narrative form which will accommodate these necessarily 'difficult' discourses, Woolf constructs her circadian experiment, I suggest, in the form of a textual labyrinth. A circular model of identity, space and structure, which would later become so essential to the Surrealists' creative and political enquiries into the architectures of the unconscious, the labyrinth is valuable for Woolf because, within it, conventional notions of time, space, subjectivity and consciousness are disorientated and decentred. Furthermore, standing in opposition to the term 'architecture', which is synonymous with state authority and patriarchal oppression, the labyrinth emerges as a radical physical and psychological space in which official male-authored versions of post-war history and culture are held up to critique.

'What a lark! What a plunge!': Mrs Dalloway's London

Stepping out onto the streets of London, Mrs Dalloway steps into a labyrinth of memories, stories and histories in which the past and the future are intermingled with the present in a continuous flow of narrative time: Clarissa's recollections of summers at Bourton cut across misremembered snippets of conversation with Peter Walsh in the vegetable patch; these distance voices and places imbricate, in turn, her more recent thoughts on her Westminster neighbours, the War and which flowers to buy for her party. Standing in stark contrast to the order and logic which govern her physical manoeuvres through the Modernist city – its surface territories are clearly demarcated and defined (Westminster, Victoria Street, Arlington Street, St James Park are all sign-posted along the way) – our protagonist's psychological peregrinations reveal an unconscious urban labyrinth of chaos and possible critique.

Mrs Dalloway's shifting thoughts and disjointed observations map, for instance, the intrusive presence of London's key architectural features: 'Big Ben strikes. There! Out it boomed. First a warning, musical; then the hour, irrevocable. The leaden circles dissolved in the air' (4). As Jeremy Tambling argues, the repeating presence of Big Ben's 'death–like' chimes throughout the course of the novel's events is, like the state itself, all-powerful and all-pervasive; 'Time's expression is not so much the existential enemy in this novel as a part of the language of state-power which is felt to be threatening and minatory' (59). While patriarchal ideology asserts itself audibly and visually (the phallic architecture of Big Ben looms over Westminster) across Woolf's post-war landscape, it also manifests itself in the absent presence of the War dead. In the novel it is the 'poor mothers of Pimlico' (20), not their sons, who stop to observe the stealth-like movement of the Royal car – 'the enduring symbol of the state' – as it moves down Bond Street. The bodies of the fallen sons have been recast, instead, into monuments of 'bronze heroes' (20) and other patriarchal symbols of 'the War' (11), of 'the dead, of the flag; of Empire' (18) which the bereaved mothers can merely stand before.

Mrs Dalloway's repeated observations that concerning the war having ended, 'The War was over . . . but it was over; thank heaven – over' (5) gestures nervously to a post-war society which is still very much alive to, and disorientated by, the realities of death and displacement. The overlapping psychological narratives of Mrs Foxcroft, Lady Bexborough, Moll Pratt, Mrs Dempster, Septimus and Rezia Smith, and Clarissa Dalloway give the lie, for instance, to male-authored narratives of post-war recovery and progress. Mrs Foxcroft's story of bereavement, it emerges, is also a cruel tale of sexual difference and political prejudice: 'that nice boy was killed and now the old Manor House must go to a cousin' (5). Emotionally bereft and economically dispossessed by the patriarchal law of primogenitureship, this female survivor is doubly displaced by the masculine fiction of war. Moll Pratt's threatened act of dissent against the Royal car, meanwhile, gestures to a concealed history of patriarchal colonialist politics in war-torn Ireland. In protest against the 'flowing corn and the manor houses of England' (18), she 'would have tossed the price of a pot of beer – a bunch of roses – into St James Street out of sheer light-heartedness and contempt of poverty' (19) if the authoritarian eye of the law had not been 'upon her, discouraging an old Irishwoman's loyalty' (19). Although the panoptic gaze of the state closes down this potential instance of physical rebellion, Moll Pratt's story has, nevertheless, been allowed to surface psychologically; the mobilizing narrative perspectives of Woolf's textual labyrinth have generated a creative and critical space for a female colonial subject to at least make her agitating presence known.

Woolf's characterization of Septimus Smith, a traumatized war veteran who is silenced and marginalized by male-authored processes of post-war reintegration and recuperation, marks another radical critique of official patriarchal narratives. In her seminal study of sex and the social construction of madness, *The Female Malady* (1977), Elaine Showalter points out how Woolf attempts to 'connect the shell-shocked veteran with the repressed woman of the man-governed world through their common enemy, the nerve specialist' (192). More than any novelist of the period (and drawing on her own experience of psychiatric treatments), according to Showalter Woolf 'exposed the sadism of nerve therapies that enforced conventional sex roles [. . .] Septimus's problem is that he feels too much for a man [Evans]. His grief and introspection are emotions that are consigned to the feminine' (193). Showalter says in a post-war climate in which questions of 'masculinity' had been thrown into crisis (193), Woolf 'feminises' Septimus Smith by placing him within a double-discourse of trauma and homosexuality. Woolf writes:

> Tears ran down his cheeks [. . .] Men must not cut down trees [. . .] There was his hand; there the dead. White things were assembling behind the railing opposite. But he dared not look. Evans was behind the railings! (24–5)

The horror of this passage resides in the way in which physical signs of death and violence are eclipsed through psychological suggestion. In Septimus's traumatized vision, the trees are monstrously surreal embodiments of dismembered soldiers: human body parts – arms, legs, trunks, heads, hands – are displaced into the branches and stems of malleable, anthropomorphic trees which stretch out of the shadows of death towards the warming sun. Woolf's depiction of soft, assembling biologies that threaten to seep through the cracks and fissures of the city's hard, geometric architectures (its pavements, railings, ramparts, park benches) sets up a tension between ideologically contrived surface narratives of post-war history and the dialogic labyrinth of repressed memories, histories and sexual desires. Man-made architectures or patriarchal discourses which are constructed in order to contain and paralyse historical trauma and memory might just no longer hold, Woolf suggests, because death and desire will always return to force a confrontation.

Woolf makes a dramatic feature of the tension between official surface narratives of history and unconscious counter-historical energies in the section in which the advertising aeroplane writes a series of indistinct messages across the sky. What is particularly striking about this passage is the way in which the vertiginous presence of the aeroplane (as it swirls, loops, drops and soars across the London skyline) distracts the onlookers from the slow and linear progress which the Royal car makes across the city streets: 'Suddenly Mrs Coates looked up into the sky [. . .] Everyone looked up! [. . .] (and the car went in at the gates and nobody looked at it)' (20–1). The enduring symbol of the state is notably relegated to parentheses as the aeroplane triggers a series of associative thoughts and criticisms in the onlookers' minds. For Mrs Dempster, the aeroplane is a symbol of escape: 'Hadn't she always longed to see foreign parts?' (27–8); it is an opportunity to flee, psychologically at least, from a 'hard life' of male alcoholism (her son), infidelity ('Every man has his ways' [27]) and sexual dissatisfaction. For the 'seedy-looking non-descript man carrying a leather bag [. . .] stuffed with pamphlets' (28), meanwhile, the aeroplane's sudden appearance over Ludgate Circus initiates a moment of critique: pausing on the steps of St Paul's Cathedral, this anonymous political activist, another physically and psychologically displaced figure (Woolf specifies he is 'without a situation' [28]), holds the state's seductive theory of national belonging through physical and political sacrifice up to scrutiny.

For Septimus, of course, the presence of the aeroplane triggers a series of traumatic memories and disorientating visions in which he believes the 'smoke words languishing and melting in the sky' (21–2) are somehow 'signalling' (21) to him:

> Happily Rezia put her hand with a tremendous weight on his knee so that he was weighted down, transfixed, or the excitement of the elm trees rising and falling, rising and falling . . . so proudly they rose and fell, so superbly, would have sent him mad (22).

In this passage, Woolf sets up a narrative contest between a male-authored psychiatric discourse which is designed to restore balance and a vertiginous female narrative of madness. For Septimus, psychological recovery is not to be found in the distractions offered by 'the music hall' and 'cricket' (25). Neither is it to be found in Sir Ian Bradshaw's ideologically demarcated parameters of 'a sense of proportion' (96). Indeed, the Specialist's prescribed 'rest cure' merely perpetuates feelings of physical and psychological isolation in Septimus because, in the name of male stoicism, the 'feminised' soldier is refused the opportunity to bear witness to the horrific material and mental realities of war. Subsequently, Septimus's trajectory throughout the course of the novel is not one of linear and rational progress, but one of dizzying descent: 'For now it was all over, truce signed, and the dead buried [. . .] He could not feel [. . .] he was falling, the bed was falling' (87). Despite Rezia's desperate efforts to secure her husband with the weight of her hand, Septimus experiences repeated feelings of falling throughout the course of that 'one day in June' until he makes his final plunge onto 'Mrs Filmer's area railings' (149). Leaping from a patriarchal psychiatric system that failed to comprehend the traumatic psychological realities of post-war survival, it is with some irony that Septimus Smith finally obeys the 'masculine' laws of gravity and jumps to his death.

Case Studies in Reading 2: Key Theoretical and Critical Texts

Bryony Randall

Chapter Overview

The range of work that has taken place in Modernist studies over the last 25 years is impossible fully to represent by making any kind of selection among the critical texts available. What this chapter aims to do, then, is to give the reader a more detailed flavour of a number of very different critical works, all of which have been highly influential in their own way, and to show how one might engage with the arguments they put forward. Having said this, it is notable that these books were all published between the late 1980s and late 1990s, a period during which the rejuvenation of Modernist studies gathered momentum. Thus, while they often take radically different positions on what constitutes Modernism, how to approach literary texts, and the politics of literary criticism, these works were among those which laid the foundations for the exciting developments that have characterized the last decade of Modernist literary study. Whether prompting commendation or condemnation, they each continue to serve as key points of reference for the vibrant, contested, diverse world of Modernist studies at the start of the twenty-first century.

Peter Nicholls, *Modernisms: A Literary Guide* (1995)

Under an apparently neutral title, *Modernisms* in fact signals, in the single letter 's', the nature of its important intervention in Modernist studies. Suggesting that Modernism might be plural, that there could be more than one 'modernism' or that Modernism might be defined in a number of different ways, *Modernisms* challenges the 'caricature of Modernism as monolithic and reactionary' that, Nicholls suggests, was a product of 'the recent enthusiasm for things *post*modern' in the 1980s and early 1990s. Like a child rebelling against its parents, so the argument goes, postmodern discourse needed to define Modernism in wholly negative terms; and in order to clarify its relationship to what it was rejecting, it needed to describe Modernism as homogenous, identifiable as a coherent movement, and conservative in tendency.

Nicholls's book leaves this 'caricature' of Modernism in ruins, and instead, in twelve wide-ranging chapters, it draws our attention to the incredible diversity within Modernist literature – indeed, expands received notions of what might be considered 'modernist'. So, while chapters such as 'Modernity and the "Men of 1914" ' and 'Other Times: The Narratives of High Modernism' address the canonical figures of Modernism (Joyce, Eliot, Pound, etc.), the book begins in the mid-nineteenth century with an analysis of a poem by Baudelaire. This instantly challenges the idea that Modernism proper appeared in a short window between about 1910 and 1925 – or even, in a more expanded timescale already favoured by many at this point, between about 1890 and 1940. Further, Nicholls's 'guide' takes us well beyond the Anglo-American horizon; the first half of his book concentrates almost exclusively on European Modernisms, covering French Symbolism, Italian Futurism, French Cubism, Russian Futurism and (mainly German) Expressionism, and addresses numerous neglected or forgotten figures as well as the expected major ones. Thus, Nicholls presents us with a vastly expanded conception of Modernisms, encouraging us to question assumptions about how, where and when, Modernism was. But he also indicates continuities within this diversity, constantly making connections between apparently disparate literary products, linking them via routes through what he calls a 'conceptual map' (viii) of Modernisms.

Key routes through this 'map' – recurring concepts or issues – include the relationship between language and object, as well as that between art and society, and the figuring of gender, in Modernist writing. Nicholls's Introduction sets us off on a number of these routes. Here, Nicholls produces a reading of Baudelaire's 'To a Red-haired Beggar Girl' showing how the poem moves beyond the poet's apparent identification with the beggar girl, ultimately reinforcing the distance between poet and his subject: 'It is as if there are two voices at work in the poem: one which sympathizes with the girl and expresses admiration for her "natural" charms, and another which simply takes her as an occasion for a poem' (2). The poet is genuinely attracted to the girl, but ultimately her attraction lies in the fact that she is a subject of poetry, and her body 'prompts [the poet] to create the ironic distance which is the foundation of this particular aesthetic' (3). Nicholls concludes that 'Baudelaire's way of making a representation of the feminine the means by which to construct an ironically anti-social position for the writer contains in germ many of the problems of the later modernisms' (3). So here Nicholls sets out what it is about Baudelaire's poem that he regards as 'modernist' – broadly, the figuring of politics (whether 'anti-social' as here or otherwise) through gender – which will set the tone for his analyses of those 'later modernisms'.

Nicholls makes his critical approach clear in his preface: 'It is [the] translation of politics into style, and the tensions it reflects between the social and the aesthetic, which are the main subject of the following pages' (vii). That is to say, Nicholls is interested in the political aspects of Modernism not, or not only, in terms of the political *content* of these works, or indeed of the avowed political affiliations of the figures he discusses – Nicholls does mention these, but more or less in passing. Rather, his concern is to explore the textual manifestations of political concerns. So, for example, disillusionment with politics at the end of the nineteenth century meant, says Nicholls that 'all the rules of normal communication must now be broken if the relation between art and society was to be significantly transformed' (25). Writers who that aimed to 'escape the confines of a degraded social world', but who did so in language that more or less conformed to the linguistic norms available, 'bear the traces of that world, even as they curse, repudiate and try to transcend it' (24). This need to 'break the rules' resulted in French Symbolism, and Nicholls goes on to show how poets such as Rimbaud and Mallarmé produced a poetics that resisted reincorporation into atrophied political structures (for Symbolism also see Day).

We can see the way in which Nicholls handles the relationship between an 'overt' politics and one at the level of 'style' if we turn to his thesis about the relationship between gender and politics in Modernist discourse. Nicholls concludes his chapter on the late nineteenth-century aesthetic movement of decadence by describing the emergence within this movement of a discourse linking the materiality of language with the body and (therefore) femininity. While exhibiting strongly misogynistic tendencies, decadent writing also celebrated this 'materiality' of language, and in so doing, Nicholls suggests, implied 'a guilty and fascinated sense of the male's feminisation'. 'Such habits of thought', he says, 'would provide a sort of deep structure for the subsequent waves of Modernism, eliding "politics" with "sexual politics" [. . .] and then construing the resulting tensions at the level of artistic "style" ' (62).

Nicholls picks up this argument in his next chapter, on the texts of Italian Futurism. The 'first definitively modernist movement' (76), Italian Futurism 'made the whole context of an emerging modernism a strongly gendered one' (88). But this is not only insofar as it articulated a particular brand of misogyny, most famously in its manifesto which stated that 'We will glorify war – the world's only hygiene – militarism, patriotism [. . .] and scorn for women' (88). Nicholls draws our attention to this statement, but does not consider it to be the last word on Italian Futurism and gender. Firstly, Nicholls observes that, apparently contradicting this 'scorn for women', Marinetti (the leader of the movement), 'developed an equally outspoken propaganda on behalf of some feminist concerns [including] the facilitation of divorce, universal suffrage, and the right to equal salaries' (88). Nicholls argues that this apparent contradiction needs to be seen in the wider context of Futurism's 'desire for a transcendence of the "merely" human' (89); it is not so much women, or femininity, that Futurism has a problem with, but the very existence of sexual difference.

Secondly, and perhaps more importantly for Nicholls, 'the repudiation of the feminine was [. . .] more clear-cut at the cultural level: here "woman" provided the symbolic focus of an attack on those attitudes towards language, subjectivity and sexual difference which seemed to characterize a Symbolist or decadent poetics' (89). The forms of Italian Futurist art (verbal and visual) emphasized speed, hardness, dynamism, action and the public, in absolute contrast to the features of that earlier poetics. Here we can indeed see how sexual politics emerges at the level of style; one might say that Italian Futurist misogyny is directed not just, or even particularly, at actual women, but at this excessive, nostalgic, passive, feminized aesthetic. There are dangers in pushing Nicholls's argument too far, and disavowing the misogyny of texts so inflected entirely; Nicholls is at pains to cut off such a reading by repeatedly acknowledging where misogyny is present, effectively saying 'this is misogynist, yes, but we need to look beyond its misogyny', in, for example, his discussions of Expressionist theatre, Percy Wyndham Lewis's *Tarr* and Antonin Artaud's Theatre of Cruelty. This perspective of Futurism also, in turn, reveals its broader political stance, vilifying the female body and all it stands for insofar as 'it is the traditional focus of desire and *deferred* pleasure' [my emphasis] (90). Resisting this deferral of pleasure, the movement rather revels in the present, rejects repression and embraces the technologies – the machines – of Modernity. It is thus an example of what Nicholls calls 'ecstatic' Modernism, which *celebrated* Modernity, as against 'the Anglo-American version [which] developed in part as a *critique* of modernity' (166). Its politics involved an affirmation of early twentieth century capitalist society (or at least, some of its aspects) rather than a repudiation thereof.

One of Nicholls's aims is to show how Modernist discourses tended to be dominated by masculinism. His chapter on the 'Men of 1914' (Pound, Conrad, Lewis, Eliot, Joyce) follows this thread through the work of the canonical Anglo-American Modernists, and shows how they also engage with gendered discourses, but with different political implications. So, for example, Nicholls argues that while Lewis's *Tarr* rejects sexual desires as a kind of 'suicide', this is 'not primarily because it entails a surrender of the masculine to the female will, but because the romantic pursuit of the "other" proves in fact to be the pursuit of the "same" ' (187). We are reminded of Nicholls's opening analysis of Baudelaire, where the poet must insist on the difference between himself and his (female) subject. This is not least because Baudelaire's beggar-girl 'is self-presence incarnate', representing a dangerous (from the poet's perspective) lack of self-awareness or ability to 'command [. . .] two voices'; this self-awareness is at the heart of the poet's self-definition, and his 'separateness from the social world of which he writes' (3). The ideal of separateness is, according to Nicholls, exposed by Lewis as under threat from Modernity, and Lewis's political position reflects this: 'the doubling and symmetry within [Lewis's] narratives testifies [. . .] to the narcissism which he locates as the structural compulsion of democratic (or communistic) societies for which the other must always prove to be the same' (87). A rejection of sexual desire, then, operates as a kind of metaphor (although this term inadequately represents the complexity of the relationship) for Lewis's rejection of democracy, in a Modernity where 'in finding itself elsewhere, the subject experiences a loss of the borders of the self' (187).

It is, however, precisely this 'loss of the borders of the self' that some of Lewis's contemporaries aim to explore, even celebrate, in their work. In a chapter entitled 'At a Tangent: Other Modernisms' Nicholls discusses writers such as, most importantly, H.D. and Gertrude Stein, whose work *pursues* a 'fantasy of sameness' (202). Nicholls is again careful not to essentialise sexual difference here. Certainly, it appears relevant that H.D. and Stein were women, while as we have seen the Modernisms Nicholls has discussed so far were overwhelmingly dominated by men. However, Nicholls wants to propose that the work of these authors 'constitutes not simply another kind of Modernism ("feminine" modernism) but rather a deliberate and often polemic disturbance within the canonical version' (197). He argues that their 'literary reactions' to masculinist Modernism are in fact 'best define[d] as forms of "anti-modernism" '. We might pause here and consider the implications of suggesting that this work is 'anti-modernist', particularly now that Stein and H.D. are entering the 'modernist' canon (if undergraduate reading lists are anything to go by). Does this help us to maintain a distinction between writers such as Pound and Stein, who might both appear on a university course on 'modernism' but whose work differed in almost every respect? Does it work to remind us that there were experimental literary tendencies that ran counter to the (supposedly dominant) Modernism of the 'men of 1914'? Or does the term 'anti-modernism' risk reinforcing the potential ghettoisation of writers like H.D. and Stein as peripheral to the main area of interest, 'modernism'?

Careful attention is needed here to what definition(s) of Modernism are in play; Nicholls's thesis is, after all, precisely that there is no single definition of Modernism. At the end of this chapter, Nicholls again signals the kind of 'modernism' he is working with here, where he argues that Virginia Woolf's *Orlando* (for Woolf, see also Baxter, Murray, Paddy, Stinson and Wilson) and Djuna Barnes's *Nightwood* 'seem to stand outside "modernism", effecting as they do such a fundamental break with the gendered aesthetics of previous avant-gardes' (222). The scare quotes around 'modernism' here alert us to the fact that Nicholls wants to retain a sense of the term as in flux, unfixed. But we also see that in *this* context, Nicholls is referring to the strand of Modernism that works with an oppositional model of gender relations. By this definition, we might indeed agree that *Orlando* and *Nightwood* stand 'outside' Modernism. If so, however, where *do* they stand? Are they postmodern? Avant-garde? And do they stand to fall out of critical view if they are placed beyond the pale of 'modernism'; or, on the other hand, do they gain in value precisely by throwing into relief the 'gendered aesthetics' of (this strand of) Modernism? How one answers these question will depend on whether one sees 'modernism' as a descriptive or an evaluative term: does attaching this label to certain texts immediately, whether intentionally or otherwise, imply a privileging of these texts as particularly worthy of critical attention? Or is it simply a way of drawing a line round a set of texts, so that we can see the wood for the trees, without implying any value judgment? Nicholls's fluid map of 'modernisms' encourages a critical approach that will not solidify into one of the other of these positions, always insisting that we keep that term, 'modernism', in mental scare quotes.

Marianne DeKoven, *Rich and Strange: Gender, History, Modernism* (1991)

Rich and Strange forms part of an identifiable movement in the history of Modernist literary criticism. An anthology edited by Bonnie Kime Scott, *The Gender of Modernism* (1990), redrew the map of Modernism by bringing to light numerous female authors who had hitherto been forgotten or ignored, and was published the year before DeKoven's book; the first volume of Sandra Gilbert and Susan Gubar's reassessment of twentieth century women's writing, *No Man's Land*, had also just appeared. Part of DeKoven's book is contiguous with the project of rediscovery and revaluation at the heart of these works, arguing, for example that we understand Charlotte Perkins Gilman's *The Yellow Wallpaper* and Kate Chopin's *The Awakening* – texts not previously seen as particularly, or at all, 'modernist' – as participating in the 'modernist narrative' she sketches out in her book. It is a sign of the influence of work such as DeKoven's that the appearance of either of these texts on a reading list for a class on Modernism would not now raise many eyebrows.

DeKoven's work is an explicit revision of the New Critical approach to and canonization of Modernism in the 1940s and 1950s. New Criticism, a movement initiated in the USA, was characterized by 'close reading,' paying detailed attention to the formal attributes of a particular text, and tended to involve limited attention to the context or history either of the text itself, or of the reader. It is also credited with (or, depending on one's viewpoint, should be castigated for) defining 'modernism' as a literary movement, proffering Joyce, Eliot and Pound as its exemplary figures (for Eliot see also Baxter, Murray, Paddy and Stinson). By contrast, DeKoven is 'interested in the connection, within the general sea-change of twentieth-century modernity, between literary modernism and political radicalism' (4) – explicitly placing these texts in their general cultural context. Interestingly, however, while DeKoven convincingly challenges the New Critical masculine Modernist canon, she approaches the texts through that close textual analysis which so characterizes the New Criticism. Indeed, she acknowledges the invaluable influence of New Criticism in 'making us *see* [. . .] the riches yielded by close readings of literary form' (6). Her approach is, therefore, very different from that of, for example, Rainey (see below, and see also Baxter, Murray and Thacker) in that there is limited reference in her work to *specific* historical and cultural events. Her focus is on how close analyses of texts can reveal to us the submerged ambivalences and tensions that, she argues, characterize literary Modernism.

That term 'submerged' reflects the primary metaphor that DeKoven uses to link her close readings: that of the sea, or water more generally. This metaphor is drawn in part from the work of one of her major theoretical influences, the French theorist Luce Irigaray. The first chapter of *Rich and Strange* provides a reading of Irigaray's work that expresses DeKoven's approach to gender. DeKoven explains and approves Irigaray's reading of the history of gender in her *Speculum of the Other Woman*. Broadly speaking, Irigaray's argument forms part of the (now familiar) feminist project of exposing the binary structure that governs the construction of gender in Western culture: male and female, masculine and feminine, man and woman are placed in a binary and hierarchical relationship to each other, where the masculine dominates. DeKoven expands on this slightly, affirming Irigaray's argument that 'Western culture has been created by masculine self-representation, which is driven by the necessity to produce an image of the self-same, and therefore to suppress the feminine, particularly the maternal. The maternal feminine [. . .] is the repressed other of Western culture' (27). Irigaray explores the manifestation of this repression in key texts of Western philosophy, and thus by implication challenges this binary structure. And one of the ways in which this 'maternal feminine' is characteristically represented is as formless, fluid, watery – hence DeKoven's use of the 'sea-change' metaphor to allude to her broader project of reassessing and revaluing the 'feminine' in these texts, and in Modernism.

DeKoven emphatically endorses Irigaray's exposure of the binaries upon which gender has historically been constructed, but she does not agree with Irigaray that a potential alternative 'feminine economy' of gender, eschewing binaries, would be characterized by 'multiplicity and diffusion' (30). While seeming to provide an escape from binary structures, 'multiplicity and diffusion' are themselves, DeKoven argues, in a binary relationship with the dualistic, binary model! Therefore, these ideas fall back into the binary model they are trying to resist. The alternative that DeKoven proposes, and that she argues characterizes Modernist texts, is the maintenance of an ' "impossible dialectic" [a term she takes from the poststructuralist feminist critic Julia Kristeva], simultaneously acknowledging dualism and repudiating both its hierarchical imbalance and its rigid self-other exclusivity' (30). This idea of holding two positions at once is a familiar one to readers of the Modernist text as something characterized by ambivalence and ambiguity. But this is more than simply an interesting textual characteristic, DeKoven argues. It means that Modernist texts also do important political work, in terms of sexual politics, as it is only this maintenance of simultaneous positions that 'offers (in a term crucial to Irigaray, as we will see) a *passage* out of our masculine economy of representation, given the fact that we are now inevitably located within it and can only see a passage out within its terms' (30). (This last point will particularly appeal to those who find the implications of some feminist theory problematically idealistic. The idea of totally breaking with binary structures in order to set up a new world of gender relations can be difficult to imagine in practice, even if viewed as desirable as such. Beginning where we are, as it were, thus seems to offer a way of being progressive without requiring the (impossible?) annihilation of all existing structures.)

What, then does DeKoven mean by this *'passage'*, crucial both to Irigaray and DeKoven's own book? This concept provides DeKoven with a means of expressing the simultaneity that she wants to emphasize as a key aspect of Modernist literature. Described in characteristically biological terms by Irigaray as a ' "*[f]orgotten vagina*" ', it is a ' "go-between" ' (37), neither in one place nor the other, both an entrance and an exit, neither outside nor inside, but constituted by movement and transition. So we retain, inevitably, a dualistic aspect in that the passage must be between two positions, but the relationship between these positions is now no longer hierarchical, with one term dominating the other. Rather, as DeKoven concludes, the relationship becomes 'a simultaneity enabled by the open "passage" between [binary terms, which] opens into the modernist text' (37).

Before moving on to look at what DeKoven does with Modernist texts, we should note her indebtedness to the theorist Jacques Derrida, specifically insofar as she takes a particular Derridean coinage to describe the relationship between Modernism and Modernity. The question of whether Modernism celebrates Modernity – the actual modern world around it and its forms – or resists it, continues to be a question for literary critical debate. Critical responses will depend, of course, on how one identifies 'modernity' and what aspects of it are under scrutiny – as we have seen in Nicholls's discussion of 'ecstatic' versus pessimistic Modernisms (see above 91–5). DeKoven argues that 'Modernist formal practice has seemed to define itself as a repudiation of, and an alternative to, the cultural implications of late nineteenth- and early twentieth century feminism and socialism' (4) that is these particular aspects of Modernity. Her contention is that 'on the contrary, modernist form evolved precisely as an adequate means of representing their terrifying appeal' (4), and that it 'enacts in the realm of form an alternative to culture's hegemonic hierarchical dualisms, roots of those structures of inequity that socialism and feminism proposed to eradicate' (4). In other words, DeKoven detects in Modernist literary form an acknowledgement, perhaps even despite itself, of the failures and faultlines in society that the moderni movements of feminism and socialism set out to challenge. DeKoven labels this paradigm '*sous-rature*', a concept coined by the Derrida, which might be translated as 'under erasure'. This idea can be visually represented as a word which has been crossed out, because it is discredited or inadequate, but which remains legible, because we cannot do without it. So, DeKoven's argument goes, Modernist texts, rather than representing *either* a celebration of the radical changes taking place in society, *or* a rejection of them, rather display an 'irresolvable ambivalence' (20), signified by the concept of *sous-rature*. Crucially, however, DeKoven argues that it is not just that we can find unresolved contradiction in Modernist texts (since we might be able to do that in all kinds of different texts), 'but that modernist writing *constitutes itself* as self-contradictory' (24). DeKoven uses the example of Proust's *A la recherche du temps perdu* to illustrate her point: in this text, the protagonist-narrator Marcel's particular aesthetic and philosophical position is both affirmed and undermined. It is precisely the narrative's refusal (or inability) to uphold one position over the other that characterizes this text as Modernist, by DeKoven's definition.

Having set up her approach, the next four chapters 'analyze [. . .] pairs of female- and male-signed modernist literary texts', tracing this *sous-rature* through them. DeKoven argues that the ambivalence these texts display towards radical social change is differently inflected according to the gender identity of the author; or, more precisely, according to whether the text is 'male' or 'female-signed', a designation which minimises the risk that a judgment about a historical individual's gender identity is being made from the outside. DeKoven's terminology is striking, since many women continued to write under male pseudonyms in this early Modernist period. As it happens, this does not apply to any of the writers DeKoven addresses; it would therefore be interesting to consider how her argument might be brought to bear on, for example, Mary Chavelita Dunne, an experimental writer working at around the same time as Charlotte Perkins Gilman and Kate Chopin, but better known as George Egerton and thus, in DeKoven's words 'male-signed'.

At the heart of DeKoven's argument is a clear distinction between the work of male and female authors: 'Male modernists', says DeKoven, 'generally feared the loss of hegemony the change they desired might entail, while female Modernists feared punishment for desiring that change' (4). This thesis is most strongly articulated in DeKoven's chapter on Gilman and Henry James where a careful close reading of Gilman's *The Yellow Wallpaper* and James's *The Turn of the Screw* and their patterns of freedom, containment and power, concludes with the assertion that 'In *The Yellow Wallpaper*, a female-signed text fearing what it desires, female capitulation is damnation; in *The Turn of the Screw*, a male-signed text desiring what it fears, female (and subaltern) victory is damnation' (63). This kind of formulation is characteristic of DeKoven's book and makes her thesis throughout clear, as she shows how male- and female-signed texts engage with the same kind of issues but in different, indeed often (as here) completely opposite ways. (One might argue that DeKoven's precisely balanced formulations themselves risk falling back on the binary structures that DeKoven wishes to resist – an inevitable side-effect, perhaps, of 'beginning where we are'?) Similar conclusions are drawn from her analyses of Gertrude Stein's 'Melanctha' alongside Joseph Conrad's *The Nigger of the Narcissus*, focusing on tropes of race and childbirth, and then of Conrad's *Heart of Darkness* alongside Virginia Woolf's *The Voyage Out*, where the Irigarayan concept of the passage plays a particularly important role (for Conrad see also Baxter, Murray, Paddy, and Stinson).

Here, DeKoven argues that 'Conrad and Woolf use the classical journey plot, the voyage of discovery [. . .] sending their protagonists [. . .] on an anti-heroic return to the terrifying heart of desire, the maternal origin of life that generates in these texts disillusionment and death' (85). This is an important statement of DeKoven's sense of what is 'modernist' about these texts, reworking traditional or 'classical' plots in the context of that 'revolutionary horizon' of feminism and socialism. But they are not simply reversals of the traditional *Bildungsroman* plot; certainly, the protagonists move towards 'disillusionment and death', but this is not a straightforwardly linear progress toward the 'maternal'. Instead, DeKoven reads 'the metaphor and plot device of the voyage that dominates both texts' as 'inscribing into representation the Irigarayan vaginal passage, the possibility of link and movement back and forth between the masculine and the feminine' (85). So it is not that DeKoven suggests a straightforward 'feminisation' of narrative in Modernist literature, on the contrary, what is crucial is that there is movement between masculine and feminine which serves to undermine or at least challenge the assumptions on which this binary structure is based.

For example, in *The Voyage Out* DeKoven reads a couple of key scenes between the two young lovers at the centre of the story, which take place in the 'womblike' setting of the jungle (129), while on a 'passage' down a river (and in one case also down a jungle path) (127), as articulating alternatives to the patriarchal, imperialist structures of the Western society which these two characters resist, to a greater or lesser extent; in particular, the structure of 'bourgeois' marriage (127). However, this resistance is ultimately co-opted as the young couple return to the society from which they came, and thus to its rules – it is, DeKoven ultimately implies, bourgeois marriage itself that brings about the tragic end to this book. DeKoven shows us how both *The Voyage Out* and *Heart of Darkness* allude to or explore alternatives to the dominant structures of their particular social context, seeming to offer a different way of organizing the world. While she concludes that ultimately both end by being 'defeated by the old text', the existing patriarchal, imperialistic structures, it is crucial that in the course of these novels '[t]he passage, however, was opened, and through it two modernist narratives were born' (138).

In her next chapter, DeKoven discusses a pair of texts – Conrad's *Lord Jim* and Chopin's *The Awakening* – for whom the preoccupations of race, gender and class are less explicit than in the texts discussed so far, and suggests that here, 'as in high modernism, modernist ambivalence and the historical referents to which it is a response are suppressed and reinscribed primarily in form' (139). (Here, her broad point resembles Nicholls's main thesis, about the manifestation of politics and especially sexual politics in the form of Modernist works, although the two critics differ greatly in their choice of texts and their theoretical approach.) DeKoven then goes on to show how her argument holds for texts of 'high modernism' where DeKoven argues '[t]he revolutionary impulse of modernism came to reside entirely in the realm of form' (188). Working at a fast pace through numerous canonical Modernist texts, DeKoven explores the ways in which these texts evince a concern at some level with questions of race, sex and class. Ezra Pound's 'In a Station of the Metro' provides a particularly condensed instance of this (for Pound see also Murray, Paddy, Stinson, Thacker and Wilson), and DeKoven shows how this poem evokes a threatening feminine (maternal) sexuality, a democratized mass culture and the modern city, and yet attempts to contain or counter those threatening presences: 'The fate, the position, of history and of woman are the same: simultaneously enabling, necessary, defining, and also negated, rejected, countered by an extremely equivocal masculine ahistorical poetic transcendence – literally, *sous-rature*' (190). DeKoven's sustained and attentive close readings here almost constitute step-by-step guides for how one might test out her approach on any Modernist text.

Houston A. Baker, Jr, *Modernism and the Harlem Renaissance* (1987)

Early in *Modernism and the Harlem Renaissance*, Houston A. Baker notes 'a change in Afro-American nature that occurred on or about September 18, 1895' (8). This is a reformulation of Virginia Woolf's famous assertion in 'Character and Fiction' 'that on or about December 1910, human character changed' (421). The 'Harlem Renaissance' generally refers to the various activities of numerous Afro-American writers, singers and artists working and living in the Harlem area of New York in the early decades of the twentieth century, especially Key figures such as Alain Locke, W.E.B. DuBois, Langston Hughes, Nella Larsen, Zora Neale Hurston and Claude McKay. Given Baker's destabilization of the term, the words 'Harlem Renaissance' should be regarded as if they appear in scare quotes throughout this discussion. Baker's intertextual reworking of Woolf signifies a radicalization of the latter's version of Modernism in terms of both content and form. First, he reorientates the reader coming to his book in search of 'modernism' by locating its foundational moment not, as readers after Woolf have been encouraged to do, around 1910, but around a specific event in 1895, the date of Booker T. Washington's address to the Negro exhibit of the Atlanta Cotton States and International Exposition. It is clear, then, that Baker's book will not only address texts of a specifically Afro-American provenance, but also encourage a complete reorientation towards the concept of 'modernism'. Secondly, by appropriating and reformulating one of the most celebrated utterances in the Anglo-American Modernist canon (one of those moments, like Ezra Pound's 'make it new' or T.S. Eliot's 'objective correlative' where we see Modernists in the process of self-definition) Baker performs one of those two approaches which he will claim in this book is characteristic, definitively so, of African-American Modernism; namely, here, 'mastery of form'. Baker's book constituted a profound challenge to received notions about both Afro-American and Anglo-American Modernism, presented in a form which itself enacts what it describes, and in so doing required Modernist literary studies both to take account of the implications of the works of Afro-American Modernist writers for established Anglo-American paradigms of Modernism, and to acknowledge the existence of alternative conceptions of 'modernism' which decline to acknowledge the privileging of Anglo-American and European models.

In another parallel with Woolf, *Modernism and the Harlem Renaissance* grew, like *A Room of One's Own*, from oral presentations – lectures or seminars. Orality, and specifically *sound*, are crucial aspects of the Modernism that Baker observes in the so-called Harlem Renaissance. So-called, because, as Baker notes 'there was no "Harlem Renaissance" [. . .] until *after* the event' (xvii) – just indeed as there was no 'modernism' (identified as a coherent movement) until after the event, when the New Critics began to define it in retrospect. Therefore, says Baker, his discussion is not aimed at ' "Saving the Harlem Renaissance" ' (xvii). Instead, he describes his project as offering 'what is perhaps a *sui generis* definition of *modern Afro-American sound* as a function of a specifically Afro-American discursive practice' (xiv).

Baker's discussion is founded on a rejection of the critical assumption that the Harlem Renaissance was a 'failure'. He argues that this assessment is based on judging Afro-American cultural and literary products of the early twentieth century against an Anglo-American notion of Modernist 'success', and that a reorientation of perspective is needed. The work of Eliot, Joyce, Picasso, Pound *et al.* is often assessed as 'successful' or otherwise insofar as it challenges the traditional modes of artistic representation in the West prevalent at the end of the nineteenth century. But Baker repeatedly reminds us that this kind of resistance to earlier aesthetic forms is completely inappropriate to an understanding of the products of the Harlem Renaissance. Perhaps the most persuasive articulation of this argument can be found towards the end of the book where Baker notes that 'what exists on the antecedent side of black modernity is not a line of stodgy, querulous and resistant premoderns but a universe of enslavement' (101). Baker argues that privileged Anglo-American writers were in a position to concern themselves with such questions as 'Are we happy? Are we content? Are we free?' because '[s]uch questions presuppose at least an adequate level of sustenance and a sufficient faith in human behavioural alternatives to enable a self-directed questioning' (7). By contrast, Afro-American writers were emerging directly from a context of slavery and impoverishment, where the single overwhelming concern was one of mere survival. This is the inheritance with which Afro-American 'modernist' writers are dealing, argues Baker.

This inheritance informs one of the most criticized aspects of the Harlem Renaissance: that is, the prevalence of traditional (Western) aesthetic forms, together with an apparent compliance with racist norms. Writers such as Countee Cullen, Claude McKay and Booker T. Washington have been castigated by later critics for apparently remaining within the forms and expectations of a (white) culture which not only is not their own, but has been the vehicle of their oppression. But Baker argues that there is a much more subtle process at work in, for example, Washington's *Up from Slavery*. Simply in order to survive, to keep his racially mixed audience 'tuned in' (30), Washington needed to reproduce some of the 'sounds' of the minstrel mask – the sanitized, infantilising 'blackface' racial stereotype with which a white audience would have been familiar and comfortable. He 'masters the form' of minstrelsy in order to make what he is saying acceptable to a potentially hostile audience, reproducing a racist discourse. Without this 'mask', Baker implies, Washington would have been susceptible to the marginalization, oppression, indeed violence, to which blackness was subjected at this time. Indeed it is, says Baker, 'the mastery of the minstrel mask by blacks that constitutes a primary move in Afro-American discursive modernism' (17). Thus, rather than attacking Washington, Baker encourages us to see the strategies at work in this text as part of a necessary struggle for survival. Similarly, Baker defends Countee Cullen's use of 'traditional' verse forms by asking what his reception would have been among his community had he come out with something sounding like *The Waste Land* (86–7), and reminds us that Cullen 'gained white American recognition for "Negro poetry" at a moment when there was little encouraging recognition in the United States for *anything* Negro' (86). What is important, Baker argues throughout, is to be heard – for the *sounds* of Afro-American discourse to be audible.

These sounds were made audible, then, on the one hand through this 'mastery of form', but also, and perhaps more importantly, through what Baker calls the 'deformation of mastery'. This gesture is a more obviously radical one, involving notions of display rather than concealment, and the production of sounds that are challenging to those who are outside the ground from which they emanate – sounds thus characterized by outsiders (here, non-black culture) as 'deformed'. Baker argues that writers such as Paul Lawrence Dunbar and W.E.B. DuBois exemplify this strategy. Provocatively, given its racist associations, Baker uses the vivid image of gorilla 'display' (playing on the homophone 'guerilla') as an instance of this 'deformation of mastery' fully at work (49). Where the guiding spirit of the 'master of forms' is the minstrel mask, that of the 'deformation of mastery' is the African mask, an African ancestral past (56).

Modernism and the Harlem Renaissance concludes with a discussion of Alain Locke's *The New Negro of 1925*, a collection which, Baker argues, constitutes no less than 'the first fully modern figuration of a nation predicated upon mass energies' (91). The Modernism of the Harlem Renaissance is, we are again reminded, oriented around survival, and in particular here the definition and survival of a black nation. Of crucial importance is Locke's inclusion of spirituals and other songs – both their lyrics and the tune, in full musical notation; DuBois had done the same in his *The Souls of Black Folks* (1903). This is perhaps the most obvious example of the manifestation of the *sound* of Afro-America in a 'deformation' of accepted critical or aesthetic forms – the insistence that spirituals and folk songs be recognized as nation-building, at the same level of discourse as the other more traditionally accepted literary or philosophical discussions included in these texts. Perhaps more importantly, they present a challenge to the assumption that this traditional discourse is a 'level' to which a culture must aspire in order to be legitimate.

Baker's own text emulates DuBois's and Locke's in its inclusion of photographs, frontispieces, songs and also family anecdotes – 'deforming the mastery' of the traditional academic work. His references to Afro-American Modernism as a 'family affair' (xvii), with a nod to Sly and the Family Stone, stands in interesting relation to the characterization of Anglo-American Modernism as either arranged around relatively isolated individuals, inassimilable in their unique genius, or (increasingly in more recent Modernist scholarship) around coteries – Bloomsbury, of course, but also the coteries of the little magazines, networks of patronage (as discussed by Rainey) and so on (for Bloomsbury, see also Murray, Paddy and Stinson). However, alongside this unusual *sound* – the sound of Baker, an academic, telling us about his father's career, his uncle's evocation of Washington, and so on – a 'mastery of forms' is also apparent. This is not only insofar as much of Baker's work operates according to recognizable norms of academic literary criticism, but more specifically in the way that Baker deploys the language and tactics of poststructuralism. Even when not explicitly evoking the names of figures such as Jacques Derrida, Julia Kristeva and Roland Barthes (founding poststructuralist critics), Baker performs some spectacular poststructuralist analyses of his chosen texts, playing with terms such as mask, conjure, nonsense, vale/veil and marronage, to demonstrate their resonance – their *sounding* – around Afro-American discursive practices. While acknowledging the substance of Baker's poststructuralist analyses, one could at the same time consider the extent to which this deployment of poststructuralist discourse participates in the 'mastery of forms' (postmodernism arguably being a dominant literary critical 'form' of the late 1980s) necessary to ensure that Baker becomes, and remains, 'heard' by his literary critical peers.

Baker is, it seems, no great fan of Anglo-American Modernism. First, he explains, he does not feel the 'intimacy and reverence' (7) towards, for example *Ulysses*, that many readers appear to feel – perhaps, he suggests, because his identity as an Afro-American means that the questions this Modernist text is taken to raise, posited as the questions at the heart of life, do not apply, or do not apply so acutely or in the same way, to him. We might ask what this implies for, say, a white British person's understanding or response to the work of, for example, Jean Toomer or Zora Neale Hurston. Of course, Baker does not suggest that we can get nothing at all from the literatures of other cultures, but does his emphatic articulation of his lack of a particular emotional response to a text imply a fundamental segregation (to use a loaded term) at the heart of literary appreciation? Baker goes on to elaborate on his objection to much Anglo-American Modernism by complaining of its lack of political, social impact – 'Surely it is the case that the various isms' of the first decades of British and American modernism did not forestall wars, feed the poor, cure the sick, empower coal miners in Wales (or West Virginia), or arrest the spread of bureaucratic technology' (13). This observation has two possible implications. First, it seems to suggest that, by contrast, the products of the Harlem Renaissance *did* play a part in bringing about material change. Secondly – and Baker alludes to this – there is the implication that Anglo-American Modernism could, even should, itself thus be seen as a failure; as the poetry that, in W.H. Auden's words, 'makes nothing happen'. However, what is at stake here is precisely the point Auden is grappling with in his poem: should art be evaluated in terms of its effects in other arenas, its capacity to change the world in concrete, measurable ways ('forestall wars, feed the poor')? Or is there a danger that art thus understood becomes merely a vehicle for political or ideological positions?

Returning to Anglo-American and British literary history, Baker also suggests that it is difficult to conceive of scholars devoting enormous energy to explicating the ' "failure" of modernism' (13) in the way that he sees scholars wringing their hands over the 'failure' of the Harlem Renaissance. The general point Baker is making about this internalized oppression, where black critics start from the premise that Afro-American art had 'failed', is an important one. However, there have in fact been numerous critics who do precisely what Baker says, from various perspectives. Georg Lukács famously castigates Modernist literature for its distortion of social reality, and is only the most prominent figure in a strand of criticism wary of modernism's (potentially fatal?) associations with fascism; later critics like Alan Wilde and Ihab Hassan attack Modernism for its damagingly conservative, indeed reactionary, tendencies, against the progressive potential of postmodernism. From a different political position, Lionel Trilling and Daniel Bell have expressed anxiety precisely about the detrimental effect of Modernist literature on the dominant social order. Baker's assertion, then, invites the literary critic to consider the general question of what might constitute the 'failure' of an aesthetic movement, and where Modernism's own failures and successes might be seen to lie.

One final question to ask of Baker's work is the extent to which its arguments are, as he himself suspects, 'sui generis' (xiv), or unique to this particular work of criticism. While the Afro-American inheritance of slavery and segregation, and the terms Baker identifies as central to its texts (mask, nonsense, marronage, etc.), clearly need to be seen as specific to the artistic and cultural context he discusses, can we read his tropes of 'mastery of form' and 'deformation of mastery' across to other subaltern groups – to women's writing, working-class writing, queer writing? What are the political implications of this? And to what extent do the tropes proposed by Baker apply specifically to the products of the early twentieth century? It goes without saying that these questions return us to the broader issue of what constitutes the Modernist canon. What makes Baker's work particularly intriguing is the way it invites us to revise and keep revising 'the canon', at the same time as proposing a whole new paradigm for understanding the literary products of the early twentieth century which does not even aspire to their inclusion in that (Anglo-American) canon, or to assessment in terms of the values and categories that the works of that canon seem to propose.

Lawrence Rainey, *Institutions of Modernism: Literary Elites and Public Cultures* (1998)

In some ways, Lawrence Rainey's book marks a return to a more traditional approach to literary criticism, invoking concepts of literary and aesthetic value (such as 'greatness') which have been treated with suspicion in most recent critical work. But it has also inaugurated a new strand in Modernist studies, one which resists the stereotype of Modernism as hermetically sealed off from 'vulgar' questions of finance and marketing, and instead draws our attention to the intimate relationship between Modernist literature and the financial, social and cultural structures that made its production and in particular its dissemination possible.

Rainey begins by clarifying his position in relation to the Modernism/mass culture debate. While there is a long history of critical work which constructs Modernism as strictly segregated from popular culture, Rainey argues that this does not accurately reflect the cultural context of the early twentieth century. In a move characteristic of his approach throughout, he identifies a number of historical events which, in his view, exemplify 'the growing complexity of cultural exchange and circulation in modern society' (2): the piloting of the *Daily Mail*, the construction of the Coliseum in London, and the first appearance of the word 'middlebrow'. These events, Rainey contends, 'point to an institutional field of cultural production being rapidly and radically transformed into one more variegated and complex than the rigid dichotomy that between "high" and "low" allows.' (3). Modernism, Rainey argues, participates in this institutional field in a much more knowing way than previously acknowledged. 'Modernism', he suggests, 'marks neither a straightforward resistance nor an outright capitulation to commodification, but a momentary equivocation that incorporates elements of both in a brief, necessarily unstable synthesis' (3).

While, as we shall see, Rainey generally eschews textual analysis in this volume, concentrating instead on describing the social and financial structures surrounding the production of a text, he does provide one particularly vivid textual example to illustrate his challenge to the received wisdom about the relationship between Modernism and popular culture: 'Leopold Bloom, the protagonist of *Ulysses* who concludes his first appearance in the novel by cleansing himself of faeces with pages torn from the popular weekly *Tit-Bits*, epitomizes the modernist contempt for popular culture' (2). Part of Rainey's project is to *revise* this model of Modernist 'contempt' for mass culture, and thus we are implicitly invited to return to this example afresh. That Bloom wipes himself with *Tit-Bits* seems, on one level, to express a fairly emphatic contempt for the paper and perhaps, by extension all it signifies. But on the other hand, it also involves an intimate and necessary relationship between Bloom and *Tit-Bits* – Bloom *needs Tit-Bits*. Is the evocation of popular culture in much Modernist literature – think of *The Waste Land, Ulysses* or *Between the Acts*, the poetry of William Carlos Williams, or the work of Jean Toomer – a textual symptom of modernism's need for popular culture, its reliance thereon, even if in order to define itself against it? Indeed, might the defensive attitude towards popular culture found in many (though not all) of these texts reflect an anxiety about precisely the kind of reliance on strategies of mass-marketing that Rainey argues is central to the very production of Modernism as a concept?

In what follows, Rainey explores how 'institutions of modernism', which he defines as 'the structures that interpose themselves between the individual and society' (6) (for his purposes, things like publishing houses, magazines, individual patrons of the arts and so on), operated in the production and dissemination of Modernist literature. In his first chapter, he examines Ezra Pound's 'steps towards art as public practice', following the 'collapse of the "courtly" structure of cultural production' (29) – financial backing from wealthy individuals – that had previously supported him. The 'failures' of Pound's projects up to 1914, notably Imagism and the magazine *Blast* (both indeed short-lived), represent, according to Rainey, a failure to respond to the new 'institutions of mass culture' whose operations precipitated 'a permanent collapse of all distinctions between art and commodity' (38). The solution that Pound ultimately identified, Rainey suggests, was 'to accept [. . .] the status of art as commodity, but simultaneously to transform it into a special kind of commodity, a rarity capable of sustaining investment value' (39). The Modernist artwork becomes, therefore, part of mass culture in that it is identified, and identifies itself, as a particular kind of commodity.

This idea of the Modernist artwork as a rare artefact and potential invest-ment is central to Rainey's arguments. In the next two chapters, Rainey presents a detailed account of the financial contexts of the production of

James Joyce's *Ulysses* and T.S. Eliot's *The Waste Land*, replete with lists of figures, sequences of dates and even a couple of tables. He also discusses the implications of these contexts for the way in which these texts have been received, assessed and entrenched as cornerstones of Anglo-American literary Modernism. In his discussion of *Ulysses*, the emphasis is on the dissemination of the text in a limited edition, priced beyond the means of the 'ordinary reader'. By contrast with the old-school systems of direct patronage, of the kind that had initially supported Pound, the publication of *Ulysses* had the 'effect of turning every purchaser of the edition into a quasi-patron, someone directly supporting the artist himself' (53). Moreover, the way in which *Ulysses* gained notoriety through its scarcity value has implications, Rainey argues, for assessments of its aesthetic value. To illustrate this, Rainey cites Pound's description of *Ulysses* as a 'sound investment', reading this phrase as a metaphor for 'genuine literary achievement'. 'Pound does not articulate the nature of the connection between these two orders of value, between his aesthetic claim and his assertion about monetary value,' Rainey notes, 'but their juxtaposition works to elide the two into a single category or to suggest that the second justifies the first, that an increase in the monetary value of the first edition works to justify claims about the artistic or literary value of *Ulysses*' (71).

While his analysis of *The Waste Land* also focuses on concrete details of the text's publication, according to Rainey 'the publication of *The Waste Land* marked the crucial moment in the transition of Modernism from a minority culture to one supported by an important institutional and financial apparatus' (91). The various institutions through which a Modernist text got into print – journals of various sorts, private, limited or commercial editions – were, Rainey suggests, sufficiently well-established by this point for Eliot, who 'fully [. . .] understood the protocols of avant-garde publishing' (103), to play the various possible publishers off against each other. In so doing, Eliot sought to ensure that his poem was, in Rainey's words 'successful, yet not too successful' (104); reaching a sufficiently wide audience to make an impact, yet not reaching so wide an audience (or the wrong type of audience) to risk its being ill-received.

The various negotiations involved in the publication of *The Waste Land* are detailed in order not only to emphasize the immense sums that were, by this point, at stake in the Modernist literature industry, but also to reiterate a provocative claim Rainey also makes in the chapter on *Ulysses*, namely that 'the effect of modernism was not so much to encourage reading but to render it superfluous' (56). Rainey draws attention to what he calls 'the illusion that "art" or "the poem" or "the text" had been the central concern of participants [mainly publishers or financiers] whose decisions were consistently made when as yet they had not read a word of the work in question. And not without reason, for the text was largely irrelevant' (106). We can see what Rainey means by this dramatic statement where he argues that having traced 'the experience of those who actually engaged in modern textual production' we are led to consider an alternative kind of reading from the one usually associated with Modernist literature, namely close textual analysis. 'Indeed, if we named it [this alternative kind of reading] in their honour,' Rainey suggests, 'we could call it the modernist principle of reading and formulate it thus: The best reading of a work may, on some occasions, be one that does not read it at all' (106). This dramatic assertion importantly draws our attention to the idea that 'close reading is itself a historical form of activity [. . .] and that other kinds of reading are and have been practiced – not least among them the not-reading that was practiced by the editors of *The Dial* [in which *The Waste Land* was finally published]' (106).

Rainey immediately pulls back from this bald statement, acknowledging that it would 'doubtless be misleading' (106). Nevertheless, his readers will have noticed that 'a reading of a work [. . .] that does not read it at all' reflects Rainey's own approach in this book. Rainey acknowledges from the outset that '[s]ome readers, especially those with literary critical training, will find far too little of the detailed examination of actual works that is sometimes held to be the only important or worthwhile form of critical activity', but defends his position by stating 'I reject the idea that history or theory are acceptable only if they take on the role of humble handmaiden to the aesthetic artefact' (6). This statement might be put into interesting dialogue with other aspects of Rainey's approach, such as his assertion of 'basic ideas about the relative autonomy of artistic judgment, or about the relative independence of artistic quality' (147), which would seem to impute some kind of privilege to the 'aesthetic artefact'; or his insistence on analyses of form as the key to identifying the 'greatness' or otherwise of a text – or a writer. To what extent does it damage Rainey's argument that, while he insists that assessment of formal qualities is that which is lacking from some strands of contemporary literary criticism on Modernism, he produces such formal analyses himself only in brief snatches?

It is worth, then, dwelling on a moment when Rainey does do some 'detailed examination of [an] actual work', to controversial effect, in his last chapter, on H.D. In brief, Rainey argues that H.D. has been erroneously canonized by literary critics too quick to embrace writers simply on the basis of their oppressed or marginal personal identity – crudely, for political rather than aesthetic reasons. H.D., Rainey implies, is particularly apt to be reclaimed by this critical tendency because of her status as female and lesbian, her associations with a black artist, sympathy for Jewish causes and so on (148). The 'institution of modernism' at play here is patronage. The crucial moment in H.D.'s life came, says Rainey, in 1918 when she met the heiress

Bryher (Winnifred Ellerman): 'In Bryher, H.D. found first a lover, then a friend. More important, she also found a lifelong patron of endless bounty' (148). Guaranteeing to provide financially for H.D. for the rest of her life, Bryher, in Rainey's account, did more harm than good; insulating H.D. from the need to 'engage in an active or genuine dialogue with her contemporaries' (155), Bryher's patronage only ensured that H.D. became a 'coterie poet', ultimately producing works for a very limited circle of friends. Rainey presents H.D. as an object lesson in 'the risks inherent in the modernist culture of patronage, the culture that sustained but may also have ruined her career' (168).

Rainey therefore argues that H.D.'s work is not of a sufficient quality to justify her reclamation as an important Modernist writer (most notably by Susan Stanford Friedman). He does so in part by producing a formal close reading of H.D.'s poem 'Leda' alongside Yeats's 'Leda and the Swan', in which H.D.'s poem comes off very badly. Yeats's text is 'plural', Rainey argues, where H.D's is 'monologic' (consisting of a single voice or perspective); Yeats 'prob[es] discordant extremes of experience' where H.D.'s 'terrain of sensibility seems more restricted' (160) (for Yeats: see also Baxter, Paddy, Stinson, Thacker and Wilson). While coherent in themselves, these assessments (like any close reading, certainly) rest on several assumptions: that plurality and dissonance are necessarily of greater value than monologism or restricted sensibility; or that a less combative, more 'level' or 'soft' (to use terms from H.D.'s poem) tone is inappropriate to a rendering of this particular mythic incident; or that H.D.'s poem *is* in fact 'monologic' and 'restricted'. Thus, when Rainey asserts that much of H.D.'s later poetry is 'irreparably flawed' (168), and of limited interest to the critic, he is evoking a poetic standard which nevertheless remains more or less implicit in his own work, and from which other readers might dissent.

This discussion takes us, finally, to the question of canonicity, and how Rainey's work might be seen in terms of the 'canon-expansion' tendency in recent Modernist studies. On the one hand, Rainey's focus on the holy trinity of Anglo-American Modernism – Joyce, Pound and Eliot – seems to reinforce the old canon rather than challenge it. On the other hand, Rainey's exploration of the practical ways in which certain texts came to hold such a central place in the Modernist literary landscape – the marketing strategies surrounding the publication of *The Waste Land* and *Ulysses* – encourages scepticism about the necessary or intrinsic qualities of these texts, as Rainey himself notes (without actually suggesting that their aesthetic qualities are therefore evacuated). Further, his very approach – his focus on apparently peripheral details, accumulation of facts about the finances of publishing houses, the family histories of art patrons, the obstacles lying in the way of a person trying to access archives in a foreign country and so on – seems to imply a shifting of focus from what had previously been seen as the 'centre', that is, the text itself, closely read, to the 'margins' – the previously parenthesised practical details of money and contacts and business negotiations. This general shift of focus, from centre to margins, is itself a critical gesture that might resonate far beyond the concerns of this particular book. In any case, Rainey's work constitutes a dramatic intervention in and disruption to previous assumptions about what, literally, makes a Modernist text.

7 Key Critical Concepts and Topics (Including a survey of major critical figures)

David Ian Paddy

Chapter Overview

Introduction

To encounter Modernism as a movement is to venture into a puzzling maze, its coordinates including apparently difficult literature and art. To glimpse the vast, ever-expanding expanse of critical responses to Modernism perhaps only heightens feelings of disorientation, and a fear of incomprehension. The aim of this chapter is to identify a series of critical themes and intellectual figures that may help the reader orient themselves in a difficult field. Included are a variety of perennial images and issues that have interested readers and critics of Modernism for many years, as well as notions that have drawn more interest in recent criticism. The first part of the chapter provides an examination of these key concepts of Modernism: the city, cultural sterility and renewal, empire and crisis, gender and identity, Modernism and form, sexuality, and time and flux. Further orientation may come from looking at the second section on key figures, which provides information about pivotal thinkers and writers, such as Charles Darwin (see also Baxter and Wilson), Sigmund Freud (see also Baxter, Stinson, Thacker and Wilson), Karl Marx (see Paddy below and Stinson) and Friedrich Nietzsche (see Paddy below), who exerted a tremendous influence on the ideas and practices of Modernist literature (for Nietzsche see also Murray and Stinson). This current section offers tips in traversing the maze of Modernism.

Critical Concepts

The City

Although cities have been a staple phenomenon of history, with the polis serving an important function for the majority of civilizations, the rapid transformation and growth of cities – in scale and quantity – in the nineteenth and twentieth centuries turned them into vital sites for Modernism. In one sense, this is a very simple matter. Most Modernist writers and groups found the city to be the ideal place to live, meet and test out daring new projects. It was the locus of intellectual and artistic activity, a place where the urbane and bohemian could build a hothouse for creativity. The city was the place to be modern.

Picture the Dadaists with their cacophonic Cabaret Voltaire in Zürich, Bloomsbury's cultured zone of studios, museums and libraries, or the movable feast of artists – Ernest Hemingway, James Joyce, Gertrude Stein, Ford Madox Ford and many more – gathered in Parisian salons and cafés (for Bloomsbury, see also Day, Randall and Stinson). Naturally, the metropolis also became the setting for a large number of important Modernist texts. What would Modernism be without Alfred Döblin's Berlin, Joyce's Dublin, Franz Kafka's Prague, Robert Musil's Vienna or Langston Hughes's New York?

There are of course notable exceptions. Modernism resided just as well in William Faulkner's Yoknapatawpha County and the colonial outposts of Joseph Conrad. (See Empire and Crisis below; see also Baxter, Murray, Randall and Stinson.) Still, Modernity is largely defined by urban experience and the city occupies Modernism's centre stage. In *Modernism: A Guide to European Literature 1890–1930*, Malcolm Bradbury argues that 'In many respects the literature of experimental Modernism which emerged in the last years of the nineteenth century and developed into the present one was an art of cities' (96). More than simple setting, the city is important to Modernism for the challenges and opportunities it offers. The city, this rapidly changing space of movement, crowds, consumerism, technology, architecture and a dizzying vortex of novel experiences, transformed modern writing by placing great demands on the means of representation.

Charles Baudelaire describes modern man as a flâneur, milling amidst the crowds, an urban dweller and mover soaking in the experience of 'the ebb and flow, the bustle, the fleeting and the infinite' (105). Yet, for many others in the nineteenth century, it was industrialization, which brought more and more people to the cities and transformed the nature and experience of the city that drew writerly attention. Novelists like Charles Dickens, in *Hard Times* (1854), and Elizabeth Gaskell, in *North and South* (1854), as well as social observers like Friedrich Engels, in *The Condition of the Working Class in England* (1844), examined the effects of industrial life on the new masses of workers living in the cities. In these works, urban existence is a largely dark affair; the city is a place of danger and despair; masses flung together in slavish, dehumanizing work, living in bare, dirty, smelly hovels. The cities of Modernism never quite lose this patina of filth and danger – Joseph Conrad's *The Secret Agent* (1907) and T.S. Eliot's *The Waste Land* (1922) make this clear (for Eliot see also Baxter, Murray, Randall and Stinson) – yet they also clearly possess more positive qualities of excitement, the thrill of speed, novelty and shopping.

If the city of the nineteenth century novel is largely a backdrop used to explore larger social themes of class inequity, poverty, crime and corruption, a number of Modernist novels bring the city to the foreground to make it a primary character, a complex living being. In the Modernist novel, the city also becomes an opportunity to examine central Modernist concerns of consciousness, perspective and time. Vital examples here are Virginia Woolf's experiment in the psychical life of London, *Mrs Dalloway* (1925) (for Woolf, see also Baxter, Murray, Randall, Stinson and Wilson), and James Joyce's gritty realistic and mythic mappings of Dublin, *Dubliners* (1914) and *Ulysses* (1922).

As Clarissa Dalloway walks through London, her mind is revealed to us as a labyrinth of thoughts and reminiscences, yet as she entangles the past – images from childhood – and the future – hosting plans for tonight's dinner party – her mind is open to a constant bombardment of images, smells and sounds of the city around her. She experiences it as a joy of explosive sensoria, often infused with the technological and commercial, as she hears a car backfire and sees a plane sending out an advertisement in smoke, and she herself crosses the streets in search of a florist. In the 'Aeolus' chapter of *Ulysses*, Joyce formalizes Dublin as a textual landscape; Bloom's experiences in and out of the newspaper offices are transcribed in the manner of journalistic conventions. This reinforces Peter Fritzsche's claim in *Reading Berlin 1900* that the newspaper became one of the guiding texts that helped modern citizens navigate the difficult, fragmentary terrains of the city.

The city posed a challenge to modern artists. How best to represent the mass conglomeration that also held such a dizzying multiplicity of views and voices happening simultaneously? These rationalized mazes of disorienting alleyways and upward-moving buildings held within them masses of individuals with their intersecting histories, experiences and perspectives. How best to capture the novel sensations of the city? The sociologist Georg Simmel thought the city a place that demanded a blasé attitude from its denizens, in order to cope with its excesses, yet modern artists also understood that the city gave them the greatest opportunities to respond in kind to its motley brew of flux and speed with radical innovations in the means of representation (for Simmell and the city see Day).

Cultural Sterility and Renewal

There is an air of apocalypse that permeates Modernism. Impatient manifestoes are filled with declarations of artistic end times. For the Futurists, museums were nothing more than cemeteries. Antonin Artaud thought Shakespeare to blame for the pitiful state of modern theatre. In 'Surgery for the Novel – or a Bomb' (1923), D.H. Lawrence asks, 'Is the novel on his deathbed, old sinner? Or is he just toddling round his cradle, sweet little thing?' (517). Bold statements all. Yet, for any true believer, apocalypse need not be a negative thing. Although the end of times brings destruction, it also brings revelation, renewal and rejuvenation, as the things and values of the past come to an end and a new age is born. Modernism made extreme demands of culture. The avant-garde's predilection for manifestoes is grounded in a desire to declare contemporary culture dead, yet each movement thought itself uniquely equipped to bring about its successful rejuvenation. If Yeats worries in the first stanza of 'The Second Coming' (1922), 'Things fall apart; the centre cannot hold; / Mere anarchy is loosed upon the world', he begins the second stanza by insisting, 'Surely some revelation is at hand' (184). Perhaps everything is dying and 'blood-dimmed', but in a new art's complex visions, some message may be read and made redemptive (184).

With a new century on the horizon, writers of the 1890s wrote with a sense of dark foreboding. The fin-de-siècle era was witness to a wide range of documents calling attention to a perceived sterility in modern culture. Some assumed decay and decline without a possibility of renewal, which resulted in a nihilistic outlook (rooted perhaps in Schopenhauerian philosophy or doom-ridden characters like Dostoevsky's underground man and Turgenev's Bazarov). For others, a belief in cultural sterility produced an attitude of Decadence, which encouraged an indulgence in the pleasures and pains of the end times. Figures as diverse as J.K. Huysmans, Comte de Lautréamont, Villiers de l'Isle-Adam and Oscar Wilde sought to remove themselves from the world and find a home in a realm of pure aesthetics. Describing Théophile Gautier's sense of Decadence Peter Nicholls says it 'expresses the inner logic of a modernity which has reached the terminal point in a cultural parabola already traced by the ancient civilizations. Like them, the modern period has exhausted itself in the search for ever greater sophistication and intensity of experience' (45). Yet, beyond the nihilists and Decadents, there were others who presumed grand hopes for the new century. Modern culture might be sterile or doomed, but such decline might be a hope in disguise, a clearing ground for creating a whole new world. Notably, the period also saw the growth of scientific romances with their visions of technological apocalypse, total war and utopian regeneration.

Much of the language and assumptions underlying the various beliefs in cultural sterility and renewal relied upon an adaptation of Charles Darwin's evolutionary biology to art and culture. What if cultures, like species, thrived or declined in an unfolding contest of the weak and strong? The criminologist Cesare Lombroso looked at human physiogonomy to decipher the faces of degenerates in a society, the criminal types who would only pass on their criminal traits if uncurbed. Building on Lombroso's theories, Max Nordau, author of *Degeneration* (1883), argued that modern authors and artists were also degenerates, and popularized a theory that the decadent tendencies of modern art in fact reflected diseases of the mind and body, an idea taken up by the Nazis in their exhibitions of degenerate art. Certainly sickness of body and spirit became a favourite topic among some modern artists, notably Thomas Mann in *The Magic Mountain* (1924) and *Death in Venice* (1911) and Franz Kafka in numerous short stories. The architect Adolf Loos, in arguing for a radical new building practice, described older practices, reliant upon impure ornamentation, in terms of criminality and disease, while the philosopher and historian Oswald Spengler argued that modern civilization was like a dying body or species on its way out.

Modernism was built upon and sustained the fin-de-siècle's twin impulses of degeneration and regeneration. Many artists, despite their varying theories and manifestoes, thought Modernity a crippling force, but new aesthetic forces were capable of rejuvenating society. Like Friedrich Nietzsche, they felt that the destruction of the constraining values of the past could unleash new freedoms. Consider one of the most famous phrases that have come to define Modernism, Ezra Pound's 'Make it new' (for Pound see also Murray, Randall, Stinson, Thacker and Wilson). While this certainly speaks to the importance of novelty and experimentation within the formal realms of Modernism, the demand to 'make it new' also speaks to a general assumption of the era that certain social and cultural traditions and mores belonged to the past, no longer worked for the present, and must be discarded in favour of new ideas and values. D.H. Lawrence did not consider that writers like Joyce and Proust showed the way forward, because their writing through abstraction, leaves the readers disconnected from the natural world, and genuine emotions which Lawrence so valued. From him this was the real sin of modernity, whereas T.S. Eliot, in *The Waste Land* (1922) attempts to represent notions of cultural sterility, exactly through an abstract citational collage, thinking such a strategy might yet return the moderns to a lost common moral ground or common knowledge lost in the fragments of modern life. As differing as the writers of Modernism were in their viewpoints they shared a common language of crisis and a need for art as the means of regeneration.

Empire and Crisis

The Modernist era has at times been thought of as a period of decadent formalism, an era of difficult works unmoored from the gravity of the world. It's as if Stephen Dedalus's declaration in *Ulysses* (1922), 'History . . . is a nightmare from which I am trying to awake' (42), has been taken as the non-ironic voice of Modernism itself, and the Victorian era, which had embraced the Condition of England novel, had drifted into an ether of art-for-art's sake. Yet history and politics clearly shaped and resound throughout Modernist art. The era of Modernism was coincident with not only Women's Suffrage (see Gender and Identity below) but also the later phases of colonialism and the start of the decline of the British Empire. Tensions over the nature and purpose of the Empire were already evident in the nineteenth century, writ large in the division of opinions between Prime Ministers Disraeli and Gladstone. The nobility or moral bankruptcy of imperialism grew as an explicit or implicit topic in a number of Modernist works. While the most notable, and most frequently discussed texts are Joseph Conrad's *Heart of Darkness* (1899) (and *Nostromo* [1904] to a lesser degree) and E.M. Forster's *A Passage to India* (1924), the empire makes its appearance known in the most canonical of texts, as in *Mrs Dalloway* (1925) and *The Good Soldier* (1915), for instance. While a growing body of postcolonial literature develops exponentially in the second half of the twentieth century, it is important to observe how the crisis of empire found its way into the content and form of Modernism.

To what extent did Modernist works perpetuate the ideologies of empire and imperialism? As discussed above in 1975, Achebe spawned a rich debate about Conrad's *Heart of Darkness* potentially representing a racist viewpoint that endorses the hierarchical and dehumanizing attitudes of imperialism (see Baxter). Subsequently, a number of critics have appealed for a more nuanced or complex reading of Conrad's novella, although many follow Achebe in drawing attention to the imperial context and subtext of Modernist works.

One of the more troubling aspects of Modernism was its reliance on the 'primitive' in drawing inspiration from the arts of the 'Third World', mined and stripped for more urbane, 'civilised' purposes. Exhibitions and collections of works from Africa and Asia became inspirational for modern artists looking for means of breaking from the traditions of Western realism. African masks shape the abstracted faces of Picasso, while Gauguin's flat planes of colour originate in his Polynesian voyages. The modern drama of Yeats and Artaud de-contextualized gestures from Japanese and Indonesian dramas to produce a new stylized theatre, while the Expressionist theatre of Oskar Kokoschka relied on a primal other of the id to come and disturb the safe ego of the Occident. As Bill Ashcroft, Gareth Griffiths and Helen Tiffin specify in *The Empire Writes Back*, 'African artefacts, then, together with art-works from such apparently "similar" cultures as New Guinea, the South Sea Islands, the North American Indians and Inuit, New Zealand Maoris and Australian Aboriginals were viewed as examples of cultures "preserved in time", of the primitive and aboriginal impulses common to all men' (157–158).

However, to think of Modernism's relation to empire is not only to think of the West's uses and abuses of the colonial other, but also to think of Modernism as something happening beyond the launching pads of empire – Britain, the US and the continent – for important Modernisms were being produced in those lands being mined for inspiration, Asia, Africa, South America, Canada and the Antipodes. The vibrant and varied scenes of Latin American Modernism are especially notable in this frame. Such zones have also produced a liminal figure like Katherine Mansfield, whose writing in the context of New Zealand, raises critical questions about her position as a colonial and/or colonizing subject.

While Conrad and Forster offered complex moral observations on the empire 'out there', another set of writers showed an imperial crisis closer to home. Irish, Scottish and Welsh writers challenged English hegemony and made greater devolutionary moves toward Home Rule. In 1899 in 'The Irish Literary Theatre' William Butler Yeats declares 'All literature and all art is national' (268), as a way of insisting upon Ireland's separate status. Language – that central topic of Modernist literary art – became a vexed question of identity and power in relation to nation and empire for writers in the Celtic lands (Yeats and Joyce in Ireland, Hugh MacDiarmiad in Scotland, Saunders Lewis and Kate Roberts in Wales, Henry Jenner in Cornwall). Yet, even these issues are not simply or clearly defined, given Joyce's mockeries of Ireland and the Gaelic League, Samuel Beckett's Molloy declaring, 'Tears and laughter, they are so much Gaelic to me' (37), and Flann O'Brien's ludicrous take on Finn MacCool in *At Swim-Two-Birds* (1939).

In Modernism's wake, a full range of postcolonial literatures would emerge, as would, in the writing of George Orwell and Graham Greene, a literature of international politics. But, Modernism itself had already begun to reflect – sometimes consciously, sometimes unconsciously – on empire as institution and as a more nefarious force that had come to rule a way of seeing people and the world. For even if, say, Virginia Woolf never contributed a novel concerned with India, in a work like *Three Guineas* (1938), she understands the subtle alliances of empire, patriarchy and war as social and psychological forces of oppression. If empire was beginning to fade, imperialism certainly was not.

Gender and Identity

For many years, in the wake of Modernism, an image persisted of the literary Modernists as a select group of bold, daring men – Ezra Pound, James Joyce, T.S. Eliot, Joseph Conrad and D.H. Lawrence. Such adventuresome individuals were depicted as standing against the herd, noble pioneers forging new frontiers. Over the past few decades, though, more attention has been given to the number of women who played vital roles in the many movements of Modernism. Virginia Woolf has of course long been one of the central stars in the Modernist firmament, but so many other women were experimentalists and innovators who changed the shape of modern literary art. A brief roll call could include Gertrude Stein, H.D., May Sinclair, Dorothy Richardson, Katherine Mansfield, Rebecca West, Djuna Barnes, Mary Butts, Charlotte Mew, Jean Rhys, Elizabeth Bowen, Olivia Moore and Kate Roberts. Other women, such as Sylvia Beach, who ran the Shakespeare and Company bookstore in Paris, played important roles as editors, patrons and publishers.

Not merely the symptom of the changing tides of criticism, the recent attention to the women of Modernism points back to a crucial fact about Modernism's historical moment. As Marianne DeKoven notes in *Modernism and*

Gender, 'The period from 1880–1920, within which Modernism emerged and rose to preeminence as the dominant art form in the West . . ., was also the heyday of the first wave of feminism, consolidated in the woman suffrage movement' (174). Coming in the wake of the Victorian 'Woman Question' and during the fight for the vote, Modernism occurred in a period reverberating with debates about the nature and fate of the New Woman. While the moderns continued to reflect, like their Victorian forebears, on the utility and morality of gender roles assigned by religion, law and commerce, they also reflected profoundly on the individual experience of gender, probing into the internal, psychological experiences that defined each individual, which led them to contemplate critically upon the very ideas of masculinity and femininity.

Pushing beyond the demands of the Suffrage movement, Mina Loy urges in her 'Feminist Manifesto' (1914) that 'NO scratching on the surface of the rubbish heap of tradition, will bring about *Reform*, the only method is *Absolute Demolition*' (611). In a manifesto crammed with thoughts of child rearing, eugenics and 'superior women', Loy demands not simple recognition for women, but a plunging into the depths of what is meant by masculine and feminine: 'Leave off looking to men to find out what you are *not* – seek within yourselves to find out what you *are*' (611).

Not content with the issues of legal representation raised by the suffragettes, a number of Modernist writers contended with that other form of representation; that is, thinking in terms of aesthetics, they asked how one captures the truth of the changing dynamic of men and women's social and psychological experiences. In *A Room of One's Own* (1929), Virginia Woolf speculates upon the reasons for the small canon of great women writers. Economic and educational conditions represent her primary answers, but she is still left pondering whether women writers would merely replicate a man's perspective or if they could produce a distinctly feminine voice and aesthetic.

E.M. Forster's fundamental distinction in *Aspects of the Novel* (1927) between flat and round characters comes into play here. To individuate a character and not merely replicate types, a writer must reflect deeply on the individual make-up that distinguishes a character, and, for many Modernists, this meant looking deep inside the character. Giving intense attention to consciousness and perspective raised questions about the nature of being – Are men and women different in their essential being? – epistemology – Do men and women see, perceive the world through different ways of knowing? – and language – Do men and women speak and write in the same language? Arguably, Virginia Woolf and Dorothy Richardson developed a feminine voice through their use of stream of consciousness, but how can such a voice be differentiated from the stream of Molly's thoughts in the final chapter of Joyce's *Ulysses*?

Modernism's concordance with the period of Suffrage alerts us to the former's interest in the nature of gender and identity. Suffrage aimed to help women find their voice and assert an identity – and the sheer number of women contributors to Modernism is testament enough to this – but Modernism's interest in the flux of experience and the unconscious forces running beneath and against consciousness also poses a challenge to notions of stable voices and identities. Immensely influential to the later French feminist theories of gender proposed by Hélène Cixous, Luce Irigaray and Julia Kristeva, Modernist texts showed how the complexity of gendered identity demands new modes of representation and deep questions about what it means to be a man or woman, masculine and feminine, and whether such qualities are essential and biological states of being, or historical and personal forces in flux.

Modernism and Form

Joseph Conrad begins the preface to his novel *The Nigger of the 'Narcissus* (1897; 1967) with these words, 'A work that aspires, however humbly, to the condition of art should carry its justification in every line' (160). This humble urging is eminently important to the development of Modernism, for Conrad here makes the simple, but demanding claim that fiction should be an art form, not merely an entertainment or medium for moral instruction, and that as an art form it needs to be deliberate in its formal construction. To make fiction artistic would entail a dramatic shift of attention from the story itself to the means of its presentation, at times giving more attention to *how* something is said than to *what* is said.

Modernism was an artistic movement, or group of movements that foregrounded formal concerns to a degree rarely or perhaps never seen before in art. While all art must necessarily consist of form and content, Modernist artists often made form a central component of a work's content, or, as Samuel Beckett says of James Joyce's *Finnegans Wake* in 'Dante ... Bruno . Vico .. Joyce': 'Here form *is* content, content *is* form.... His writing is not *about* something; *it is that something itself*' (503).

Such an increasing concentration on form and aesthetic autonomy originated in Symbolism and the Aesthetic Movement. Inspired by Charles Baudelaire, the French Symbolist poets Stéphane Mallarmé and Arthur Rimbaud sought an art rife with unconventional symbols and imagery that would leave the reader momentarily suspended within a fresh metaphor's novelty, rather than in the comfort of familiar imagery (see also Day). Caught in suggestion and mystery, the reader of a Symbolist work is meant to pause in the process of signification in an effort to loosen the referential function of language. Building on Walter Pater's aestheticism, Oscar Wilde, in the preface to *The Picture of Dorian Gray* (1891), insisted that 'All art is quite useless' and that 'to reveal art and conceal the artist is art's aim' (xxxiii–xxxiv). Together, the principles of Symbolism and the Aesthetic Movement influenced such artists and critics as those of the Bloomsbury Group, particularly the theories of Clive Bell, and helped art become free of its duty as mere mirror for the world outside art.

Such a focus on form posed a challenge to the dominant nineteenth-century traditions of realism and Naturalism because it drew attention to the necessarily constructed nature of any representational act. The Russian Symbolist, Valery Briusov, writes, in 'Against Naturalism in the Theater' (1902; 2001), 'To reproduce life faithfully on the stage is impossible. The stage is conventional by its very nature' (73). Impressionists and Expressionists and other movements undermined Naturalism's assumption that the external world could be described objectively, and emphasized instead the subjective perspectives that occluded any direct access to the world. In so doing, these new artistic practices gave more attention to art as a tool that shapes and creates a world rather than merely documents an external one.

At the same time, the strange formal experiments of Modernism, while reacting against realism, paradoxically forged new and more complex forms of realism. For instance, while the digressive, suggestive and associational sentences of stream-of-consciousness writing clearly depart from the clear and explicit linear logic and chronology of the nineteenth century realist novels, the novels of Joyce, Woolf, Richardson and Faulkner could be regarded as providing a more realistic depiction of human thought processes and how the world is perceived and experienced.

Being more attentive to form, Modernist writers developed an expanded paint box of tools and techniques that enabled them to enrich the works composed on writerly canvases. Experiments in point of view, such as multiple perspectives, unreliable narration and an increased use of free-indirect discourse, were useful for portraying the complexities of human psychology, the filters of consciousness and the relativity of truth. Fascination with the relativity of time brought about bold explorations in narrative sequencing, which generated deliberately confusing narratives that looped and moved against time's arrow (see Time and Flux). Language became musical – an artistic tool in itself, not merely servant to a message – be it in the multilingual flourishes of Joyce or the fragments of Gertrude Stein. Overall, the reader of these Modernist works could not help but notice the way language, syntax, narrative structure and point of view were being brought to the fore and employed in new, self-conscious ways that may initially seem to spoil a simple story, but upon reflection gave it a richer complexity. Given a modern world that felt increasingly chaotic, Modernist artists concentrated on form as a means of capturing that chaos or providing a sense of order the world was felt to lack.

Sexuality

Breaking from the prescriptive mores of Victorian society, the moderns explored sexuality with a brave new frankness. There was a rising bohemian culture that encouraged a lifestyle alluded to by Virginia Nicholson as experiments in living. The early twentieth century saw a new spirit of sexual liberation, in which open discussions of sexual matters sometimes led to open relationships. This was particularly true of the Bloomsbury Group. The endorsement of free love in the early 1900s stemmed from the new freedoms of the New Woman and Margaret Sanger's innovations in birth control, even if, like the sexual revolution of the 1960s, open relationships often benefited men more often than women. A freer sexuality for women was explored in books like Grant Allen's *The Woman Who Did* (1895) and H.G. Wells's *Ann Veronica* (1909). Yet the depiction of the more 'open' woman was often ambiguous. From Gustave Flaubert's *Madame Bovary* (1857) and Henrik Ibsen's *Hedda Gabler* (1890) up through Joyce's Molly and Saunders Lewis's *Monica* (1930), sexually free women were caught on an edge of celebration and condemnation, as were their authors for depicting them as such.

Breaking from the Victorians, Oscar Wilde insisted that art is not moral; the aim of the author is not to be moralistic. Yet it might be fairer to say that the artists of Decadence and the Aesthetic movement, far from abandoning morals, were, in the spirit of Nietzsche, challenging the sanctity of traditional values in order to generate more vital contemporary values. From its earliest days, Modernism became famous, or infamous, for graphic representations of sexual acts not previously depicted in popular fiction, and which succeeded in shocking the bourgeoisie. Masturbatory images in Joyce's *Ulysses* (1922), sordid affairs and unconventional acts in D.H. Lawrence's *Lady Chatterley's Lover* (1928), the erotic writings of Anaïs Nin, and the Sadeian perversions of Georges Bataille, were scandalous contributions to literature, often for simply showing on a page things commonly done off the page, or for flaunting convention by celebrating acts publicly condemned as immoral.

Outside the pages of literature, Modernist artists themselves were exploring the nature of sex and challenging conventional moral assumptions about what constituted legitimate sexual relationships. While some, like the members of the Bloomsbury Group, questioned the wisdom of monogamy, even more radical figures like the artist Eric Gill openly experimented with nudism and incest. More authors lived and wrote about homosexuality with greater honesty, despite homosexuality being illegal in Britain until 1967. Despite the controversy of the trial of Oscar Wilde in 1895, more discussion and depiction of homosexual life occurred in the literature of Modernism, most notably in the works of Gertrude Stein, Ronald Firbank, Djuna Barnes, Radclyffe Hall, Vita Sackville-West and Sylvia Townsend Warner. Still, an author as well known as E.M. Forster felt the need to delay publication of his overtly gay novel, *Maurice* (1971), until after his death.

An increased attention to matters of sexuality and sexual identity can be attributed to the popularization of the writings and ideas of Sigmund Freud. Freud's pioneering work in psychology gained notoriety for its revelations about the latent sexual content underlying the most seemingly innocent expressions and behaviours. Yet, however radical a notion like the Oedipus complex may have seemed at the time, Juliet Mitchell notes that it was in actuality a 'conservative stopper' for the more shocking conclusions about the sexual desires of children, 'if one was to argue at all for the child's incestuous desires then at least these had better be for the parent of the opposite sex' (10). Freud's theories emerged in the wake of other ideas that claimed to provide a scientific perspective on sexuality as act and personality. The development of sexology introduced a taxonomic approach to sexuality, classifying and categorizing a wide variety of behaviours. Works in sexology, like Richard Freiherr von Krafft-Ebing's *Psychopathia Sexualis* (1886), in which he coined the terms sadism and masochism, and Henry Havelock Ellis's *Sexual Inversion* (1897), the first medical study of homosexuality, may have depended upon reinforcing a notion of normative sexuality, but they also exposed to the light a range of non-normative activities not usually discussed in polite society. While Michel Foucault, in *The History of Sexuality* (1976–1984), demonstrated that more discussion of sexual matters led to more classification, and thus more containment and regulation, it is also possible to say that these discussions meant a turn from regarding monogamous heterosexual functional missionary sex as the only game in town.

Time and Flux

Even the most casual glance at a work of literary Modernism might make it clear to the reader that something happened to time. No longer an arrow aiming straightforward into the future, time became jumbled and fragmented, pushed and pulled in all directions. Inspired by figures as diverse as Albert Einstein, Henri Bergson and Sir James George Frazer, Modernist writers no longer regarded time as a linear given (for Einstein see Stinson and Wilson). It was now relative to human perspectives, subjective as well as objective, experienced out of sequence or in multiple sequences, and in and out of history. Common to many Modernist fictions are s narrative techniques that distort temporal teleology, so as to fragment space-time to create an impression of an apparently non-linear experience, where the past may be encountered seemingly simultaneously that is intersecting later events such as in Woolf's *Mrs Dalloway* (1925) and William Faulkner's *As I Lay Dying* (1930). In such texts this conveys an individualist, impressionistic sense of the world and its interconnections, an intensity of the sense of moments of being inter-related by memory with the intensity of ongoing current experience. Clearly, in short, one of the most significant transformations that Modernism brought to literature was its radical ruminations on how to represent time in literature. The modern world was now regarded as having a more complex sense of time and space, especially in urban experience, so that new forms were required. The clear, linear movement of time used to structure the realist novels of the nineteenth century no longer seemed acceptable.

Henri Bergson's developed the concept of *la durée* (duration), which involves a distinction between an objective sense of time associated with clocks and a more fluid sense of subjective time, the plastic duration of the mind in which time seems to slow down or speed up, at odds with objective time's regulated intervals. This is most famously illustrated in Woolf's *Mrs Dalloway*, in which Clarissa Dalloway's single day is seen primarily through the loose and associative trails of her mind – the past and future commingling with the present – yet it is occasionally brought to order by the regular tolls of Big Ben. Bergsonian notions of time as memory-infused duration can be found throughout a great many Modernist works, wherever, like Proust's made-leine, a single focus explodes into myriad directions by the force of association and layers of memories overwhelm the present.

Although misappropriated in many ways, Albert Einstein's work on rela-tivity offers a convenient metaphor for understanding the relative nature of time. His special theory of relativity (1905) demonstrates that there is no abso-lute frame of reference in the observation of an event. Hence two events which appear to occur simultaneously to a particular observer, may seem to do so separately for another observer. No frame of reference is available to establish which of the observations is correct. Drawing on Einstein's funda-mental discovery that space has a fourth dimension of time, Modernist writers extended this notion in speculative directions, such as time appearing to move faster in the city than in the country, or at different rates for different people, especially actors versus viewers. In the course of Joseph Conrad's *The Secret Agent* (1907), which concerns an attempt to blow up Greenwich Observatory (and thus Greenwich Mean Time), time slows down, then speeds up, especially around the main event of the bomb going off, which seems to go off again and again in the novel as it is experienced separately by different characters.

Sir James George Frazer's monumental *The Golden Bough* (1890, revised variously to 1936) studied the rituals, symbols and figures of 'primitive' civil-izations, which became a source for numerous writers interested in the creative uses of myth. T.S. Eliot was at the forefront of regarding the import-ance of a presence of myth in Modernist works, notably in his own *The Waste Land* (1922) and James Joyce's *Ulysses* (1922), as well as David Jones's

In Parenthesis (1937). Such works used ancient or classic mythologies as a stabilizing ground or as raw material to weave through fragments of modern life. Modern works are then given significance for being situated in a broad expanse of mythic time or felt diminished by being severed from this epic scale of time. Such a conception of time has a correlation with Charles Baudelaire's claim in *The Painter of Modern Life* (1863), 'Modernity is the transient, the fleeting, the contingent; it is one half of art, the other being the eternal and the immovable' (106).

The Marxist Georg Lukács was especially critical of Modernist literature's loose play with time, for he felt that in gesturing toward mythic time or emphasizing subjective time, the Modernists were ridding literature of history and thus disavowing its ideological work for bourgeois play. Yet a counter claim can be made that in Joseph Conrad and Ford Madox Ford's unconventional sequencing of events in time, Virginia Woolf's exploration of the mind's fluidity in 'moments of being' and Joyce's experience with time compressed and drawn out, Modernist writers were making readers more conscious of the nature of time and of how it shapes identity, human relationships and one's relation to the world.

Critical Figures

Charles Baudelaire (1821–1867)

French poet and critic, author of the infamous collection of poetry, *Les Fleurs du Mals* (1857). Baudelaire inspired the Symbolist movement, especially the poets Stéphane Mallarmé and Arthur Rimbaud, in fostering a poetry open in its portrayal of sexual and morbid subject matter, exploratory in sensory and sensual experiences, and suggestive rather than direct in its imagery. As a critic, he offers influential observations on modern art, the city and modernity in *The Painter of Modern Life* (1863) and defines modernity and modern art as consisting of two halves – the eternal, immutable and the temporary, contingent. Modernity can be characterized by flux – constant change – yet enduring values of truth and beauty could be found within that flux. Modern art finds the eternally beautiful in the temporary, the fashionable, and the fleeting world. Baudelaire also writes of the flâneur – a bohemian figure who takes advantage of the anonymity and fluctuating nature of the modern city, and who merges with the crowd to better observe its multifarious exhibitions.

Clive Bell (1881–1964)

English art critic who was a central member of the Bloomsbury Group, and husband to Virginia Woolf's sister, Vanessa Stephen. With Roger Fry, who coined the term Post-impressionism, he helped organize a seminal Post-impressionist exhibition in 1912. Bell's principles of art, stated most dramatically in his essay, 'The Artistic Problem' (1919), embody the boldest expression of English aestheticism. In many ways, Bell's ideas have come to stand in for, perhaps too much so, the aesthetic principles of the Bloomsbury Group. Bell stresses that a work of art is a unique and autonomous phenomenon. In 'The Artistic Problem', he states, 'A work of art is an object beautiful, or significant, in itself, nowise dependent for its value on the outside world' (103). Elsewhere in *Art* (1914) he put this even more boldly, 'To appreciate a work of art we need bring with us nothing [from life] but a sense of form and colour and a knowledge of three-dimensional space' (27). In addition, by countering a Romantic ideal of the artist pouring his or her emotions directly on the paper or canvas, Bell asserted that the central matter of the 'artistic problem' is how to provide an adequate and controlled expression of a prior emotional experience. Hence for Bell it is not enough to feel something to be artistic. Rather one has to be skilled at studying emotion and understanding of form to know how to transpose the emotion into artistic work. He adds in 'The Artistic Problem' 'Automatic writing will never be poetry, nor automatic scrabbling design' (106). Bell's aesthetic theories were obviously inspirational within the Bloomsbury Group, notably setting the tone for Woolf's essays, 'Mr Bennett and Mrs Brown' and 'Modern Fiction'. Additionally, Bell helped prepare the ground for many subsequent formalist theories in Britain.

Henri Bergson (1859–1941)

French philosopher whose ideas on time and the mind were influential for Modernist authors such as Virginia Woolf, Marcel Proust and William Faulkner, as well as fellow theorists such as William James. Merging psychological, scientific and philosophical interests, Bergson practiced a form of dualism in terms of major philosophical issues such as the relationship between the body and soul, and the brain and mind. In *Matter and Memory* (1896), he argues that matter should be studied in relation to memory, and states in the introduction that he 'affirms the reality of spirit and the reality of matter' (9). In this he challenges the dichotomous positions of mechanistic philosophy (Descartes) and idealist philosophy (Berkeley). Additionally, his approach brought together the physical and the metaphysical, which proved to be of great interest to Modernists who were exploring the ways an inner spirit interacted with an objective, external world. Bergson's development of concepts like *la durée* (duration), *élan vital* (vital force) and *l'evolution créatrice* (creative evolution) reflect his interest in a philosophical methodology rooted in intuition, from which he could claim that reality is experienced largely through subjective forces. Richard Tarnas in *The Passion of the Western Mind:*

Understanding the Ideas That Have Shaped Our World View (1991) links him with William James, Edmund Husserl and Martin Heidegger, for shifting attention from an 'objective' world to a study of 'being', to an emphasis 'on the lived world of human experience, on its unceasing ambiguity, its spontaneity and autonomy, its uncontainable dimensions, its ever-deepening complexity' (374). Bergson's influence is often strongly felt in Modernist writers who contemplate the nature of consciousness, perspective, time, memory and self, providing as he does a philosophical ground for the subjective turn in Modernist literature.

Charles Darwin (1809–1882)

An English naturalist who is immensely influential in terms of his studies of evolution and natural selection, most particularly in *On the Origin of Species* (1859) and *The Descent of Man* (1871), Darwin indirectly challenges theological visions of the universe, demonstrating it is governed more by chance than divine plan, while equally unsettling humanistic, anthropomorphic notions that *homo sapiens* are the most important species on the Earth. His observations and taxonomies of nature, therefore, had tremendous reverberations beyond his field of study. The theory of natural selection resulted in both the Victorians and subsequent generations in a revision of their fundamental preconceptions about the nature and purpose of humans in relation to history and the cosmos. Most importantly, the theory of evolution postulates the possibility that that nature is neither static nor permanent, but is contingent and full of elements constantly in contention. Darwninism has been open to broadly divergent interpretations. Some Marxist social theorists found comfort in the notion that nature is itself subject to history; other social theorists adapted evolution – particularly the notion of the 'survival of the fittest' – as a justification for racialist hierarchies and eugenics.

Albert Einstein (1879–1955)

German theoretical physicist whose theories of relativity, special and general, shook the foundations of classical physics and indirectly influenced new ways of thinking about and representing time and space in Modernism. Interpreted in a general sense Einstein's special theory of relativity challenged the notion of an absolute frame of reference. His theory encompassed a notion of simultaneity, which demonstrated that two events, apparently simultaneous to one observer, will not necessarily be so for another in a different place (due to time differentials and other variables). Again no absolute frame of reference exists, highly influential in terms of Modernist artists who arguably misapplied such theories to notions of the individual's immediate perception of time, space and perspective. In objecting to Niels Bohr and Werner

Heisenberg's work on quantum mechanics, Einstein famously objected 'God does not play dice'.

Sir James George Frazer (1854–1941)

British anthropologist, whose work, *The Golden Bough* 1890 which was revised variously, culminating in 13 volumes (1936). Frazer's work was widely read and inspirational for many outside the anthropological field. This comparative study demonstrated the commonalities of a vast group of rituals, myths and symbols across a wide range of cultures and time periods, exemplifying the evolution of cultures from 'primitive' to modern, while simultaneously implying the structural similarity of paganism and modern Christianity. Jeremy MacClancy places Frazer in the 'ritualist school' of anthropology, which believed 'myths were post hoc rationalizations, used to explain rituals whose original meaning had been long forgotten' (80). Frazer's comparative studies of myths and religions proved to be a great source of inspiration for Modernist writers interested in the potency of ancient myth and folklore employed in a modern context. This is most evident in T.S. Eliot's *The Waste Land* and James Joyce's *Ulysses*, but Frazer's influence can also be felt in the work of W.B. Yeats, David Jones and Robert Graves.

Sigmund Freud (1856–1939)

Austrian founder of the psychiatric school of psychology, Freud became notorious for revealing latent sexuality beneath the surface of rational civilization. Together with such notions as the Oedipus complex and polymorphous perversity this spawned a new literary frankness in the depiction of sexuality. His schema of human identity – the ego, id and superego – had a monumental influence far wider than the field of psychology, in the Modernist period on writers as diverse as Ford Madox Ford and André Breton. Freud's account of human identity centres upon a decentred mass of desires and drives, a complex set of forces – consciousness, conscience and the unconscious – in motion and tension. One of his earliest major works, *The Interpretation of Dreams* (1900), demonstrates how the activities of the mind may be read and interpreted, and set out a latent structure which gives thought content its significance. One might access the unconscious layer of the mind (the other two being the conscious and preconscious) through dream analysis and dialogue with the subject being analysed. He explains that the seemingly incoherent dream-world is in fact governed by an underlying logic, with dream thoughts converted into dream content by processes of condensation and displacement. Freud later subdivided the unconscious to include the descriptive, the dynamic and the systemic aspect. Generally, he regarded individuals as motivated largely by sexual or libidinous desires, often repressed. In his view humans perversely fixated on objects (or others as objects), a notion at the heart of his idea of the Oedipal and Electra Complexes (projected upon the father and mother). In the Modernist era Freud's work acquired legitimacy initially because his 'talking cure' was so effective with treating shell-shocked or traumatized soldiers Like Darwin, Marx and Nietzsche before him he provided intellectuals and artists with a new vocabulary – narcissism, the uncanny, the death drive, the pleasure principle and repetition compulsion – and in essence radicalizes what it meant to be human, offering new ways of conceiving and portraying human psychology. Freud's work has fundamentally affected fiction and its interpretation, with characters, for instance, tending to be more multilayered and internally contradictory, their significance often implicit given they are mostly unaware of the dynamics underlying their speech or actions, which can both be understood in terms of unconscious desires and repressed motivations.

William James (1842–1910)

American psychologist and philosopher, who became one of the major figures of American pragmatism. His studies in epistemology, perception and the nature of inner life, in works such as *The Principles of Psychology* (1890, two volumes), became immensely influential on early Modernism. Although the first use of the term 'stream of consciousness' is credited to May Sinclair in a review of Dorothy Richardson's work in 1918, it is commonly understood that this notion of consciousness as a stream of associational flux, subjectively guiding and shaping our interaction with the world, stems from James's work. Novelist Henry James was William's brother and Gertrude Stein his prize-winning student, which suggests the possibility of William's direct as well as indirect impact on the shaping of Modernist literature, particularly in its emphasis on the complex inner landscapes of human thought.

Adolf Loos (1870–1933)

Austrian architect whose ideas and work were influential on Modernist architecture. His famous creed, 'Ornament and Crime' (1908), is an exemplary Modernist manifesto in the extreme demands it makes on the practice of building. He urged architects to rid buildings of unnecessary, non-architectural elements, to create something akin to autonomous architecture; placing an emphasis on simplicity and primary elements. Such principles would prove inspirational for the Bauhaus movement as well as later artistic movements in minimalism (referred to by many as Brutalist). In 'Ornament and Crime', he relies on a language of degeneration and sterility: 'But the man of our own times who covers the walls with erotic images from an inner compulsion is a criminal or a degenerate' (77). Artists who rely on ornament

Figure 6: The Isokon building in Lawn Road, Belsize Park, London NW3.
© Philip Tew 2008

are sterile degenerates, but renewal is possible: 'cultural evolution is equivalent to the removal of ornament from articles in daily use' (78). In these
ways, he can be seen as adapting the ideas of Max Nordau for a revitalized
architecture.

Karl Marx (1818–1883)

German philosopher and political economist who aimed to turn German
Idealism on its head, stating famously in *The German Ideology* (1846): 'In direct
contrast to German philosophy which descends from heaven to earth, here we
ascend from earth to heaven' (154). Rather than conceive of human lives being
governed by abstract universals, which then shaped the particulars of life,
Marx insisted on a materialist approach that demonstrated that life is shaped

by historical forces. Human lives are defined by work, but the type and nature of work changes over time, and along with changes in the modes of production come radical transformations in the way humans relate to themselves, each other and their environment. Humans are organized into classes that determine not only the type of labour they do and the positions in life they hold, but also their very consciousness: 'The ideas of the ruling class are in every epoch the ruling ideas' (172). Unique to the capitalism of modern society is a relentless dynamic of change, a constant churning and undermining of values, so that in the *Communist Manifesto* (1848) Marx & Engels declare famously that 'all that is solid melts into air' (476). Modernity, therefore, is defined by uncertainty and flux. Yet, for Marx, this also meant that capitalism produces a potential for self-destruction. In his many works Marx continued to produce a model of social life structured by relations of power but also subject to the tides of history. Two of his central concepts are 'alienation' and 'commodification', where in a capitalist society human relations and possibilities are reduced by the market disillusioning people and limiting most of their lives to matters of monetary exchange as if reduced to objects. Also, influential conceptually is his essay 'The Uncanny.' Marx's influence on Modernism shows directly in the work of socialist writers like George Bernard Shaw and H.G. Wells, the aesthetic theories and practices of Bertolt Brecht, and the criticism of Georg Lukács, but also indirectly in the work of a number of Modernist writers who pursue an interest in the experience of alienation and change in modern society.

Friedrich Nietzsche (1844–1900)

German philosopher whose unconventional approaches to philosophy took slow root in their course of influence across the twentieth century. Perhaps made famous or infamous for the notion of the *Übermensch*, Nietzsche's extended influence stems from his radical critique of morality as well as his innovative approaches to writing. Stylistically he departs from the conventional lengthy, focused discourses of philosophical monographs, working instead in an aphoristic mode of insightful and paradoxical fragments, wherein he fused logical (Apollonian) and passionate (Dionysian) discourses, taking on, in *Thus Spoke Zarathustra* (1885), a voice of prophetic, messianic qualities. His work is greatly concerned with the vacancy of modern culture. Often labelled a nihilist, Nietzsche in fact provides analyses and criticisms of the nihilistic nature of modern culture itself. Modern culture's values were for him sterile and demanding rejuvenation. Such rejuvenation could come through self-realization and a hard-thought critique of modern values and institutions. Nietzsche thought man should not be weighed down by idealized pasts or borrowed systems of thought. In works like *Beyond Good and Evil*

(1886), he expresses his view that morality was in fact an expression of power, merely the force of group beliefs, and not an innate set of truths. Against the repressive systems of politics, religion and law (which impose suffering on the individual and demand ascetic habits of denied living), Nietzsche insists upon embracing life, freedom, passion and an individually derived morality. All of which reinforced Modernism's re-evaluation of Victorian morality and its quest for new forms in which to express radical new values.

Max Nordau (1849–1923)

Hungarian author of the controversial and influential work, *Degeneration* (1883; 1998). This seminal work which declares the cultural sterility of European art and society in the later nineteenth century was built in part upon Cesare Lombroso's work on physiogonomy and degeneracy. Where Lombroso claims that a criminal's nature could be detected in his face and that a society's welfare depends upon being able to identify the degenerates, who passed on criminality as they bred, Nordau extends that argument, saying that 'Degenerates are not always criminals, prostitutes, anarchists and pronounced lunatics; they are often authors and artists' (22). Nordau was influential in his attempts to see art as a product of neurological conditions, sometimes linking art to popular notions of the time – 'neurasthenics, hysterics and mattoids. This will be, in the near future, the condition of civilized humanity, if fatigue, nervous exhaustion, and the diseases and degeneration conditioned by them, make much greater progress' (24). In some sense, Nordau adopts Darwinian principles for a theory of art and culture, in that sterility and stagnation equate with an evolutionary failure of a species to adapt and evolve.

Georg Simmel (1858–1918)

Founding German sociologist whose work, 'The Metropolis and Mental Life' (1903), analyses the social and psychological effects of life in the modern city. Simmel argues that the city offers an individual tremendous freedom yet it also threatens the very nature and experience of individuality: 'one nowhere feels as lonely and lost as in the metropolitan crowd' (1950, 418). Unlike rural experience, which encourages close and enduring relationships, life in the city isolates individuals and cuts them off from others. To survive, city denizens must develop a blasé attitude to survive the onslaught of stimuli and sensations, which also means that the life of the city may be cold, distant and largely mental and abstract, as distinct from the close and emotional life of the country.

Oswald Spengler (1880–1936)

German philosopher and historian who argues in his work that that history can be seen and understood in terms of grand cycles and structural phases. Most famously, he applies a biological conception to social systems, declaring that civilizations, like human bodies, undergo inevitable phases of birth and decline. In his most influential work, *The Decline of the West* (1918–1922), released notably in the wake of the Great War, he claims that Western civilizations had entered a phase of irreversible decline. According to his account individuals refute common principles or goals, rejecting traditional rules and regulatory principles. He describes as decadent, simply reflecting the *zeitgeist* or changing styles.

8 Changes in Critical Responses and Approaches

Gary Day

Chapter Overview

Interpretation of Modernist art and literature has emerged as a veritable industry. When James Joyce wrote *Ulysses* (1922) the first copy of which, incidentally, was brought into England by the critic F.R. Leavis (1896–1975), he was not just penning a masterpiece, he was also offering employment to literary scholars for generations to come. Here was a novel radically different from its nineteenth century predecessors. It wasn't just that it broke taboos in describing bodily functions, or that it had a mythic structure or that it had a complicated relationship with Irish nationalism. What made it stand out was its linguistic ingenuity. Joyce declared war on English because it was the language of the colonizer. 'The language in which we are speaking is his before it is mine', muses Stephen Dedalus in *A Portrait of the Artist as a Young Man* (1914) during a conversation with the Englishman who is dean of studies at his university. 'I cannot speak these words without unrest of spirit. His language, so familiar and so foreign, will always be for me an acquired speech' (159) (for Joyce, see also Stinson).

And so Joyce lays siege to its syntax, mines its diction with Irish terms and lays waste its grammar. The result can be exquisite, as is seen in *Ulyssses*: 'Perfume of embraces all him assailed. With hungered flesh obscurely he mutely craved to adore' (ibid.: xlii). But it can also be enigmatic. Joyce's coinings and joinings of words, his suspension of punctuation, his unfinished sentences and, above all, his ambition to make language approach the condition of music make some pages of *Ulysses* appear more like clues for a cryptic crossword than parts of a story. 'Pearls: when she. Liszt's rhapsodies. Hissss' (1992: 330).

An Old and New Approach

The problem with which the reader is confronted here, namely how to interpret this piece of writing, is a common to number of Modernist works. The poetry of T.S. Eliot (1888–1965) and the novels of Virginia Woolf (1882–1941) appear not just difficult but downright obscure. Why should this be? John Carey in *The Intellectuals and the Masses: Pride and Prejudice Among the Literary Intelligentsia, 1880–1939* (1992) famously suggests that such writers felt their cultural authority threatened by the spread of democracy and responded by making their art an exclusive affair. This is not an entirely convincing argument. Since these same artists felt that the new reading public, beneficiaries of the 1870 Education Act, were not interested in their work, it is difficult to see what was to be gained by making it even less appealing to a wider audience.

One of the first serious investigations of modern art was Edmund Wilson's *Axel's Castle* (1947). He sought to make it intelligible to a wider audience, which implies *contra* Carey, that the reading public were interested in what artists were doing. Wilson argued that the literary movement represented by Yeats, Eliot, Joyce and others has its roots in the French symbolism of the late nineteenth century which itself goes back to romanticism. From the mid-eighteenth century we can detect a move away from classical ideals of balance, order and proportion towards originality, imagination, nature and emotional expression, culminating in the romantic emphasis on self rather than society, on subjective rather than objective truth.

James Longenbach argues that 'Modernism makes most sense when we understand it as part of a continuum beginning with the *Lyrical Ballads*' (100), one of the key works of the Romantic Movement. The advertisement for the volume, published in 1798, makes a number of claims that will later be echoed in modern manifestos. For example, the majority of poems 'are to be considered as experiments' and that ordinary language is to be adapted for poetic purposes (2005: 49), very comparable in certain ways to the intentions outlined in the 'Preface' to *Some Imagist Poets: An Anthology* (1915) which admits its 'principles are not new' (vi) expounding the view that the poet in free verse should 'use the language of common speech [... always the *exact* word' [emphasis in original]] (vi) while reflecting passionately the 'artistic value of modern life' (vii). In his 1800 Preface to the collection, Wordsworth further notes that his 'principal object was to make the incidents of common life interesting' (ibid.: 289). Joyce could have made that claim for *Ulysses* and his desire 'to forge in the smithy of [his] soul the uncreated conscience of [his] race' (1952: 257) also had its roots in the romantic support for national self-determination.

After romanticism came realism, a feature of nineteenth century English writing. It arose partly because of a feeling of dissatisfaction with the effusiveness of romanticism which, in addition, appeared to have little to contribute to understanding the problems of industrial society. Scientific advance was also a spur to the development of realism. The theory of evolution, in particular, suggested that human beings were the products of heredity and environment, very different to the exalted conception of man found in romanticism. French writers such as Émile Zola (1840–1902) created a literary style that reflected these changes. Naturalism, as it became known, sought to document the social and economic influences on behaviour with an almost photographic attention to detail. Many naturalists wrote for the theatre, the most well known being Henrik Ibsen (1828–1906), but the return in his later plays of the supernatural creatures that can be found in his early ones suggests the limitations of a wholly naturalistic explanation of character (Wilson, 1947: 10).

The reaction to naturalism in France was known as Symbolism, which was to have a much wider influence in Modernist circles. We can trace the origins of this particular movement back to Edgar Allen Poe (1809–1849) and the French poet essayist and translator Gérard de Nerval (1808–1855), the pen name of Gérard Labrunie. Poe believed that a poem should express a single mood or emotion and that every element of the poem should be subordinated to that end. He was also interested in the affinities between poetry and music arguing that 'indefiniteness' in both produces a spiritual effect.

This idea was central to the aesthetic of Stéphane Mallarmé (1842–1898) who in 'Crisis in Poetry' stipulates that artists should avoid the precise delineations of naturalism, of such *'description'* in favour an arbitrariness, of *'evocation, allusion, suggestion'* [emphasis in original] (40), and he was also insistent that poetry was a form of music. Labrunie suffered periodic bouts of insanity but believed, even in his lucid periods, that we cannot separate dream from reality which, incidentally, was the basis of surrealism. It, too, was a reaction to a world in which as André Breton (1896–1966) says in the first surrealist first manifesto (1924), that although 'the reign of logic' (9) persists self-evidently 'experience itself has found itself increasingly circumscribed' (10). Breton maintains that surrealism stood for the freedom of the imagination, or 'the actual functioning of thought' (26) something which

Joyce tries to capture in the stream of consciousness style, though he was not a surrealist.

In his book *The Symbolist Movement in Literature* (1899), Arthur Symons (1865–1945) argues that the symbol is an incarnation of the infinite, claiming that the modern poet's self-conscious use of symbols distinguish him from his predecessors (3). Only in such a transcendent form can life be validated and 'all art worth making, all worship worth offering' (175). Such a sensibility also characterizes other Modernist genres, with Woolf, for example investing water with a great deal of symbolic value in novels like *To the Lighthouse* (1927) and *The Waves* (1931). She uses symbols in a personal way which is quite different to how they were used in the past. Dante's *Divine Comedy* (1308–1321), for instance, assumes knowledge of the symbols of both Christianity and courtly love (for Woolf see also Stinson, Murray, Baxter). One of the characteristics of modernity is the absence of a symbolic system expressing common beliefs and values. In its place we have arbitrary symbols, chosen as Wilson says by the poet 'to stand for special ideas of his own' (20). One major, overarching reason for such hange was the industrial revolution, which over-turned many of the social, religious and political beliefs in which civilization had previously been rooted.

So far, then, we have two critical approaches to Modernist literature and art. Both take as their point of departure its notorious difficulty. Carey states that this is due to the elite trying to maintain their position, while Wilson traces it back to earlier literary movements, suggesting that the poetry of Eliot and the prose of Joyce are not so bewildering once we place them in this wider con-text. Both critics concentrate on the stylistic features of Modernism but each explains them in a different way, one doing so in social terms, the other in terms of literary history.

As the twentieth century progresses, more and more interest focuses on the social rather than on the artistic aspects of Modernism, although surely the two cannot really be viably separated. When Wilson talks about French Symbolism as an intensification of the romantic emphasis on the individual, he is also saying something about the increasingly atomized nature of modern existence. However, while we cannot separate art from the social one must be wary of conflating the two, something very easy to do if one is examining a text such as *To the Lighthouse* solely in terms of its representations of gender. Then the temptation is to forget that it is precisely the notion of repre-sentation that is at issue in modern art (as it is in politics too, incidentally). Remember that the suffragettes, for instance, were agitating for the right to vote, to have their views represented in Parliament. Classical authors might argue that one aim of art was to imitate nature, but there is nothing in Aristotle or Horace to guide writers about how they should portray such radical developments. A new form of social organization required new forms of expression. Consequently, as the artist and critic Roger Fry (1866–1934) says the painter does not seek to 'imitate life but to find an equivalent for it' (Kolocotroni: 190).

After the good deal of criticism that has been devoted to explicating the nature of the literary and artistic forms that appeared in the early twentieth century, attention is now shifting from reading Modernist works to examining how they were promoted, circulated and discussed, all of which helps establish their status as objects set apart from the mass society. Here perhaps a key work is Lawrence Rainey's *Institutions of Modernism: Literary Elites and Public Culture* (1998). There is still, though, much work to do, for as Aaron Jaffe points out recently, 'the full range and extent of the practices that regulate Modernist cultural production remain one of the principal blind spots of contemporary criticism' (6).

The City and Human Character

Although Woolf declares famously 'that on or about December 1910 human character changed' (1994: 160), even before that time artists had begun to notice that the old idea of character as a coherent, consistent entity was in crisis. The Swedish playwright August Strindberg (1849–1912), for example, declared in his 'Preface' to *Miss Julie* (1888) that his heroine was a 'modern character', that is, she was 'an agglomeration of past and present cultures, scraps from books and newspapers, fragments of humanity, torn shreds of once fine clothing that has become rags [she is] a human soul patched together' (Kolocotroni: 116). This anticipates Lawrence's description of the self in 'Why the Novel Matters' as a 'curious assembly of incongruous parts' (536) and the broken selves of *The Waste Land* (1922) who can connect nothing with nothing. (1978: 74).

What, though was the reason for this change in the conception of character? There is no single answer. The work of Darwin, Marx, Nietzsche and Freud had begun to alter the conception of what it meant to be human. Darwin argues in his work that man is not created by God, but descends from apes; Marx claims that it is not consciousness that determines existence but social and economic existence that determines consciousness; Nietzsche demands a revision of all values, that one should learn to think beyond good and evil, while Freud declares that human personality was essentially neurotic because of the thwarted development of one or more of the sexual instincts (For Freud see also Wilson, Stinson, Paddy). The condition of life in the cities, meanwhile, affected perception and psychology. The German sociologist Georg Simmel (1858–1918) makes the point that the tempo of life becomes much quicker in the urban environment than the rural one. The bustling boulevard places far greater demands on the senses than a stroll down the village street. Coping with a constant barrage of stimuli, deciding which to accept and which to reject, means that the city dweller has a more heightened consciousness than his country counterpart. The life of the latter is based on the unconscious rhythms of emotion and feeling, while that of the former is based on the intellect which operates at the farthest 'remove from the depths of personality' (Kolocotroni: 52–3). That is to say, the need to defend the mind against an army of impressions leads to the over-development of the rational faculty and the under-development of the affective, aesthetic and ethical ones. Some artists tried to heal this split, or, to use Eliot's phrase in 'Metaphysical Poets,' 'dissociation of sensibility' which he, incidentally, traced back to the seventeenth century (64), by recourse to myth. So too, of course did the Nazis with their appeal to a German *volk*.

According to Simmel, the difference in psychic organization between the inhabitants of the city and those of the country results in a different approach to relationships. Those who live in the city treat people as means to an end while those who live in the country treat them as ends in themselves. However, the city-dweller's treatment of others is not just a product of a new form of perception, but also of capitalism. Mind and money are closely intertwined. 'The economy and the domination of the intellect', writes Simmel, share 'a purely matter of fact attitude [towards] persons and things' (Kolocotroni: 53). Moreover, each concentrates on general characteristics, ignoring individual ones.

Simmel elaborates on the nature of commified alienation in the modern age. In his view the purely intellectualist person is indifferent to all things personal because, out of them, relationships and reactions develop which are not to be completely understood by purely rational methods – just as the unique element in events never enters into the principle of money. Money is concerned only with what is common to all, that is with the exchange value which reduces al quality and individuality to a purely quantitative level (53).

Moreover by his account the nature of work in modern society also fosters certain qualities that help condition social interaction, whether in an office, a shop or a factory, employees are required to be punctual, to calculate correctly and to be exact in their dealings with customers. Simmel argues that these modes of behaviour are imposed on the individual from without and that they stifle those 'irrational, instinctive, sovereign human traits which seek to determine [him] from within' (54).

The combination of the city's assault on the sensory apparatus and capitalism's refashioning of human psychology produces three distinct attitudes. The first is what Simmel calls a 'blasé outlook', the second is a cloak of reserve and the third is a desire for self-display (55, 58). The blasé outlook is the result of sensory overload. The individual is no longer capable of reacting to new stimulations and responds by cultivating an indifference to them. He comes to experience the distinction between things, and therefore things themselves, as meaningless. This attitude is also related to the circulation of money which, with its indifference to quality, 'becomes the frightful leveller, hollow[ing] out the core of things, their peculiarities, their specific values, and their uniqueness and incomparability in a way which is beyond repair' (55).

The attitude of reserve is a reaction to the numerous encounters that characterize city life. While it is possible for those who live in a small town to respond fully to those around them, this is not the case in the city where such openness would cause a person to be 'completely atomized internally [and] to fall into an unthinkable mental condition' (55). To prevent his inner self from being worn down by acquaintances, casual contacts, advertisers and all those officials who demand proof of identity, the individual must play a role or wear a mask. However, the preparation of a face to meet a face is tinged with resentment. The other is perceived as a threat because he is always poised to invade the self and so the relation between the two is marked by hostility as well as distance.

Since the individual is in danger of disappearing in mass society he feels the need to assert his identity, to separate himself from the crowd. But how can he do this and still maintain a necessary air of reserve? How can he signal himself yet remain secret? The metropolitan type, one might say, wants to be noticed but not known. Indeed, he hardly knows himself: his mind may have penetrated the mysteries of the atom but it has not peered into the recesses of his heart. He is a one-dimensional creature, with an over-developed intelligence and under-developed emotions, more caricature than character. Perhaps this accounts for the particular type of self-display found in the city; fantastic, eccentric, extravagant, precisely the sort of behaviour, in fact, that we find in Dickens (1812–1870).

Modernists on Art

Simmel's description of how the urban conditions perception and psychology provides another context for understanding modern art. Indeed, the role of the metropolis in shaping the character of Modernism later becomes a staple of critical discussion. Yet, long before such responses, contemporaries were aware of the relation between the experience of the city and the experience of art. The essayist and critic Walter Pater (1839–94), for instance, in the 'Conclusion' in *The Renaissance: Studies in Art and Poetry* ([1986] 1873) written in 1868 makes the rapid fire of stimuli the basis of aesthetic appreciation. For him one lives in a swirl of sights, sounds, smells, tastes and textures. The attention is captured for a moment before it is seized by something else; 'impressions of the individual mind [. . .] are in perpetual flight' (151). Some of these impressions are more valuable than others but because, as Pater says, 'our failure is to form habits' (152), and so one misses the diamond sparkling in the dirt. Pater believes in a requirement to be more observant, to learn to discriminate between impressions, since some are choicer than others, capable of stirring the sense, exciting the mind or reviving jaded spirits. Art is a way of arresting such moments so that we can appreciate them properly. 'Art comes to you', writes Pater, 'proposing frankly to give nothing but the highest quality to your moments as they pass, and simply for those moment's sake' (153).

One can trace the influence of Pater's thinking in at least two Modernist writers, Ezra Pound (1885–1972) and Woolf. Pater's description of philosophy as that which makes us see things afresh parallels Pound's advice to the artist to 'make it new', a sentiment echoed by the Russian literary critic Viktor Shklovsky (1893–1984) who in 'Art as Technique' says that it is precisely the task of art that 'removes objects from the automatism of perception' (13) and 'exists [so] that one may recover the sensation of life' (12). Pater also advises that one should realize impressions as vividly as one can and Pound too stipulates that the poet must render as clearly as he can the image he portrays (see Kolocotroni et. al. 1998: 373–79). The stipulation that poetry should aspire to exact expression recalls Simmel's point that precision is required in all areas of modern life. More generally, one might classify the type of poetry that Pound promoted, Imagism, as in accordance with the presentation of 'an intellectual and emotional complex in an instant of time' (ibid.: 374) as directly related to Pater's view that all 'Experience, already [is] reduced to a group of impressions' (151). Imagism is the elevation of an impression into art. Pater's observation that each impression is that 'of the individual in his isolation', and that each individual's mind remains 'a solitary prisoners [in] its own dream of a world' (151) encapsulates much of the atomized nature of existence in the modern world. Since the city is the major source of our impressions, Pater's remark also implies that symbolism's characteristic mix of fantasy and reality is not merely an aesthetic principle, but a symptom of urban existence.

Pater's influence on Woolf is evident in 'Modern Fiction' in her remark that the mind receives, at every moment, 'a myriad of impressions, trivial, fantastic, evanescent, or engraved with sharpness of steel', and that these impressions come 'from all sides' (160). This observation becomes the basis of her fiction and also features in her theory of the nature of women's writing. She adopts a fragmentary form, or to use the technical term a 'stream of consciousness' to convey impressions of thought, of experience in her fiction. The term was coined by William James in his *Principles of Psychology* (1890) using it in an attempt to capture the way one perceives the world. It also suggests something of the way in which one's mind is too complex to be known, perhaps even by the reflexive individual. Pater says that inevitably one is surrounded from experience by 'that thick wall of personality through which no voice has ever pierced' (151).

In *Mrs Dalloway* (1925), the eponymous heroine muses that not even husband and wife can ever really know one another (120). In *To the Lighthouse*, Mrs Ramsay reflects in similar fashion about her husband (95–6), but concludes that 'she loved him,' something he knows without words being expressed (142). Mrs Dalloway realizes that even self-knowledge is fleeting, far from final, inconclusive (43). Similarly, The self, muses Mrs Ramsay, is a 'wedge-shaped core of darkness, something invisible to others' (72). Given this one should be wary of seeing the stream of consciousness as an expression of identity. Indeed, in Woolf's novels, one person's inner voice sounds much the same as another's. In terms of tone, rhythm and diction, it is hard to tell Mrs Dalloway and Mrs Ramsay apart, perhaps inevitably for as Desmond MacCarthy observes in *Criticism* (1932): 'The moment we dig down to the semi-conscious thought stream in human beings, individuality tends to disappear. It is in actions, gestures and habits of speech that character is revealed' (171). Is there nothing positive to be said about the stream of consciousness? Certainly it represents mainly the dramatization of how individuals are isolated in their own psyches, but it might also be regarded as an assertion of the integrity of the internal life in the face of external constraints, its fluidity in marked contrast to the fixed nature of action in, say, the factory. This is possible, but to complicate matters Freud suggests that the inner life is as ferociously determined as the outer one.

In the Modernist period, the problem faced by thinkers and artists, then, was how to be an individual in the modern world. Indeed, for D.H. Lawrence (1885–1930), this is the challenge of modernity. In *The Rainbow* ([1915] 1995), Ursula, the central character, puts it this way: 'How to become oneself, how to know the question and answer of oneself when one was merely an unfixed something-nothing, blowing about the winds of heaven, undefined, unstated' (264). The romantics define themselves in relation to nature but Modernists define themselves in relation to the city. Nature enlarges the individual by connecting him to something greater than himself, but the city diminishes him, dispersing him across a range of discourses from work to citizenship. One element of the many experiments of modern art is an attempt to reclaim the self from these narrow representations. As early as 1860, the French poet Charles Baudelaire (1821–67), posited the figure of the dandy as one solution to what he considered to the conformist culture of the city. The dandy, he wrote 'is above all, the desire to create a personal form of originality within the external limits of social convention' (Kolocotroni: 108). And yet the dandy did not reveal himself through his self-display any more than did Simmel's metropolitan inhabitant. His pleasure comes from 'causing surprise in others, and the profound satisfaction of never showing [himself]' (ibid.).

The answer to the question of how to be an individual, then, is paradoxical. To exhibit oneself is simultaneously to hide oneself. As this is precisely the condition of the city-dweller as described by Simmel, it seems there is no solution to the problem, merely its restatement. The situation of the self in the city, revealed and concealed, is a factor in some Modernist literary criticism manifesting itself in discussions of style. A.R. [Alfred] Orage (1873–1934), best known for his editorship of *New Age* magazine, which was devoted to discussions of politics, literature and art, says that style had a personal and an impersonal aspect. It is at once the signature of the individual and yet has no defining features. Literature, writes Orage, in 'The Art of Reading,' 'has neither class distinction nor distinction of dialect; but is what we call plain English' and its purpose is to 'restore [language] to speech in a purified and universal instead of local form' (1935: 23). The critic John Middleton Murray (1889–1957) devotes a whole book to the subject of style reflecting the import-ance of the term in the Modernist lexicon, if not in our own. Unlike in Orage's commentary, there is no tension between the personal and impersonal in Murray's analysis. The two are brought into a perfect balance. He states that when it is said that a writer has style, 'we are referring to a quality which transcends all personal idiosyncrasy, yet needs personal idiosyncrasy in order to be manifested. Style, in this absolute sense, is a complete fusion of the personal and the universal' (1930: 7–8).

Romantics and Classicists

Some Modernist writers such as Desmond MacCarthy (1877–1952), a literary journalist and member of the Bloomsbury group favoured personal art, while others like the poet T.E. Hulme (1883–1917) preferred the impersonal sort. In his 'Introduction' to the catalogue of the first Post-impressionist Exhibition in Britain (1910),[1] MacCarthy writes in 'The Post-impressionists' that the differ-ence between the Impressionists and the Post-impressionists was that the former wanted to render objects in a new way whereas the latter wanted 'to express emotions which the objects themselves evoked' (175). The techniques the artists used to do this, for example the use of vivid colours, gave the paintings an unnatural quality, which upset the spectators, as did the 'primi-tive' element in a number of these pictures. Hence the need for critics to explain the significance of these innovations to a wider public, which must have annoyed artists since, according to Carey account, they wanted their work to remain impenetrable.

Whereas MacCarthy positioned Modernist art as a return of romanticism. In contrast, Hulme regarded it as the revival of classicism, defining romanti-cism as a belief in man as a creature of infinite possibilities of man whereas classicism looked upon man as a 'fixed and limited animal whose nature is absolutely constant' (Kolocotroni: 179). In his analysis, the romantic view of society was of 'an oppressive order' denying man the opportunity to realize his full potential, as opposed to the classical view that, without restraint, man was capable of nothing 'decent' (ibid.). Hulme's claim in 'Romanticism and Classicism' that the coming age would be classically inclined is partly based on his observation that 'there is an increasing proportion of people who simply can't stand Swinburne' (ibid.: 182), a nineteenth century poet writing in the idiom of a decadent romanticism. Swinburne represented, for Hulme, all that was wrong with modern poetry: it was always 'moaning or whining about something or other' and it pointed 'to a beyond of some kind' (ibid.). In its place, he proposed a poetry based on the classical principles of reserve, restraint and limit; a poetry of accurate description not 'the expression of some unsatisfied emotion' (ibid.: 183).

Hulme and Pound were both closely connected with Imagism, a mentor of Eliot, editing *The Waste Land* (1922). Given the proximity of such influences perhaps unsurprisingly in 'Tradition and the Individual Talent,' which was to become a renowned essay, Eliot voices ideas similar to those of Hulme and Pound. Eliot too saw poetry 'not [as] a turning loose of emotion but an escape from emotion . . . not the expression of personality, but an escape from personality' (43). Eliot's removal of the self from the realm of art mirrors its removal from other areas of modern society. The scientific manager was not interested in the workman as an individual but as tool to increase production.

Eliot expounds his 'impersonal theory of poetry' in 'Tradition and the Individual Talent,' which introduces another approach to modernity: its relation to the past. Eliot argues that in order to appreciate an artist comparison must be made to his predecessors. European literature, which is what Eliot means by tradition, is an arrangement of works that is complete in itself. The introduction of a new work modifies this arrangement 'so the relations, proportions, values of each work of art toward the whole are readjusted' (38). What makes a writer traditional, Eliot continues, is that a sense of the past contributes acutely to an awareness of the present, not just in terms of their difference but also of their similarity.

Published in 1919, one year after the end of the First Word War, Eliot's essay has two purposes. The first is to confer the authority of tradition on Eliot's own poetry which was, in some quarters, as John Harwood explains in *Eliot to Derrida: The Poverty of Interpretation* (1995), regarded as frivolous and even fraudulent (92–5). The second is to restore a sense of continuity between past and present which had been shattered by the War. Although mass slaughter had killed off the enlightenment idea that history was the record of human progress, Eliot attempts to show that still intact was the relation between the past and the present, each nourishing the other. Europe may have been divided by politics but it was united by culture. And if this culture could be integrated into contemporary life, civilization would be renewed (For Eliot, see also Baxter and Stinson).

Futurism and Dada

Others disagreed, most notably the leader of the Futurist movement, Filippo Tomasso Marinetti (1876–1944), who writes in the *Futurist Manifesto* (1909) 'We will destroy the museums, libraries, academies of every kind' (42) and celebrate in song 'the multicoloured, polyphonic tides of revolution in the modern capitals' (42). Marinetti expresses the belief that appreciating art of the past was irrelevant, and what matters is the future. In his own, inimitable words 'admiring an old picture is the same as pouring our sensibility into a funerary urn instead of hurling it far off, in violent spasms of action and creation' (42). It is hard for contemporary readers to take Marinetti seriously. He wants his face 'smeared with good factory muck' and plaster himself with 'metallic waste' (41) then, when aged 40 in 10 years, he wants to be thrown into 'the wastebasket like useless manuscripts – we want it to happen!' (43). There's a great deal in this vein, excessive, enthusiastic, all of it sincerely meant. And that's precisely why it can be seen as comical. However, in other ways it also remains disturbing. The Futurists want to 'glorify war' and art itself is a force of destruction, being cruel, violent and unjust (For Marinetti, see also Stinson).

The fascist dimension of Marinetti's thought is considered in detail by Andrew Hewitt in *Fascist Modernism: Aesthetics, Politics and the Avant-Garde* (1993). Nevertheless, Marinetti is not a sophisticated thinker, with something innocent in the manner in which he expresses his opinions. He reacts to the idea that art should be a knowing, self-conscious activity. He severs art from its traditions and attaches it to the machine, making it a form of energy rather than a mode of enquiry. He defines art as 'nothing but violence, cruelty, and injustice' (43) describing a speeding car crash bringing 'the white-hot iron of joy' (41). Through such speed and danger he can evoke and vye with the *Winged Victory of Samothrace*, a sculpture of the goddess Nike (Victory) still displayed in the Louvre and considered by many as one of the artistic high points of antiquity. Marinetti is not the only one to pull art from its pedestal. Romanian born French poet Tristan Tzara (1896–1963), author of various manifestoes, the first being the *Dada Manifesto: 1918* (1918), is equally impatient with the reverence shown to tradition. He writes in the first manifesto 'The new artist protests . . ., (7) and 'I am against systems; the most acceptable system is that of having none on no principle' (9). Dada is part of the avant-garde which, unlike high Modernists, sought to overcome, not stress the separation between art and life.

Both the Futurists and the Dadaists treat culture with contempt. Like the Futurists, the Dadaists believed as Tzara writes that 'there is great, destructive negative work to be done' (12). However, unlike the Futurists, they did not ally art with that great force of modernity, the machine. Instead they identified it with life itself. Anything could be art from a sneeze to singing in the bath. The Dadaist opened his heart to all creation and, like some of the post-impressionists, valued African art.

To summarize, the Modernist approach to art arises out of the intellectual developments of the nineteenth century and particularly the experience of the city, which alters the nature of the self and how it perceives the world around it. There are fundamentally two approaches to the self in modern literature. The first is a revival, in a modified form, of the romantic view of the self; the second is the recovery, again in a modified form, of a more classical view of the self. Both approaches are related to an urban existence. The emphasis on self-expression can be seen as a protest against the anonymity of mass society and the emphasis on self-restraint as a reflection of the impersonal forces governing modern society. There are also two basic approaches to art, both of which can be argued to be responding to the advent of the metropolis. The first regards art as a specialized activity that, while not part of daily life, has a bearing on it. The second is the abolition of the distance between art and everyday daily life, integrating it into our routines. And, once again, the first view attempts to protect art from being absorbed into commodity culture, while the second recognizes that if art is to have a cultural role it must be more integrated in the quotidian.

Such a distinction seems neat, clear cut, but, of course, the actual situation is very far from being so. The approaches to self and to art are highly complex and difficult to categorize simply. Formal experimentation can be related to self-expression, as in Post-impressionism, or to its opposite, as in the case of Imagism. And, as Lawrence Rainey argues, 'the question of aesthetic value is inseparable from commercial success in a market economy' (54) (for Rainey see Randall, Murray). In other words, one cannot make a clear distinction between artists who distanced themselves from the wider culture and those who did not. Eliot chose to publish *The Waste Land* in the *Dial* rather than the *Little Review* or *Vanity Fair* because not only did the *Dial* offer more money, it also agreed to purchase the first 350 copies of the book publication of his selected poems. Similarly, Pound's *A Draft of Canto XVI* was issued in a limited, deluxe edition which attracted investors whose aim was to sell them at a later date for a substantial profit rather than necessarily to read the poetry therein (Rainey, 43–4, 51).

This though, was not how all contemporaries approached modern art. Artists and intellectuals might discuss how art needed to change to make its audience experience the nature of the modern world, but few understood the fragmentary nature of modern poetry or the jagged lines of a cubist painting. As Harwood notes, 'almost everyone who reviewed *Prufrock and other Observations* came to the same conclusion: here was something so remarkable, or outrageous or offensive as to defy categorisation' (88). Woolf seeks clarification from the critic whose 'duty [was] to tell us . . . where we are going' (1966b: 218) but, as she acknowledged, he seems bewildered. In fact there is a case for saying that such critics did little more than extend what artists said about art. The criticism of F.R. Leavis, for example, builds on that of T.S. Eliot, in particular his notions of tradition and the dissociation of sensibility.

The View from Bloomsbury

Clive Bell (1881–1964), another member of the Bloomsbury group, does develop an independent theory of art. He is responsible for one of the classic statements of the doctrine of aesthetic autonomy, a key idea of Modernism. As he argues in *Art* (1914), the starting point of aesthetic discussion is 'the personal experience of a peculiar emotion' (1987: 6), so called because such emotion is aroused precisely by a work of art. Bell further interrogates precisely what aspect of the work of art gives rise to this emotion, concluding, 'Only one answer seems possible – significant form' (8). In painting, which is Bell's particular subject, significant form refers to the arrangement of lines and colours on canvas. The job of the critic is to point out to the public those parts of a work which unite to produce such significant form. In Bell the very process of situating form at the heart of the aesthetic experience serves to separate art from life. And another outcome is the implication that one ought to respond to form in a painting over and above its content. Woolf makes a parallel point concerning fiction in 'Mr Bennett and Mrs Brown' when she complains that Edwardian novelists weren't really interested in books themselves but in 'something outside' of them (1966a: 327). She adds that the novels of Mr Wells, Mr Bennett and Mr Galsworthy 'leave one with so strange a feeling of incompleteness and dissatisfaction. In order to complete them it seems necessary to do something-to join a society, or, more desperately, to write a cheque' (ibid., 326).

For Bell in *Art* to appreciate a work of art, 'we need bring with us nothing from life, no knowledge of its ideas and affairs, no familiarity with its emotions. Art transports us from the world of man's activity to a world of aesthetic exaltation' (25). Momentarily it is as if one leaves the immediacy and flow of life. An artist who concerns himself with lines and colours, their relations, quantities and qualities is superior to one who uses them almost as a narrative and so depict 'real life'. The former creates 'objects of emotion' while the latter uses his subject as a 'means of suggesting emotion and conveying ideas' (18). The emotion aroused by the former is far more 'profound' and 'sublime' than the latter because the contemplation of significant form raises the spectator 'above the accidents of time and place' (36). According to Bell, a painting like William P. Frith's 'Paddington Station' uses line and colour to 'recount anecdotes and indicate the manners and customs of the age' (18) but Cézanne uses them to create a state of extraordinary ecstasy and 'complete detachment from the concerns of life' (68).

Bell's account of significant form responds to a number of modern developments, first photography which has taken over the role of descriptive painting, and the camera capable of conveying far more rapidly information about the interests, manners and fashions of society than paint on canvas. He calls Frith's work 'otiose' or lacking value in comparison to the two (18). Hence art has to redefine itself if it is to retain its value. Moreover, form is a way of ordering the experience of contemporary life, which without some principle of organization appears chaotic, random and meaningless. Additionally, for Bell his concept of form provides a way of distinguishing high art from low art, although the justification for high art, that it removes one from the practical realm, risks the same charge of escapism that is often levelled at popular art forms. Much as Bell attempts to lift art out of life, the critics who follow will bring it back down to earth. In doing so, they risk losing Bell's central insight: that the value of art lies in its distance from mere existence (on Bloomsbury see Murray, Stinson).

Marxists on Modernism

The role of art in society and the relation between form and content are the staples of Marxist discussions of literature. A famous essay by Walter Benjamin (1892–1940) on the place of art in the modern world, 'The Work of Art in the Age of Mechanical Reproduction' (1936), argues that, historically, a painting has an 'aura' because originally it was unique but this 'aura' becomes dissipated in the modern world because the painting can be reproduced and viewed in many different contexts. Such a reproduction also serves to prise it from tradition where it possesses a 'cult' value, either magical or religious. The new availability of art makes it more democratic but it also lessens its overall significance. Artists respond by making their work more difficult.

Benjamin's view appears similar to that of Carey alluded to earlier. However, Benjamin's version is different, as he makes a crucial distinction between the response to high art and that made in terms of the new art of the cinema. One is absorbed by the former but distracted by the latter. However, Benjamin reverses the conventional hierarchy saying that such distraction is more valuable than contemplation. His claim is that film makes one more conscious of how one perceives in the modern world, facilitating an examination of the individual situation which can be resolved even though that may be achieved in an absent-minded way. The intricacies of the argument can only really be appreciated by reading Benjamin's text. Among the less baroque of his observations are those that suggest film helps exploration of the environment, extending the individual's understanding of the necessities that rule his life, reminding his reader that reality, like a Charlie Chaplin movie, is a construct than can be changed.

Another Marxist critic, Georg Lukács (1885–1971), objects to the stream of consciousness technique. In his comparison of its use by Joyce and the German writer Thomas Mann (1875–1955), according to Lukács, Joyce uses it merely as a formal device to give shape to the work itself, while in Mann its purpose is 'to explore aspects of [a] world which would not otherwise have been available' (1996: 142). Lukács argues that these two different uses of the technique reflect two different views of the world, one static and sensational, the other dynamic and developmental. The first he terms Modernism and the second realism. Realism focuses on the relation between self and society, Modernism concentrates on the self alone. Realism aims to depict reality, Modernism veers away from it. For Lukács, although Joyce's work may achieve epic proportions, it remains aimless and without direction.

The chief difference between realism and Modernism, however, is that the former has a perspective that shapes the narrative, enabling the artist to stress what he or she sees as the progressive forces and 'enables the artist to choose between the important and the superficial, the crucial and the episodic' (2006: 33). However, in Modernism, which lacks such a perspective, all events seem equivalent. There are two aspects to Lukács idea of perspective: objectively it 'points to the main movements in a given historical process' and subjectively it 'represents the capacity to grasp the existence and mode of action of these movements' (55). In broad terms, perspective is based on a desire for change which Modernists believe is impossible. Hence while optimism is the characteristic note of realism, Modernism is suffused with angst.

Not all Marxists were so dismissive of the Modernist interest in form. Ernst Bloch (1885–1977), for example, was sympathetic to Expressionism on the grounds that it drew 'attention to human beings and their substance, in their quest for the most authentic expression possible' (1990: 23). He also disagreed with Lukács' conception of reality. Was it really as consistent as Lukács conjectured? Could everything be explained by the workings of capitalism? And, more fundamentally was there, as Lukács insisted, such an iron divide between subjective perception and objective reality? Bloch thought not. Reality could be uneven, a fact which art could exploit to counter official versions of it. Lukács responded with the observation that reality was indeed fragmented. One only has to think of the isolated inhabitants of the city. The point, however, is 'to pierce the surface to discover ... the hidden social forces' that produce this atomized condition (ibid.: 36–7).

Theodor Adorno (1903–1969), the most rigorously intellectual Marxist critic of his generation, said that Lukács failed to understand the shaping power of artistic form. Lukács' idea of realism depended on the imitation of empirical reality, with the result that any work which did not accurately reflect that reality was deemed to be either distorted or worse, decadent. Adorno's own view was that art is not simply mimetic, that is holding up a mirror up to nature, but rather reveals what much that normal representations of the world conceal. How does it do this? Central is the autonomy of art, that is its form. The purpose of form is to arrange material from the world in accordance with its own laws. In doing so it makes rendering this material in a new way for the observer. Art does not, as Lukács claims yield knowledge, rather it alters perception.

Adorno is a difficult but rewarding writer and the following quotation opens a path into his thinking: 'It is not the office of art to spotlight alternatives, but to resist by its form alone the course of the world, which permanently puts a pistol to men's heads' (1990: 180). There is insufficient space to explore the full ramifications of this statement – concerning for instance, whether the world holds a pistol to our heads – but it does capture the essence of Adorno's concept of art, that its internal organization disturbs the 'realistic' representations of the world that run through everything from the news bulletin to the soap opera. Essentially this is the achievement of Modernist art. Its complexities, its dissonances and its refusal to resolve the issues it raises gesture to the contradictions of capitalism, for example economic enslavement and apparent cultural freedom which simmer beneath the blandness of politics and the inanities of celebrity culture. However, by showing how broken things are, art also holds out the promise that they may be mended.

One of the implications of Benjamin's essay cited earlier is that popular culture is more progressive than high culture. Cinema might teach us about the construction of reality as opposed to painting with lessons in its contemplation. The divide between 'high' and 'low' culture is also considered by German scholar Andreas Huyssen who particularly in *After the Great Divide: Modernism, Mass Culture, Postmodernism* (1986) defines Modernism in terms of its hostility to mass culture. So far as this applies to, say, *The Waste Land* there is an element of truth in the assertion. However, as Todd Avery and Patrick Bratlinger point out, 'even the most seemingly aloof Modernists engaged in attempts to teach unsophisticated readers to read in more sophisticated ways' (2003: 250).

Adorno believes that the division between mass and minority culture represents 'the torn halves of an integral freedom' (1990: 123). He takes Benjamin to task for not recognizing that capitalism has destroyed culture's capacity to develop the whole person, turning it instead into an instrument of social control one, moreover, that corresponds to the division labour. The symphony appeals to the mind, the American film to the body. One must, says Adorno, understand the relation between them, not put them in opposition. 'Only connect', as E.M. Forster said in another context.

Late Twentieth and Twenty-First Century Approaches to Modernism

An early, seminal occurrence of the term 'modernist' in the sense of artistic innovation, occurs in the title of Laura Riding and Robert Graves' book *A Survey of Modernist Poetry* (1927). True, *The Modernist: A Monthly Magazine of Arts and Letters* appeared in 1919 but this, despite its name, as Harwood indicates it was more concerned with politics than culture and was, in any case, very short-lived (31). Certainly according to Harwood there was no systematic definition of Modernism until 1942, when the American poet, novelist and critic Randall Jarrell published his famous essay 'The End of the Line' which Harwood insists must be seen in context without retrospection or hindsight (37). Jarrell listed thirteen characteristics of Modernism (and in doing so one wonders whether he alludes to Wallace Stevens' notable 'Thirteen Ways of Looking at a Blackbird' published in 1917, the same year that Eliot published 'The Love Song of Alfred J. Prufrock') but rather than the 'differentness' Jarrell perceives in the general response to 'modernist poetry' (76) he was principally concerned to show that, far from being a radical departure from the romantic tradition Modernism was its culmination, even though 'A good many factors combine to conceal the essentially romantic character of modernist poetry' (77); an insight that continues to inform contemporary criticism of the subject. Longenbach, to whom we have already alluded, notes the affinities between romantic and Modernist poetics (1999: 100) and Frank Kermode made a detailed study of their relation in *Romantic Image* (1957).

Since Jarrell's exploration of Modernism, its meanings have grown exponentially. Internationalism, experimental art, industrialism, discoveries of physical science and new forms of corporate power are just some of the senses covered by the term. Modernism refers to first a period, from approximately 1880 to 1932 with particularly intense activity between 1908 and 1920, and second to an aesthetic, even intellectual style. It possesses such strong evaluative overtones that whatever is not included within 'modernism' – even if as in the case of Georgian poetry it belongs to the same period – is automatically deemed by many critics as unworthy of interest. With importations from philosophy, historiography, theology, cultural studies and the history of ideas the concept of Modernism seems to defeat all attempts to grasp it as a whole. Nevertheless despite its reach, variety and richness of signification, Modernism has certain recurring themes to which critics return again and again; themes, moreover, which were often first raised by Modernist thinkers themselves.

As noted earlier, Modernism was in part a response to the impact of thinkers like Darwin, Marx, Nietzsche and Freud. Later, critics continue to ponder the effect of these thinkers and their continuing relevance. Christopher Butler (1994) makes Nietzsche's declaration that what we most need 'is an absolute scepticism toward all inherited concepts' (1968: 409) the foundation of his study of early Modernism. Michael Bell (2003), however, thinks that this aspect of Nietzsche's thought is more a feature of postmodern than Modernist thinking. In the early part of the century, Nietzsche was better known for his notion of the superman than for his philosophical scepticism. And his 'metaphysical claim that the aesthetic is the fundamental activity of man' (2003: 64) was further justification for the Modernist notion that the aim of art was to transcend life, not imitate it.

The advent of literary theory with its distrust of 'master narratives' that offered to explain everything meant that Marxism, which claimed that class-struggle was the key to understanding history, fell into disfavour. One of the last great studies of Modernism from a Marxist point of view is Marshall Berman's *All that is Solid Melts into Air: The Experience of Modernity* (1981). Marx does not show us a way out of the contradictions of modern life but he does, argues Berman, give us a more profound appreciation of them. As an example of what he means consider the following image from the *Manifesto of the Communist Party* by Marx and Engels: 'The bourgeoisie has stripped of its halo every activity hitherto honoured and looked up to with reverent awe. It has transformed the doctor, the lawyer, the priest, the poet, the man of science into its paid wage labourers' (Marx and Engels, 1973: 38). The halo is a symbol of religious experience not religious doctrine and, as such, it suggests that life has a spiritual as well as a material dimension (For Marx, see Paddy).

Yet it is precisely this spiritual dimension, however one chooses to define it, that is ignored by capitalism, which to paraphrase Marx and Engels, profanes all that is holy. Berman suggests that Marx views this development in two ways. First, he is dismayed that life should be stripped of meaning, that all restraints on self-interest should be lifted and, second, he is delighted that the removal of 'the halo' 'brings about a condition of spiritual equality' (1981: 115). The bourgeoisie may have power of the proletariat, but they lack the spiritual authority enjoyed by the previous ruling class, the aristocracy. Benjamin adapted Marx's insight about the halo for his account of how the work of art loses its aura in the modern world. But, as considered above, Bell believes art does stand apart from existence, a radiant object that answers to our spiritual need. They are both right. It is another example of the contradictions of modernity, contradictions which make it both thrilling and terrifying, contradictions which says Berman, drive people apart but which can also draw them together 'ready to grasp new human possibilities, to develop identities and mutual bonds that can help us hold together as the fierce modern air blows hot and cold through us all' (ibid.: 129).

Baudelaire wanted the experience of modernity, the contingent and the fleeting, to be the basis of a new aesthetic, one that stood in marked contrast to the view that the classical world had fixed the standards of what counted as god art for all time. The city was the Modernist arena for Baudelaire as it was for Simmel, its random collisions finding artistic expression in collage or surrealism which Breton, defines as when one 'relives with glowing excitement the best part of childhood' (39), a knowledge abjuring pattern and convention (40), a assertion of 'complete nonconformism' (47). Later commentators also examine the nature of how the city affects perception, psychology and art. There are numerous questions. How is urban space divided? How do literary descriptions correspond to real locations? How does a middle class person cope with traversing the streets? What happens to the boundaries between self and other in the thronged thoroughfares? And more recently, what is the relation between the big cities of Modernism and empire? A useful overview of such issues may be found in a collection edited by Peter Brooker and Andrew Thacker, *Geographies of Modernism: Literatures, Cultures, Spaces* (2005). Of utmost importance in the initial phase of Modernism are the networks of cafes, cabarets, publishers and galleries in the creation of new artistic forms and values. Bradbury (1976) wonders if Modernist art is more concerned with the unreal rather than the real city. Its pre-occupation with perception leads one away from realism and into fantasy.

In contrast to the adulterous mixture of everything that characterizes the nineteenth and early twentieth city is Le Corbusier's vision of a planned urban space where there are no collisions or confrontations. The big shift in perspective is from the pedestrian who stands apart from the crowd but who is assailed on all sides, to the commuter who crosses the city by tram, train and eventually car. Man is absorbed into the mass and then precipitated out into the privacy of his own transport. Le Corbusier's epiphany occurred as he tried to take a stroll on the Champs Elysées one autumn evening in 1924, but felt threatened by traffic, as described in Berman Le Corbusier comments, 'We were in danger of being killed' (in Berman, 1981: 165). And then, instead of fear came pleasure, the pleasure of being in the midst of power and strength, for as he adds, 'One participates in it. One takes part in this new society that is just dawning' (166). Le Corbusier sounds very like a Futurist.

One criticism of Berman's analysis of Modernism concerns his focus on the individual rather than class, a strange omission for a Marxist. More generally the blindness concerning class on the part of many analysing Modernism has not troubled critics anywhere near as much as the neglect of gender. The view of Modernism as the extension of reason and the advance of science has been interpreted as 'the male master placing order on female chaos' (Frosh, 2003: 118) but, as Marianne DeKoven rightly notes: 'Modernism had mothers as well as fathers'. (1998: 175). The New Woman was also in revolt against Victorian culture, particularly Coventry Patmore's notorious 'Angel in the House' (1854), a poem he wrote in praise of his wife Emily, in which she is pictured as submissive to her husband and selflessly devoted to her children. The middle class woman of the late nineteenth and early twentieth century wanted much more for herself than to brush her children's hair and defer to her husband. As indicated earlier, she wanted to study, to work, to vote.

Mina Loy (1882–1966), an English poet, painter and dramatist and author of 'Feminist Manifesto' (1914), demanded a complete revolution in how women were perceived. They were to shake off the traditional roles of wife, mother and mistress and to realize that men and women were 'enemies' who have nothing in common except pleasure in 'the sexual embrace' (Kolocotroni, 1998: 259). Loy is writing about women in a political sense but her views, particularly the idea that women must discover themselves without reference to men, had implications for female artists. Writing in *The Egotist*, formerly the *New Freewoman*, Dora Marsden, (1882–1960) declares in a piece entitled 'I Am' that women establish a new poetic, one that will 'blast the stupefactions of-the Word' (ibid.: 332) which, as a vehicle of male power, helps keep women in subjection.

Woolf famously argues that because male writers had sculpted language after their nature, the female writer can find little inspiration in traditional literature and only in the relatively new form of the novel could she hope to bend the sentence to her purpose. However, women like the American Amy Lowell (1874–1925) were closely associated with the development of modern poetry, particularly Imagism, while others like Charlotte Perkins Gilman (1860–1935), another American, prefigured the subject and style of Kafka (DeKoven, 1999: 176). Charlotte Perkins Gilman, incidentally, also declares in *The Man-Made World, or Our Androcentric Culture* (1911) that 'neither the masculine nor the feminine has any place in art – art is human' (83). 'The greatest writers' Woolf added, 'lay no stress upon sex one way or the other' (1966b: 256). Some contemporary critics take issue with this position, seeing their task as adding to the canon of women authors. Others such as Jane Dowson in *Women, Modernism and British Poetry 1910–1939: Resisting Femininity* (2002) tend to agree with Woolf. Given that a canon is, by definition, limited, if it expands too much it ceases to have any value. Despite this, there remain difficult questions of whether some women were excluded by their contemporaries simply because of their gender. This seems unlikely because some women were included from the beginning in the Modernist pantheon, and as Woolf herself acknowledged there were as many active, well-regarded female writers as male. This suggests other criteria apart from gender at work. Those selected were often part of a larger group, sharing similar ideas about what constitutes art, which may have played their part. Most likely canonization resulted from a combination of factors, including the quality of the writing, something not dependent on gender (for Modernism and gender, see Parsons, Randall, Murray).

The novelist and first female president of the International Section of PEN (the world's only international fellowship of writers, working together to promote literature and defend the freedom to write) (Margaret) Storm Jameson (1891–1986) advocates the development of a socialist literature which shows that she, at least was aware that class was a factor in gender and indeed transcended it. The two came briefly together in Pablo Picasso's *Les Demoiselles D'Avignon* (1907), one of the paintings which announced the advent of a new age in art. The women in the painting are prostitutes and their faces resemble African tribal masks. In the late nineteenth century, social investigators compared the east end of London to parts of darkest Africa and now, in Picasso's painting, we find working class women conflated with the primitive.

The interest in 'the dark continent' is another strand of Modernist criticism. Anthropology was a product of empire and its practitioners believed, in general, that all societies were improving though at different rates. Frazer's immensely popular *The Golden Bough* (1906–15 abridged 1922) suggests that while 'primitive' societies may differ from one another in many ways, they also share certain myths, particularly that of the need for sacrifice in order that new life can flourish. Myth was the organizing power of *Ulysses* and *The Waste Land*, linking such work to a classical past or to one where humans were in more in direct contact with nature. The outcome might be framed in terms of a negative experience, because it led to terrible excess as with Kurtz in Conrad's *Heart of Darkness* (1902) (for Conrad, see also Baxter, Wilson, Stinson). In contrast, the result might be more positive because it revitalizes the spirit as Birkin explains in *Women in Love* (1920). As Bell explains in Art, meanwhile, 'primitive art' was the very model of what modern art should be because in it 'you will find no accurate representation; you will only find significant form' (22).

Bell's concept of significant form takes on a new meaning when we put it in the context of the work of Frederic Winslow Taylor (1856–1915), the founder of scientific management. The relation between Modernist literature and scientific management is discussed by James F. Knapp in Literary Modernism and the Transformation of Work (1988), and useful for a gender is Morag Shiach's *Modernism, Labour and Selfhood in British Literature and Culture* (2004). The purpose of scientific management was to improve efficiency and so increase profit. Although scientific management may not seem to have anything to do with Modernism, there are surprising parallels between the two.

Both, for example, place great emphasis on technique or form. The scientific manager is not interested in the individual worker, only that he adopts the right method for doing the job. As such, he is parody of the artist who puts form before content. Thomas Strychacz (1993) extends this idea, saying that there are striking resemblances between Modernism and professionals. Both have monopolies on certain forms of speech and procedures, both offer their expertise to only a few initiates, and both seek to mark themselves off from mass society. How that situation has changed. A perceptive recent study, *John Xiros Cooper's Modernism and the Culture of Market Society (2004)*, demonstrates that the art and lifestyle of the Modernist coteries have become the norm of mass culture. The concern with consciousness mutates into the contemporary privatized self while advertisers appropriate Modernist techniques to sell hatchbacks. *Ulysses* has gone from being a banned work, to a cult book, to being one commodity circulating among many. One can even find James Joyce's image on sale on tee-shirts.

This critique has moved from what Modernists say about their own work to the view of contemporary critics, and the major change of perspective is from examining the work in isolation to its analysis in context. Many of the themes that critics have discussed over the years were raised by the Modernists themselves which suggests that these themes, the city, mass culture, the nature of art and so on, still resonate. Despite all the critical commentary on Modernism, the story remains fundamentally the same. Arguably, Pound, Eliot, Joyce and Woolf are the central figures, the rest is sub-plot. The purpose of criticism is to better understand the past than was possible at the time and to use the past to better comprehend the present. Contemporary critics look back to the early twentieth century and find their own interests reflected back to them. Current areas of study include food, celebrity and the changing face of shop windows. The focus, though, remains on the subjects already discussed.

Finally, one must not forget that criticism is partly governed by the economics of higher education. It isn't simply that there is a need to explain Modernist art, there is also a need to increase research outputs in order to qualify for grants and gain funding to produce scholarship. The result is that criticism has a certain interest in making Modernism more obscure than perhaps it was originally in order to justify writing about. There is a danger, in short, that criticism may become as divorced from Modernism as Modernism apparently was from life.

Changes in the Canon

Alex Murray

Chapter Overview

Canonization and the posthumous identification of movements are curious processes, inevitably revealing as much about the intellectual climate in which these parameters are belatedly drawn as the period which they address. Modernism is arguably the most closely 'canonized' movement in English literature, subjected to a famously narrow identification of authors which has proved difficult to expand and explode in the years after its emergence. However, developments in literary criticism in the past 25 years has worked to interrogate this canon, identifying the ways in which its declaration and limitation was essentially conservative and narrow, seeking to expand the horizon's of Modernist criticism by calling for a more fluid, broader and actively political interrogation of the very term 'Modernism'. In what follows I highlight a number of shifts and challenges that have faced the Modernist canon, including areas such as literary theory; gender; postcolonialism; cultural economy and temporal co-ordinates, exploring those long-neglected writers who have begun to emerge, enriching and expanding Modernism as a field of critical study.

Creating a Canon

The issue of a literary 'canon' is bound up in the very institution of English literature itself. Prior to the twentieth century the study of English literature at university was isolated. Yet even as it emerged, certain authors came to appear as necessary in telling the narrative of English literature. One started at Chaucer and moved through a possible 20 authors – the greats – before concluding with T.S. Eliot and D.H. Lawrence (for Eliot see also Baxter, Paddy, Randall and Stinson). This limited range of authors that made up the English canon is associated with the development and formalization of its study at Cambridge under the control of F.R. Leavis, Q.D. Roth (later Leavis) and I.A. Richards. As the discipline expanded with the rise of 'new' universities in the 1960s and 1970s, the limitations of the canon were called into question by a number of literary critics. Indicative of this challenge to the idea of the canon is Terry Eagleton, whose *Literary Theory* (1983) seeeks to expose the ideological assumptions of the discipline. As he states ' "English" included two and a half women, counting Emily Brontë as a marginal case; almost all of its authors were conservatives' (33). While Eagleton could be accused of simplifying the issue for rhetorical effect, his point is clear: the process of 'canonization' limits and controls our understanding of the literary, usually at the expense of those who have traditionally been excluded from elite forms of cultural production.

Modernism could easily be considered paradigmatic of such a process. Yet whereas the canon of renaissance authors was controlled by those critics and educators of later generations, Modernism worked tirelessly to create and limit its own canon. When one thinks of Modernist authors, the names of Joyce, Pound, Eliot and Woolf immediately spring to mind (for Woolf, see also Baxter, Paddy, Randall, Stinson and Wilson). While one may extend the canon out to include W.B. Yeats, Wyndham Lewis, Joseph Conrad (for Conrad see also Baxter, Paddy, Randall and Stinson) and D.H. Lawrence, these writers dominate our understanding of the period. Yet to suggest that they were all widely read in their own day is thoroughly misleading. In fact Modernism prided itself on the exclusive nature of its audience, on cultivating itself as a small coterie of experimental writers who produced groundbreaking work, oriented towards a limited, highly educated, wealthy and discerning audience. While these issues of cultural capital and economy will be dealt with below, suffice to say that Modernism began with its own process of canonization.

The leading figure in this process was Ezra Pound (see also Paddy, Stinson and Wilson). On coming to London in 1908, Pound set out to make a living from writing poetry and delivering cultural lectures. He also had, for a short time, his own patron. The necessity to create a comfortable life out of the literary arts led Pound to become a prominent and vocal public intellectual, and by 1915 he had cemented himself as an important voice in English letters. Part of this process was Pound publishing the 'A Few Don'ts by an Imagiste' in 1912 which declares itself to be essentially an anti-manifesto in which Pound outlines the new movement of Imagism largely through a 'mosaic negative' in which the movement refuses to outline an aesthetic and political dogma, as the Futurists had done some years earlier. Instead Pound formulates a poetic that immediately cast itself in opposition, placing itself against the current cultural trends of its own day. While movements such as Futurism were populist, working to persuade the public at large into following its aesthetic and ideological formulas, Modernism – in the case of Pound's Imagism – worked to isolate, creating a 'canon' of those who were concerned with a specific form of aesthetic production that rejected all forms of popularism (see Rainey, 1998, 10–41).

Modernism continued in this exclusive vein, cultivating a selective and limited audience. The most widely known and representative instance of this selectivity was the Bloomsbury group that included figures such as Virginia and Leonard Woolf, the historian Lytton Strachey, Clive and Vanessa Bell, the economist Maynard Keynes, the artist Roger Fry and E.M. Forster (for Bloomsbury, see also Paddy, Day and Stinson). Many of the group met at Cambridge and developed an informal social and intellectual community in the Bloomsbury area of London. While many achieved considerable individual success, their status as an elite and informal group has become symbolic of the Modernist endeavour. Upper middle-class, highly educated and free-thinking, the group embodied the radical aesthetic and social ideas of Modernism, while maintaining a certain socio-economic conservatism. For a writer such as Woolf, the group was a microcosm of certain modernity, a radical shift in social and cultural interaction, yet one which is limited to those who are part of the small and elite world it populated. As she states in her diary after a Bloomsbury party in 1923 where she records having sat next to Walter Sickert, the painter: 'There is something indescribably congenial to me in this easy artists talk; the values the same as my own & therefore right; no impediments; life charming, good & interesting; no effort; art brooding calmly over it all . . .' (1981, 223–24). The notion here of values 'the same as my own & therefore right' suggests a certain insularity, an intellectual, social and cultural isolation. In what follows I will explore a number of shifts in the way we read Modernist texts, bringing into view a range of 'impediments' and challenges to the 'congenial' insularity of the Modernist canon.

Literary Theory

Many, if not all, of the changes to the canon are linked to the rise of a range of theoretical perspectives that have radically altered the study of English literature in the past 30 years. While specific theoretical perspectives, such as Queer theory, gender studies, postcolonialism, issues of class and cultural economy, and so forth will be dealt with below, I will provide a short explanation here of the ways in which theory has generally called into question practices of reading texts. Prior to the rise of a number of theoretical perspectives, Literary studies was dominated by what is often known as 'Practical Criticism'. This approach is concerned with generic conditions of the text, examining how, for instance, a poem fits into known metrical and rhyme forms. Coupled with this formal or generic consideration is a search for meaning. In essence the literary text is imbued with one overall meaning, usually the intention of the author, and the literary critic's role is to uncover meaning. Yet in some ways Modernism worked to destabilize both the formal features of a text, as well as the notion that there was a singular way in which a text could be read. In this way Modernism was 'auto-deconstructive', that is working to deconstruct the unity of a text through experimentation with genre. The great Modernist texts, such as Joyce's *Finnegans Wake* and *Ulysses*, or Pound's Cantos reject any sense of a singular 'meaning', anticipating much theoretical work that was to participate in a challenge to the canon.

If Modernism worked at the textual level to deconstruct traditional notions of reading and textuality, its politics were often far more conservative and questionable. While this was obvious in the case of Wyndham Lewis and Ezra Pound's infamous dalliances with fascism, the cultural politics of Modernism was undoubtedly elitist, partially sexist and deeply Eurocentric. The work of literary theory has been to explore in canonical texts the latent prejudices and practices that worked to exclude a number of writers, readers and texts which failed to fit into the canon. The result is two-fold: first, literary theory reads canonical Modernist texts, uncovering in their form and content both conscious and unconscious biases that can isolate the cultural politics of Modernism. Secondly, in drawing attention to these forms of conservatism, literary theory has provided the impetus for greater research into those marginal figures whom as a result of their gender, class or ethnic/national identity were denied the recognition that their works deserved.

Class, Cultural Economy and Modernist Elites

Some of the most important Modernist scholarship has been undertaken in recent years is by Lawrence Rainey, whose work on the cultural economy of Modernism has been vital in helping us understand the historical contexts of Modernist literary production prior to its canonization (see also Baxter, Randall and Thacker). Rainey's study *Institutions of Modernism: Literary Elites and Popular Culture* undertakes an examination of influential Modernist writers Joyce, Pound, Eliot and H.D., mapping the ways in which their work was produced for a small and elite audience. In particular Rainey focuses on three 'events' that were to give rise to some of the great Modernist texts: Eliot's *The Waste Land*, Pound's *Cantos*, Joyce's *Ulysses*. Rainey's primary contention is that Modernism, emerging at a time when the idea of the 'public sphere' had become compromised by the dominance of mass media, retreated 'into a divided world of patronage, collecting, speculation and investment, a retreat that entailed the construction of an institutional counter-space securing a momentary respite from a public realm increasingly degraded' (5). For Rainey, to understand Modernism it is essential to study how these institutions, such as patronage, functioned and in particular how they developed, economically, in opposition to mass culture. While a group such as The Futurists sought to appeal to a large audience in order to survive economically, Modernist writers such as Joyce and Eliot turned to patronage, creating an exclusive, and in some sense pre-Modern form of cultural capital through which to market their literary products and finance their careers.

While Rainey's work has been integral in calling into question how we view the cultural production of canonical writers, it is only part of a broader interrogation of issues of economy and cultural hierarchy which have challenged how literary studies is viewed, and in particular the study of Modernism. These diverse studies, which we could generally call cultural materialist, are concerned with how forms of cultural hierarchy are created, and how these levels of cultural value influence our perception of contemporary and historical cultural production. One of the major strands in this work has been to examine the ways in which Modernism treated class, both in terms of authorial identity and fictional character, working to both create a distorted image of class within literary texts and to obscure the importance of authors whose class and background were antithetical to the cultural elitism of Modernism.

One of the central facets of the revision of class is the ways in which Modernist attitudes to mass culture developed. An important text here is John Carey's study *The Intellectuals and the Masses* (1992), a polemical and at times almost hysteric critique of Modernist elitism. Carey's text, despite its excesses in expression, brought into focus the ways in which Modernism sought to denigrate an emerging educated and semi-educated middle and lower-middle class. The move in England to a legislated universal elementary education was part of a much wider trend towards an increasing literacy that, according to Carey, Modernism responded to with disdain, attempting to represent 'the masses' and its emerging culture as vulgar and corrupted. Carey plots how both English Modernist writers, as well as European intellectuals more generally, in particular Nietzsche created a binarized system of cultural value that failed to admit the far more fluid and dynamic nature of modern cultural production that was deconstructing the elitism of popular culture, providing cultural rejuvenation (for Nietzsche see also Paddy and

Stinson). Carey's work is valuable in capturing the violent rejection of the masses by the intellectual. The following quote from D.H. Lawrence, writing to Blanche Jennings in 1908 is emblematic of the extremity of this hatred: 'If I had my way, I would build a lethal chamber as big as the Crystal Palace, with a military band playing softly, and a Cinematograph working brightly; then I'd go out into the back streets and main streets and bring them in, all the sick, the halt and the maimed; I would lead them gently and they would smile a weary thanks; and the band would softly bubble out the "Hallelujah Chorus" ' (in Carey, 12). While this image takes on the air of chilling prophecy, what is most striking is that it comes from the pen of the only canonical Modernist writer whom could be described as working-class. Brought up in poverty in Nottingham, the son of a miner, Lawerence's rejection of the masses can be read as an internalization of cultural elitism. As such it represents the difficulty of uncovering a working-class writing during the period which combined experimentation with a sympathetic representation of the masses.

In this regard work still needs to be done in exploring the relation between working-class cultures and Modernism. While the work of Morag Schiac and others has brought to light the perception of class in a number of writers, little work has emerged on working-class narratives of the period and their relation to Modernism. One of the few works to attempt such an investigation is John Fordham's study *James Hanley: Modernism and the Working Class* (2002). Hanley, born into a working-class family in Liverpool worked as a sea-man before beginning his career as a writer. His work is marked by a focus on the autobiographical, with much of it drawing on his working-class upbringing. While his work is often dismissed as working-class realism, Fordham argues that Handley's work consistently engages with Modernism, and in order to fully understand the category of Modernism and that of the genre of working-class fiction it is necessary to engage with these writers who produce a productive tension between innovation and class-focussed mimetic representation. Perhaps the relationship between Modernism and class is potentially more symbiotic than has been assumed.

Gender and Sexuality

Of the Modernists, only Virginia Woolf, among female authors, has risen to truly canonical status. As many commentators have observed the Modernist canon remains a masculine domain, as was the academic world of the 1950s, 1960s and 1970s that was largely responsible for its creation. In the past 25 years a vast raft of scholarship has been undertaken to establish the striking originality and importance of a number of women writers, including Charlotte Perkins Gilman, Dorothy Richardson, Djuna Barnes, H.D., Gertrude

Stein and Elizabeth Bowen, along with those far more marginal figures who are yet to enter onto university syllabi, or to become objects of extended research such as Mina Loy, Antonia White and Nella Larson. Not only has this scholarship worked to recuperate or recover such writers and their work, it has also cast the gender politics of Modernism into a new light, calling into question more broadly how Modernism was both conservative and sexist, yet simultaneously radical in its attempts by both male and female authors to deconstruct the binarised and hierarchical forms of gender construction.

There were a number of important studies that paved the way for a feminist and gender studies. Arguably Bonnie Kime Scott's anthology *The Gender of Modernism* provides a focal point for this wave of scholarship. In it a range of critics wrote introduction to gender in the works of both male and female authors of the period, looking at both canonical and forgotten figures. As such the collection united some of the disparate foci of research that were emerging. Among these are myriad cases of both feminist critics both interrogating the gender politics of Canonical male Modernists, and of researchers resurrecting the lost work of women poets. Those critics include Susan Gubar, Sandra Gilbert, Elaine Showalter, Marjorie Perloff and Rita Felski. There is no one text or author who can stand as representative of this shift, with approaches taking a number of different positions, both in terms of theoretical approaches to gender and the scope of inquiry. Marianne DeKoven's study *Rich and Strange: Gender, History, Modernism* (1991) is an important text here, representing the poststructuralist–feminist interrogation of gender that emerged in the 1980s as a radical critique of Modernist literary studies (see also Randall). In Modernist texts, by both male and female authors, she finds a tension between welcoming changes to existing gender divisions, as well as an anxiety over the effect of such changes. Beyond this ambivalence she also sees an attempt to dismantle the binary gender constructions of the Victorian period, offering a glimpse of a more fluid conceptualization of gender (concerning gender studies and Modernism see also Parsons, Randall).

Alongside this investigation of gender politics has come a fascinating and valuable exploration of sexuality in the Modernist period. Prior to Modernism it was difficult for homosexual writers, in particular females, to openly display their sexuality, or for writers to explore sexuality more generally. Modernism saw a number of shifts in attitudes towards homosexuality. While it was hardly socially acceptable, more writers were willing to flout conventional morality, both in their works and in their public lives. The rise of 'Queer Theory' in the 1980s led to a radical re-reading of many canonical literary texts to uncover both the emergence and repression of various sexual identities. The volume *Modernist Sexualities* (2000), edited by Hugh Stevens and Caroline Howlett was important in drawing together a number of different writers in order to explore constructions of Modernist sexualities. The collection explores both canonical writers and neglected figures to create a portrait of an age in which sexualities in flux were representative of a much broader cultural move to interrogate the margins of identities, rather than positing new ones.

Postcolonialism

Modernism has always been deeply Eurocentric, and has tended to be regarded as a decidedly Western phenomenon, accounts of its scope and ambitions largely centred on the experiences of those in the Metropolises of the old world. The result is that those writers from non-European places, cultures and ethnicities have repeatedly been excluded from the Modernist canon. Postcolonial studies has sought to challenge the Eurocentrism of Modernism, seeking to explore how those writers from non-European back-grounds explored Modernist style and subject matter. Increasingly examined are those writers, who writing from far more European positions of colonial alterity, such as Scottish and Irish, worked to erode English as a language or colonial oppression. In doing so they have pointed out the ways in which Modernism sought to create a universalising vision of modern experience, yet was simultaneously keen to limit that experience to certain cultural and geo-graphic spaces. At the same time postcolonialism has worked to explore the latent 'othering' of those from outside Europe within canonical Modernist works. Writers such as Lawrence, Woolf and in particular Conrad have been interrogated for the propensity in their work to either celebrate colon-ized peoples as 'noble savages', or to adopt even more direct forms of racial discrimination (on Conrad see also Baxter, Stinson, Day).

Such a revision of Modernism based upon issues of race and colonial power has led to a de-centring of Modernism from Europe to elsewhere. The most notable, and indeed original instance of this critical work, was the delineating of the 'Harlem Renaissance'. Following the abolition of slavery, an African-American intelligentsia developed around the New York area of Harlem. The group produced a number of important writers such as Jessie Redmon Fauset, Zora Neale Hurston, Langston Hughes and Claude McKay. While the group was actively anthologized from the 1930s onwards, works such as Baker's *Modernism and the Harlem Renaissance* have been influential in placing this movement in relation to Modernism, arguing that we revise our understand-ing of Modernism, both geographically and conceptually (for a further dis-cussion see Bryony Randall's chapter in this volume). There is now also a move towards exploring alternative cultural traditions in an effort to expand our understanding of Modernism such as Stefan Meyer's study *The Experi-mental Arabic Novel: Postcolonial Literary Modernism in the Levant* (2000) which explores writers from a number of countries whose work is identifiably

Modernist, but whose intellectual and cultural heritage creates a markedly different account of Modernism. In other cases an argument can be made, as Simon Gikande has recently done in 'Preface: Modernism in the World,', that the very idea of a postcolonial literature is indebted to Modernism. He suggests that writers such as Chinua Achebe utilize the poetics of Modernism as they simultaneously challenge its cultural imperialism.

Within the United Kingdom a large amount of critical work has considered those writers who, while writing in English and from a close geographical proximity to the centre of colonial power, sought to undermine the dominant force of English as a colonial language. The centre of such a development is James Joyce and his cosmopolitan attempt to critique both British imperialism and Irish nationalism. In a recent collection of critical articles, *Semicolonial Joyce* (2000), edited by Marjorie Howes and Derek Attridge explores the idea of Joyce as a 'semicolonial' author. As Howes and Attridge state in their introduction: 'In their dealings with questions of nationalism and imperialism they (Joyce's works) evince a complex and ambivalent set of attitudes, not reducible to a single anti-colonialism but very far from expressing approval of the colonial organizations and methods under which Ireland had suffered during a long history of oppression, and continued to suffer during his lifetime. The allusion to punctuation, furthermore, reminds one that Joyce's handling of political matters is always mediated by his strong interest in, and immense skill with, language: the two domains are, finally, inseparable in his work' (3). This notion of language seeking to rupture or destabilize identifies the parasitic force of Joyce's work, whereby the English language is corrupted and in doing so radically altered. These revisions of Joyce from the perspective of postcolonial studies work to challenge the notion of an 'English' canon that attempts to appropriate and domesticate a linguistic and cultural alterity that lurks at its very heart. In addition to Joyce, Scottish writers such as Hugh MacDairmid who challenged ideas of a Modernist, English, urban elite by focussing on the politics and poetics of place, as Scott Lyall's recent study *Hugh MacDiarmid's Poetry and Politics of Place: Imagining a Scottish Republic* (2006) has shown. Undoubtedly much work remains in exploring the lesser known figures of Scottish and Irish Modernism in order to expand our understanding of such alternate Modernisms.

Perhaps the most influential aspect of the postcolonial challenge to Modernism has been the re-reading of Modernist texts with an eye to both latent and explicit forms of cultural 'othering'. Undoubtedly the most famous instance of this has been the critical reception of Joseph Conrad's novella *Heart of Darkness*. The postcolonial re-reading of this novel was lead by Chinua Achebe's seminal essay 'An Image of Africa: Racism in Conrad's *Heart of Darkness*,' published in 1977 (see Baxter and Paddy). In it Achebe suggests that Europe has had a constant need to construct 'Africa as a foil . . . as a place of negations at once remotè and vaguely familiar, in comparison with which Europe's own state of spiritual grace will be manifest' (252). Since then the field of Conrad studies has been dominated by the presence of postcolonialism, with the novelist's considerable body of work thoroughly revised. Another Modernist writer whose construction of ethnic others has undergone interrogation is E.M. Forster, whose *A Passage to India*, long celebrated for a liberal sensitivity in its view of India has been challenged, with Teresa Hubel's work re-reading Forster's text with a view to encountering those moments in which Forster's perceived sensitivity comes up against his own limits of representing the colonial 'other'. Other figures to undergo such an interrogation are D.H. Lawrence, whose vitalism used the alterity of Africa, among other spaces to project an alternative to European modernity.

Temporal Co-ordinates

'HURRY UP PLEASE IT'S TIME'

T.S. Eliot, *The Waste Land* (46, 47)

The repeated plea from the barman in *The Waste Land* is only one among many instances of Modernist obsessions with time. Within the creation of a Modernist canon this concern is repeated as critics struggle to assert the precise temporal co-ordinates of Modernism. Did it begin on New Year's Eve 1899 when the clock struck midnight and ushered in the new century? Or was the publication of Conrad's *Heart of Darkness* earlier in 1899 in *Blackwood's Magazine*? Many take Virginia Woolf's famous formulation, stated in her essay 'Mr Bennett and Mrs Brown' of 1924 that 'on or about December 1910, human character changed' (320). Alternatively one could suggest that if Modernism was primarily an aesthetic category rather than pertaining to a particular socio-economic period then we could extend Modernism so as to include Sterne's *The Life and Opinions of Tristram Shandy, Gentleman* (1759–1767). And if the beginning of Modernism is a minefield then the ending is no better. Some suggest it was 1939 with the outbreak of World War I and the publication of Joyce's *Finnegans Wake*. Others believe it can be extended to 1941, the year of Joyce's and Woolf's death, while many believe that the true economic and cultural shifts that spelt the end of the modern period did not really occur until the end of the Second World War and the emergence of the post-war consensus in the UK. For others the delineation between Modernism/ modernity and 'postmodernism'/'postmodernity' is fallacious, an erroneous division that gives the illusion of change when we are very much trapped in the epistemological and metaphysical conundrums of Modernism.

If one had any doubt of Modernism's, and Modernist literary criticism's obsession with dates one only needs to turn to the studies produced in honour of certain years, namely 1910, 1913 and 1922. Michael North's *Reading 1922: A Return to the Scene of the Modern* (1999) has firmly consolidated that year as the epicentre of Modernism. Not that the claim had been in doubt, with the publication of the two ur-texts of Modernism, Joyce's *Ulysses* and Eliot's *The Waste Land* – in addition to Woolf's *Jacob's Room*, the year has long been recognized as Modernism's *annus mirabilis*. Pound famously posited October 30 1921 as the end of the Christian Era, when Joyce penned the final words of *Ulysses*. Willa Cather identifies 1922 as the year in which the world 'broke in two'. North goes beyond the usual histrionics, excavating the year in a much deeper and richer vein, exploring the much richer cultural and intellectual hinterland of the period as evidenced in such events as the publication of Ludwig Wittgenstein's *Tractatus Logico-Philosophicus* and the cinema of Charlie Chaplin. In doing so North argues that we need to see our own selves and our own critical practices in the light of this year, and call into question the sense that we can identify Modernism through the canon alone. Jean-Michele Rabaté has recently proposed that the year 1913 could be usefully designated as what he terms 'the cradle of Modernism'. For Rabaté the year marks not so much the final year of peace before the devastating onslaught of World War I, as is commonly held, but instead marks the explosion of globalization. Rabaté explores the cross-cultural exchange that was driving the innovation of Modernism, highlighting the shifts in global politics, the changes in technology, cross-cultural literary consumption and the awarding of the Nobel Prize in literature to the Bengali writer Rabindranath Tagore. Rabate is able to utilize an exploration of 'what it meant to be modern' in 1913 as a means of expanding our very definition of Modernism.

For both Rabaté and North, the interrogation of a single year as the epicentre of Modernism works to expand and complicate our definition of the modern. Their work is part of a much larger critical debate that has sought to call into question the ends of Modernism. The debate draws back to the 1980s when Frederic Jameson attempted to delineate postmodernism. As he famously states 'Consider, for example, the powerful alternative position that postmodernism is itself little more than a stage in Modernism proper (if not indeed of the even older romanticism); it may indeed be conceded that all the features of postmodernism I am about to enumerate can be detected, full-blown, in this or that preceding Modernism' (2000, 191) Jameson instead posits that there had been much wider social and cultural shifts that rendered the power of Modernist aesthetics to shock far less than they had in an earlier period what we see in Jameson is the recognition that between the postmodern and the modern very little, in terms of aesthetics, had changed. What little work exists in post-war literary studies concerning the continuities between the modern and the postmodern, in particular in regards to the novel seems persuasive. Writers such as Anna Kavan, Samuel Beckett or Jean Rhys, whose work cover both 'periods' can be usefully seen as examples of the flaws inherent in trying to delineate sharp divisions. Similarly the work of 'experimental' post-war writers such as B.S. Johnson, Ann Quin, Christine Brooke-Rose or Muriel Spark is arguably far more indebted to an earlier poetics than it is a prelude to a future literary style.

Conclusion

The idea of a canon – a group of texts that seem representative of a period and movement, appears to the new student the most natural of phenomena. Yet as I hope to have demonstrated here, canonicity is certainly not an organic component of the literary text. In the case of Modernism an interrogation of the canon can reveal the self-reflexive critical project of Modernism in creating its own canon as well as its inherent biases and limitations in such a process. Yet this complexity should not be seen as intimidating for those first encountering Modernism, rather it should be embraced as underpinning the vitality of Modernist studies as an exciting and dynamic area of study.

10 Gender and Modernism

Deborah Parsons

'What are some of the emerging approaches or paradigms at the crossroads of Modernist studies and gender/sexuality studies?' This was the key question posed by the symposium on *Gender, Sexuality, Modernism* held at the University of Pennsylvania in 2006. (For Modernism's relationship to feminism and gender, see also Murray). Eager to embrace new theoretical models that might hold the 'potential for exciting new research', it was yet accompanied by a marked uncertainty as to the way forward when faced with the pluralized discourses of both Modernism and feminism: 'Where are we headed, or where should we be headed, given the shifting disciplinary rubrics and divisions among feminism, literary criticism, Modernist studies, women's studies, gender studies, queer theory, and other proximate fields? What new configurations or alliances might be desirable?' The terms of this debate articulated an emerging trend in reappraisals of the place and function of feminism within Modernist studies in the new millennium, informed by a sense of gender-focussed criticism as having reached something of a theoretical impasse. At the inaugural conference of the Modernist Studies Association in 1999, for example, Susan Stanford Friedman argued forcefully in a piece later published as 'Gender, Spatiality, and Geopolitics in the New Modernist Studies' for a 'locational' feminism that would recognize issues of gender as one of a complex matrix of cultural identity markers, and lead new explorations into the global dimensions of Modernism and the spatial politics of its subsequent definition. As succeeding conferences continued to self-consciously debate 'Is There a Future for Feminist Criticism in Modernist Studies?', or, 'Whatever Happened to Feminist Criticism?', it is at the intersection of Modernism, globalism and gender that possible answers to those questions have increasingly been sought. The topic of the roundtable session at MSA 8 in 2006, 'Displaced Modernisms', and the titles of the ninth and tenth conferences *Geographies of Literary and Visual Culture* (2007) and *Modernism and Global Media* (2008), the latter calling, at the time of writing for seminars and papers of 'transnational and international aesthetic interaction, Diaspora, media in various colonial and anti-colonial projects [. . .] as well as the ways in which global media shapes racial, ethnic, gendered, classed and regional identities and affiliations', points to the locational/dislocational focus of millennial Modernist studies. This chapter aims to provide an introduction to and understanding of the history of literary critical perspectives and debates that have led up to this current juncture in Modernist studies, but also to encourage recognition of the consciously gendered and (inter)national rhetoric and debates with which the Modernist period was itself riven.

The emergence of feminist literary studies in the 1970s and early 1980s impacted radically on the academic establishment, refiguring the subject-focus, theoretical assumptions and methodologies of literary analysis, and initiating the reform of an accepted 'canon' of writers and their works. Critiquing the gendered politics that shape literary value-judgements, Anglo-American feminist criticism set out to define a specifically *female* literary tradition. 'Gynocriticism', and feminist critic Elaine Showalter defines this approach in her groundbreaking essay 'Towards a feminist poetics' (1979), as being concerned with 'the history, themes, genres and structures of literature by women', and the identification of a literary subculture that gave voice to women's feelings and experiences under patriarchy (128). Showalter's now classic study of a lineage of British women writers across the nineteenth and twentieth centuries, *A Literature of Their Own* (1977), epitomizes this endeavour, identifying over two hundred previously unknown or marginalized women writers to stand alongside the quartet of Jane Austen, the Brontës, George Eliot and Virginia Woolf, and arguing for the evolution of a tradition of female authorship and self-awareness through three historical stages (the Feminine, the Feminist and the Female), up to the 1960s.

The gynocritical project of rediscovering women writers found a ready body of work in the late nineteenth and early twentieth century period, and in the newly formed Virago Press, a like-minded publishing house with the objective of disseminating both previously unpublished or out-of-print works by 'forgotten' women writers, and literary critical studies making the case for their recognition by the academic institution. The launch of the Virago Modern Classics reprint series with Antonia White's *Frost in May* in 1978, boldly created a new canon of Modernist women writers, as readers rediscovered the works of Willa Cather, Radclyffe Hall, Zora Neale Hurston, Dorothy Richardson, May Sinclair, Sylvia Townsend Warner and Rebecca West, to name but a few. Also significant were the edited anthologies of the short fiction that typified much of women's literary production in the late nineteenth and early twentieth centuries, originally appearing in the leading literary journals and avant-garde magazines of the period; notably Showalter's *Daughters of Decadence: Women Writers of the Fin-de Siècle* (1993), which re-introduced the work of 'New Woman' writers, including Kate Chopin, George Egerton, Sarah Grand, Charlotte Perkins Gilman, Vernon Lee and Olive Schreiner, and Trudi Tate's *That Kind of Woman: Stories from the Left Bank and Beyond* (1991), which included pieces by, among others, Djuna

Barnes, H.D., Katherine Mansfield, Anaïs Nin, Jean Rhys, and May Sinclair. Showalter's *A Literature of Their Own*, Gillian Hanscombe and Virginia Smyers' *Writing for Their Lives: The Modernist Women 1910–1940* (1987), and Shari Benstock's *Women of the Left Bank: Paris, 1900–1940* (1987), were all published by Virago, as was Showalter's *The New Feminist Criticism* (1985), an edited collection of essays by both Anglo-American and European feminist critics.

Crucial as the imperative to recover the voices of women writers who had hitherto disappeared from literary historiography has been to Modernist studies, it is yet important to note that at first the pioneers of the new feminist criticism, including Showalter herself, were more than a little ambivalent about the contribution made to the 'female tradition' by *Modernist* women writers, who tended to be regarded as betraying their own often overt feminist politics in their literary works. Thus Patricia Stubbs, for example, in *Women and Fiction: Feminism and the Novel 1890–1920* (1979), accuses Virginia Woolf of a 'failure to carry her feminism through into her novels', the consequence, Stubbs suggests, of her '*aesthetic* theories' (231; my italics). Similarly, Showalter, in *A Literature of Their Own*, is intensely critical of Woolf, Katherine Mansfield and Dorothy Richardson, the principal Modernist women writers she discusses, for what Showalter describes as their preoccupation with female 'consciousness' over women's social 'experience', in a feminist withdrawal from the male-dominated world that she regards as leading 'more and more toward a separatist literature of inner space' (1977: 33). Woolf, Mansfield and Richardson, she notes, evolved 'a deliberate female aesthetic' that applied feminist ideology 'to words, sentences and structures of language in the novel' (33). According to Showalter's account, however, this was in no way a positive development, as 'the more female this literature became in the formal and theoretical sense, the farther it moved from exploring the physical experience of women' (34). 'The female aesthetic', she writes, 'was to become another form of self-annihilation for women writers, rather than a way to self-realization'. Even Woolf's feminist polemic *A Room of One's Own* (1929) is attacked by Showalter for a writing style that is 'teasing, sly, elusive [. . .] denying any earnest or subversive intention', and thus setting so injurious an example in its disguising of any clear advocacy of feminist agency on Woolf's part, that Showalter recommends readers 'remain detached' from its 'narrative strategies' (285). The 'room of one's own' that Woolf had proclaimed the enabling material resource of the woman writer, becomes in Showalter's account a claustrophobic retreat from social reality, and her advocacy of an aesthetic of androgyny a sterile denial of female sexuality. The 'feminine equivalent' to masculine realism that Richardson so determinedly pursued in the writing of her life's work *Pilgrimage*, is dismissed by Showalter as 'an end in itself, a journey to nowhere [. . .] a closed and sterile world' (258). The refusal of both to admit partisanship to any collective faith, politics or identity, moreover, signal ultimately for Showalter an evasion of the demands of others, and repression of feminist political engagement. Woolf and Richardson's writing falls short of the demands of Showalter's socio-logical feminist criticism, because their aesthetic, or 'modernist', experimenta-tion with literary focus and form, is regarded as undercutting their political duty to write angry manifestos representing women as social agents within a material world. To be both a feminist writer *and* a Modernist writer, Showalter seemed to imply, was impossible.

The theoretical naivety of Anglo-American feminist literary criticism in terms of its own ideological underpinnings is similarly taken up by Toril Moi, in her sustained attack on the theoretical bias inherent in Showalter's critique of the Modernist 'female aesthetic' in *Sexual/Textual Politics* (1985). Incredu-lous at the limits of a feminist criticism that could not find value in the writing of such self-affirmed feminists as Woolf and Richardson, Moi suggests that the fault might lie with the critical assumptions of the critics rather than the supposed ideology of the texts they were so awkwardly dismissing. The prob-lem with such Anglo-American feminism is that for all its critique of the exclusion of women from the standard narratives of literary history, feminist critics themselves retain conventional empiricist, humanist and realist notions of representation by which they revalue women's writing. They judge works by how authentically they portrayed 'real' (i.e. social) female experience, and on the basis of the assumption that literary texts *should* and *could* straight-forwardly reflect material reality. Showalter, for example, in *A Literature of Their Own* perceives women's writing as moving 'in the direction of an all-inclusive female realism, a broad, socially informed exploration of the daily lives and values of women within the family and the community' (29). This is a focus to which the impressionist narratives of a Woolf or Richardson do not conform. According to the values of Anglo-American feminist literary criticism, Moi thus argues, Modernist writers might be recognized as part of a female literary heritage, but their texts, which were non-realist, or at least unconventionally so, could not offer an effective feminist voice. Even when a number of important recuperative studies of Modernist women in the 'gynocritical' tradition did begin to appear in the mid-1980s, notably Benstock's *Women of the Left Bank* and Hanscombe and Smyers' *Writing for Their Lives*, they tend to focus attention on and discuss the professional lives of the women rather than the formal dynamics of their unconventional writ-ings. Drawing on developments in European structuralist, semiotic and post-structuralist theory, notably the deconstruction of the single unified subject, and the binary logic of concepts of 'masculinity' and 'femininity', as well as the concept of *écriture féminine*, Moi demonstrates that Anglo-American feminist criticism in fact affirmed the traditional humanism at the heart of patriarchal ideology. Politically radical, in its championing of realist literary form it was yet aesthetically reactionary. French theorists such as Jacques Derrida and Julia Kristeva, Moi explains, by contrast regarded the form of Modernist writing by writers such as James Joyce, fragmented by ellipsis or written in unpunctuated stream-of-consciousness, as inherently revolutionary, whether written by a male or female writer, because it fragments and subverts the symbolic order as constituted by language.

Moi here pursues a line of argument set out by Alice Jardine in her article 'Gynesis' (1982), in which she posits a new direction for feminist literary criticism, bringing into dialogue Anglo-American feminism, with its social-historical focus on the sex of the author and the representation of female stereotypes, and French post-structuralism, with its suspicion of mimesis and theoretical focus on the 'deaths' of the 'author' and the unified 'self'. Anglo-American 'feminism, as a concept, as inherited from the humanist and rationalist eighteenth century, is traditionally about a group of human beings in history whose identity is defined by that history's representation of sexual decidability', Jardine states, '[a]nd every term of that definition has been put into question by contemporary French thought' (1982: 58). 'Gynesis', in Jardine's terms, shifts the terms of debate from *women* to *gender* (or the *feminine*), and the focus of study from writing by and/or representations of women to the recognition and exploration of the role of gender in the master narratives and signifying practices that underpin Western society. Moi argues that gynocriticism, with its naïve faith in the transparency of linguistic meaning, fails to recognize the gendered binary system at the heart of normative 'phallogocentric' ideology, and thus also to appreciate the disruptive potential of a seemingly irrational or non-logical style of writing. The result is a literary criticism that was both essentialist and reductive. '[T]o remain detached from the narrative strategies of the text', she observes somewhat witheringly of Showalter's assessment of *A Room of One's Own*, for example, 'is equivalent to not reading it at all' (Moi, 1985: 3). At the same time, however, both Jardine and Moi warn against feminist idealization of both the essentialist concept of *écriture féminine* (or a stylistics and thematics of writing that is inherently 'female'), and the assumption of a parallel between literary or linguistic experimentation and social or political disruption. Advocating a feminist literary criticism that would combine the theoretical awareness of post-structuralist theory with the political commitment and agency of gynocriticism, Jardine and Moi pave the way for a critical turn in Modernist studies, revitalized around a re-examination of questions of gender. Interestingly in 'Twenty Years On: *A Literature of Their Own* Revisited', Showalter defends the sociological and ethnographical principals of her work, and her elevation of historical and cultural questions over philosophical or linguistic ones. While somewhat redressing her account of the ultimate frustration and failure of the 'New Woman' writers of the 1890s, whose work she had already revalued in

Daughters of Decadence (1993), she yet remains noticeably silent over the Modernists who had been the main butt of her attack.

The influence of post-structuralism turned the tables of revisionary criticism. Suddenly classical realism was no longer the preferred vehicle for literary articulations of social or political resistance, but instead deemed ideologically complicit with bourgeois, patriarchal assumptions about society and consciousness, while non-realist or unconventionally realist writing was by contrast regarded as anarchic and avant-garde in its very form, if not necessarily overtly so in content. Questions over the politics of style contribute to a perhaps broader dialogue concerning the politics of representation. As Jardine notes, '[i]n the writings of those French theorists participating in gynesis, "woman" may become intrinsic to entire conceptual systems, without being "about" women – much less "about" feminism' (Jardine, 1982: 58). The traditional canon of Modernist authors, texts and critical principles now becomes a highly contested terrain, for not only was the feminist project of recovering forgotten women writers strengthened by the ability to recognize *political* value in more formally experimental works, but the works of male writers previously regarded as the bastions of a monolithic 'high' Modernism demanded reinterpretation. Perhaps nowhere are questions over the relationship of gender, politics and aesthetic experimentation most hotly debated than in the reinvigorated field of James Joyce studies. Margot Norris' *The Decentered Universe of 'Finnegans Wake': A Structuralist Analysis* (1974), has already identified the muse author Anna Livia Plurabelle as the quintessence of Joyce's critique of the social order, an 'unsystematic and archaic' force against 'structuring, ordering principle governing societal systems' (Norris, 1974: 68). With Colin McCabe's notorious politicized revaluation of Joyce from classical formalist to revolutionary anarchist in *James Joyce and the Revolution of the Word* (1978), the writing of at least the latter half of *Ulysses* and *Finnegans Wake* is ripe for careful reappropriation by feminist critics.

Looking back from the perspective of 1987, Bonnie Kime Scott recalls that the influence of post-structuralist feminist theory, 'was inevitable for a Joycean of my generation' (Scott, 1987: xvi). As Stephen Heath observes, in an essay titled 'Men in Feminism' (1989), 'for male Modernist writers seeking an avant-garde dislocation of forms, a recasting of given identity into multiplicity, writing differently has seemed to be naturally definable as writing feminine, as moving across into woman's place' (Heath, 1989: 27). While critics such as Karen Lawrence and Suzette Henke, however, lead the recognition of a textual and linguistic errancy in Joyce's work, identified with the 'feminine', an intervention that undercuts the patriarchal social order, others are more cynical about such 'feminist re-Joyceings' over a writer who can refer to a woman as 'an animal that micturates once a day, defecates once a week, menstruates once a month and parturates once a year' (Gilbert and

Gubar, 1985: 519; Ellmann, 1959: 162).[1] Indeed Scott herself opens her *Joyce and Feminism* (1984) defensively aware that fellow feminist critics might protest that 'Joyce is disqualified by his gender [...] or that he has received far too much attention from the male establishment to require any compensatory effort from a feminist', and she is at pains to stress the gynocritical credentials of her focus on the role of women such as Harriet Weaver and Sylvia Beach in the production and dissemination of Joyce's work (3). At the same time, anticipating Moi's attack on the theoretical naïvety of Anglo-American feminism, she refuses to be limited by any single critical model of feminist criticism so far outlined. Scott's focus in *Joyce and Feminism* (1984) is largely historical and biographical, re-positioning Joyce within the context of Irish feminism, his personal and professional relationships with women, and contemporary reviews of his work by female critics (notably Woolf, Richardson, Rebecca West and Djuna Barnes), yet it is also imbued with the influence of theory, especially in Scott's observation that Joyce 'favours systems that multiply meanings, offer contraries, and are multiply voiced', and her argument that this pluralism is exemplified in 'the contradictions of Molly Bloom and the plurabilities of ALP' (206). A significant feature of Scott's study, moreover, is her emphasis on the fact that the significance of Joyce within literary debates over the relationship of writing, sex and gender was in fact nothing new, but a common preoccupation of the Modernist moment itself; her study, *Joyce and Feminism* 'does not invent or substitute a subject,' Scott asserts, 'but reclaims one that was there, too little recognized and worked, from the start' (201–2).

During the 1990s, and thanks in no small part to the work of Scott herself, the recuperative project of feminist Modernist studies begins to shift to a revisionary cultural materialism, and an examination of the gender politics with which critics can recognize key literary debates of the era that had been hotly contested. As the 1990s opened Kime Scott produced *The Gender of Modernism*, perhaps the most influential anthology to appear since Richard Ellmann and Charles Fiedelson's *The Modern Tradition: Backgrounds of Modern Literature* (1965). Ellmann and Fiedelson's selection of manifestos and statements of aesthetic principle from 'the age of Yeats, Joyce, Eliot and Lawrence, of Proust, Valéry and Gide, of Mann, Rilke and Kafka', had included only one female contributor, Virginia Woolf. As Scott famously writes in her introduction, '[m]odernism as we were taught it at mid-century [...] was unconsciously gendered masculine', the result of selective quotation and strategic anthologizing of a limited range of writers, and indeed a limited range of their work, to shape a particular strand of Modernist literary thought into a singular and increasingly dominant narrative of the period (2). In striking contrast to the limited parameters of Peter Faulkner's contemporaneous *A Modernist Reader* (1986), which in its acceptance and reiteration of this monolithic narrative entirely suppresses what had by now become a conspicuous critical debate over the 'conception' of Modernism, Scott and her 18 contributing editors set out to demonstrate the 'gender-inflected territories' of early Modernist practice, reception and definition, and in so doing redefine the reading of male and female Modernist texts alike. Scott comments, 'We suspect that Modernism is not the aesthetic, directed, monological sort of phenomenon sought in their own ways by authors of now-famous manifestos [. . .] and perpetuated in new critical-formalist criticism through the 1960s', and adds 'Modernism as caught in the mesh of gender is polyphonic, mobile, interactive, sexually charged; it has wide appeal, constituting a historic shift in parameters' (4). Two further key studies that challenge a singular, institutionalized concept of 'modernism' are Bernard Bergonzi's *The Myth of Modernism and Twentieth-Century Literature* (1986) which declares that 'The dominance of a limited canon of unquestionably great authors is to be resisted' (xiv), and Astradur Eysteinsson, *The Concept of Modernism* (1990) which insists that the avant-garde and Modernism cannot simply be conflated (4) since this would ignore the often affirmative capacity of its ability to 'shock' (223).

Resurrecting hard to find essays and reviews, diary entries and letters, as well as extracts from little known or hitherto unpublished literary works, selected and introduced by scholars articulating a diversity of feminist and literary critical approaches, *The Gender of Modernism* provides a key resource for the reappraisal of both the writings of Modernist women and the significance of gender in relation to them. An awareness of the politics and aesthetics of gender within Modernist discourse demands a rethinking of universalizing critical paradigms of the 'name and nature' or the 'mind' of Modernism, as Malcolm Bradbury and James McFarlane outline them in their influential *Modernism* (1976). 'Did the formal innovations advanced by Modernism and the phallic metaphors used to express them suit women writers as well as they did men?', Scott asks, for example. Moreover, '[h]ow did the Great War, which has generally been seen as a deep influence on Modernist view of the world, have different effects on men and women writers?' The 1920s, Scott notes, is typically represented by women writers in the anthology as 'a time of excitement and new freedoms', very different to the period of emptiness, meaninglessness and crisis with which it has been mythologized in canonical narratives of Modernist literary history (6). These are questions Bridget Elliott and Jo-Ann Wallace re-engage in their *Women Artists and Writers: Modernist (im)positionings* (1994), which draws upon the work of cultural theorist Pierre Bourdieu to again highlight Modernism as a 'discursive field' of diverse and competing agendas, shaped into a singular entity by its dominant practitioners and subsequent critics through the foregrounding of a certain set of elements which then serve to contain, suppress or simply ignore others.

Elliott and Wallace ponder whether 'formal experimentation *mean* the same thing to women and men artists, or to the women and men who viewed or read their work?', and further they ask us to reconsider, 'did women feel the same need to restore a lost cultural coherence? whose interests did "modernism" (and its critics) serve?' (6).

If *The Gender of Modernism* transmits to the reader something of the spectrum of the gender-inflected concerns of women writers in the period, and thus serves to disrupt the accepted yet limited norms by which 'what modernism was' had been previously understood, Scott and her contributors were nevertheless as bound to principles of selectivity (albeit based in alternative aims and objectives) as the editors of previous Modernist anthologies. Remaining firmly allied with the gynocritical project of recovering the voice of women writers, as the dedication 'To the forgotten and silenced makers of modernism' affirms, the discourse of gender it articulates is exclusively female in focus, notwithstanding the occasional male contributor. Despite Scott's reiteration of certain points that she makes elsewhere in *Joyce and Feminism*, insisting in the introduction of *The Gender of Modernism* that '[o]ur critical generation did not invent gender as a concept' (3), and that 'modernists themselves attached labels such as "virile" and "feminine" to the new writing as they reviewed it, attributing different meanings and values to the terms' (3), the range and diversity of gendered meaning in the aesthetic debates, projects and manifestos of the period is never fully demonstrated even in Scott's seminal text. The conspicuous absence of pieces by male writers in whose fiction and criticism gendered rhetoric is overt, and the volume's relative silence over the fluidity and/or hostility between different ideological variants of feminism at the turn of the century and through into the 1930s, or the social and psychological crisis in *masculinity* that followed the rise of women's suffrage, *fin-de-siècle* sexology, and the mass slaughter of the Great War, results in a conception of the 'gender' of Modernism that is concerned only with the 'feminine'. The identifications of creativity with the feminine by writers such as Joyce, Marcel Proust and Henry James, alliance of suffragettism and avant-gardism in the masculinist manifestos of F.T. Marinetti and Wyndham Lewis, and the more ambivalent representations of masculinity in the work of D.H. Lawrence and Ernest Hemingway, are just some of the areas of gender ambiguity that go almost entirely unrepresented. *The Gender of Modernism* consciously turns away from 'a few masters and movers of modernism' (3), thus setting out to counter any patriarchal construction of a canonical definition of Modernist writers and texts by critical scholarship of the plenitude or multiplicity of encounters, a task it admirably fulfils, but its deliberately separatist focus on women results in a failure to explore the mutual imbrication of the feminine *and* the masculine in the politics and thematics of the period, and how they cross the interests and aesthetics of both female and male writers.

In highlighting the politics of gender within Modernist studies, *The Gender of Modernism* nevertheless triggered further questions about the status of further aspects of identity 'othered' by the hegemonic New Critical enterprise, and the complex cross-referencing of gender with issues of race, colonialism, nationhood and sexuality. The questions that Scott recalls being posed by Jane Marcus on first reading the volume, however – 'How would modernism look if viewed from Africa or India or Japan? What is the patriarchal component of Eurocentrism?' – are ones with which, as Susan Stanford Friedman's call for a locational feminist Modernism with which we began indicates, Modernist studies have only recently begun to engage. No longer the ghettoized domain of a feminist literary studies, women's writing and issues of gender are purportedly an integral part of a Modernist curricula in which male and female writers may be taught alongside and in relation to each other. Yet, in the eyes of some feminist critics, this, in fact, serves to subdue women's literary voice, and contain the radical potential of feminist criticism. If, by the end of the twentieth century, 'modernism' had come to signify a set of heterogeneous Modern*isms*, as Peter Nicholls in his influential guide, *Modernisms: A Literary Guide* (1995), proclaims, their acknowledgement and study still requires championing so as not to be subsumed and subdued. Modernism, Nicholls asserts, is 'inextricably bound up with a politics of gender' (197), yet amidst the range and nuance of his delineation of Anglo-American and Continental avant-gardism, the work of a stunningly curtailed number of women writers (H.D., Gertrude Stein, Marianne Moore and Mina Loy) is relegated by Nicholls to a chapter entitled 'At a Tangent: Other Modernisms' (193). Moreover, as Marcus' cautionary questions implies, much of Modernism's 'polyphony' is yet to be explored.

Where the *Gender of Modernism* enacts a feminist revision of previous anthologies of Modernism, Scott's subsequent project offers a feminist rewriting of the genealogy of Modernism, countering the male Modernist axes and lineages identified by critics such as Hugh Kenner and Michael Levenson. In the two-volume *Refiguring Modernism* (1995), she challenges the canonically accepted authority of the 'Men of 1914' as the arbiters of a formalist Modernist aesthetics, substituting instead Virginia Woolf, Djuna Barnes and Rebecca West, whom she designates the 'Women of 1928', and the principal representatives of a '*second* rise in modernism' that she argues is significantly female and feminist in orientation. This repositioning of key Modernist personnel is then paralleled by the substitution of the figurative trope of the *scaffold*, which Scott identifies with the 'architectonic male Modernist designs' of canonical aesthetic formalism, by that of the *web*, taken from Woolf's depiction of fiction in *A Room of One's Own* as a spider's web, 'attached to life at all four corners' (62–3). In direct contrast to the canonical reading of a (male) Modernism that, to borrow from Joyce's Stephen Dedalus, positions the artist 'behind or beyond or above his handiwork, invisible, refined out of existence', Scott appeals to the assertion made by Woolf in *A Room of One's Own* that literary works are 'not spun in mid-air by incorporeal creatures' but the result, at least in part, of 'grossly material things, like health and money and the houses we live in' (63). While acknowledging that Woolf, West and Barnes all make recourse to the 'scaffold' in the style and structure of their work, and that Woolf herself regarded the 'web' as applicable to male as well as female writers, Scott's focus is on the social and material emphasis of Woolf's arachne image as a metaphor for women writers' creative process and the affiliative networks of patrons, publishers and other writers significant to their literary production (for Woolf, see also Baxter, Randall, Stinson).

Her project of refiguring Modernist aesthetics and authorship is the product, Scott admits in *Refiguring Modernism: Volume One, The Women of 1928* (1995), of 'an anxious, self-conscious, yet ill-defined era of postmodern feminist theory' for which the concepts of '[a]ndrogyny, the autonomous self, [. . .] women's literary tradition, maternal affiliations, essentialism, and the category of gender have all been superseded' (xxxi). It is perhaps thus not surprising that within its pages feminist Modernist studies seems to reach an impasse; caught between the strategies of counter-canon formation and 'a postmodern caution about difference' (xxxiv). Following the delineation of female Modernist tradition(s), anthologies and genealogies, and arguments for a 'feminine' language, what objective is left for feminist revisionary criticism to pursue? While neatly reclaiming the narrative strategies of *A Room of One's Own* for a feminist Modernist 'tradition', Scott's two volumes awkwardly reflect the longstanding split in feminist literary studies between an empiricist, social-historical concentration on the material conditions of women's writing, and the theoretical emphasis of post-structuralism. Thus, the first delineates the 'domestic and professional arrangements' within which Woolf, West and Barnes worked, Scott anxiously noting the potential alignment of a focus on close reading with new critical values, methodology and strategies of canonization, while the second offers exactly such theoretically informed, deconstructive readings of their writings. Despite the common gender identity one might consider holds together Scott's analysis, nevertheless, the particular choice of these three writers 'as central representatives of Modernist writing' seems arbitrary to say the least. If Woolf's place is indisputable, those of Barnes and West over, say, Dorothy Richardson, Katherine Mansfield (these former, identified as influential rivals by Woolf herself, placed bizarrely as 'midwives of modernism'), H.D., or Gertrude Stein are surely not. Scott's selected date of 1928, moreover, is equally idiosyncratic, chosen according to Scott's account for being a meeting point of the three writers across texts that contain representations of lesbian sexuality and coincide with the obscenity trial over Radclyffe Hall's lesbian novel *The Well of*

Loneliness (xvi). What Scott's strategy, in mimicking Lewis' earlier taxonomy, unintentionally serves to highlight is the expedient selectiveness by which both canonical and revisionist historiographies operate.

Writing in 1996 a year after Scott's *Refiguring Modernism*, Susan Stanford Friedman in ' "Beyond" Gynocriticism and Gynesis: The Geographics of Identity and the Future of Feminist Criticism' offers a succinct summary of the limits of feminist revisionary criticism within the postmodern critical era. She says 'Whether distinct or intermingling, gynocriticism and gynesis have shared an emphasis on sexual difference and a privileging of gender as a constituent of identity,' noting further that:

> For gynocriticism, the existence of patriarchy, however changing and historically inflected, serves as the founding justification for treating women writers of different times and places as part of a common tradition based on gender. For gynesis, the linguistic inscriptions of masculine/ feminine – indeed language's very dependence on gendered binaries – underlie various feminist unravelings of master narratives and discourses. (14)

Despite the political significance of both approaches for the position of women writers within academia, Stanford argues, however, their uncritical assumption of a stable concept of gender as the 'foundation of feminist critical practice' has left it 'seriously out of step' with advances in the conception of identity and subjectivity occurring across contemporary theory, exemplified by two landmark studies published in the same year as *The Gender of Modernism*; Judith Butler's *Gender Trouble* (1990) and Eve Kosofsky Sedgwick's *Epistemology of the Closet (1990)*. Both Butler and Sedgwick accused feminist accounts of gender of being ahistorical and heterosexist, retaining a humanist faith in the notion of a stable internal 'self' that identifies itself as either masculine or feminine, and assuming the correlation of sex, gender and sexuality as normative. Feminist criticism, Butler declares, whether heterosexual or lesbian in its focus, typically takes for granted a basic association of sex and gender, or the male body with masculinity and the female body with femininity, thereby reinforcing rather than refusing or subverting the fixity of binary oppositions. Undercutting the feminist supposition that female identity and female experience can be regarded as unified and universal, she argues instead that gender is 'discursively constituted', or in other words that gendered meaning is produced by rather than reflected by its signification. 'There is no gender identity behind the expressions of gender', Butler writes, 'identity is performatively constituted by the very "expressions" that are said to be its results' (25). Gender, in Butler's terms then, is something one *does* rather than one *is*, a performance rather than an essence or given, and one that may take a number of forms, in relation to history, location and circumstance. The heterosexist conception of masculinity and femininity as relating to the male and female body, respectively, is merely one of those norms, elevated to the normative and the hegemonic.

Sedgwick agrees, noting that the division of sexual acts and identities as either 'homo' or 'hetero' is the result of a historical signifying process that began in the multiple, ambiguous sexual taxonomies of fin-de-siècle culture and discourse. Examining the process by which homosexuality was increasingly homogenized and marginalized as the deviant other to a 'natural' heterosexuality, she locates the moment of inscription of this hetero/homosexual divide as the trial of Oscar Wilde for homosexual acts under the charge of gross indecency in 1895, going on to explore the subsequent anxiety over and equivocal representation of 'the love that dare not speak in its name' in the work of early Modernists such as D.H. Lawrence and Marcel Proust. Two recent studies, Joseph Allan Boone's *Libidinal Currents: Sexuality and the Shaping of Modernism* (1998) and Colleen Lamos' *Deviant Modernism: Sexual and Textual Errancy in T.S. Eliot, James Joyce, and Marcel Proust* (1998), both continue this reading of the 'queering' of gender by Modernist texts, arguing that the formal experimental strategies by which Modernist fiction attempted to represent modern psychosexual subjectivity constitute a narrative erotics of sexual/textual errancy. The effort by Modernist writers to 'construct new forms to evoke the flux of consciousness and the erotics of mental activity', Boone for example asserts, resulted in the coalescence of contemporary sexual, psychological and aesthetic discourses into a 'poetics and politics of the perverse' (19). Rather than identifying gay or lesbian Modernist counter-canons, the 'queer' reading of Modernism serves to re-read works such as Djuna Barnes' *Nightwood* (1936), reclaiming its perverse aesthetics and carnivalesque thematics from the overarching formalism by which it had been framed by T.S. Eliot's editorial hand, alongside those of Eliot himself, whose formalist method becomes, in Eve Kosofsky Sedgwick's terms found in *Epistemology of the Closet* (1990), an 'alibi of abstraction', purging the Modernist text of the taint of dissident sexuality (164). A further critique of gynocritical accounts is emerging that attempts to reconfigure Modernism in terms of overarching myths of the female subject or female writing, to shift the terms and focus of debate from *modernism* to *modernity*, and move academics away from the revision of a retrospective, institutionally-constituted canon to the historicist examination of the construction and representation of masculinity and femininity as set within the cultural and socio-political contexts of the turn-of-the-century. Published in the same year Lyn Pykett's *Engendering Fictions* (1995) and Rita Felski's *The Gender of Modernity* (1995), for example, counter the standard periodization of Modernism as definitively breaking with its immediate past, reminding that early twentieth century representations of femininity and the feminine were historically grounded in the overtly gendered rhetoric of fin-de-siècle sociology, sexology, psychiatry, suffragism and evolution/degeneration theory. As Felski observes, 'modernism is only one aspect of the culture of women's modernity', gendered rhetoric saturating representations of and reactions against feminized modernity in both the popular and experimental fictions, and the social-scientific and psycho-sexual discourses of the late Victorian and Edwardian era (25).

Both Butler and Sedgwick are widely credited as the pioneers of what has come to be defined as 'queer theory', a mode of analysis originating in the deconstruction of the heteronormative conception of gender, yet that has come to be associated with the refusal of all normative and universalising models of identity, emphasizing instead the radical potential of the perverse (in the sense of 'peculiar') and the polymorphous. Where, for Sedgwick, however, the regulation of the dissonance of homosexuality underlies the binary logic of all Western culture, Butler notes that just as 'gender is not always constituted coherently or consistently in different historical contexts', it also shifts in meaning as it 'intersects with racial, class, ethnic, sexual, and regional modalities of discursively constituted identities' (1990: 3). This extension of the argument for the performativity of gender identity to that of the situated, historical construction of identity markers more broadly, moves towards the critique of Friedman, who draws upon postcolonial accounts that have critiqued Anglo-American universalizing models of Modernism, and thereby encouraged recognition of both the national specificities and transnational scope of Modernist moments, practices and contexts, which Friedman describes as the new 'geographics of positionality'; the understanding of identity as 'an historically embedded site, a positionality, a location, a standpoint, a terrain, an intersection (even intersextion), crossroads of multiply situated knowledges' (15). Friedman's vision of a feminist literary criticism 'beyond gynocriticism and gynesis' requires exactly this acknowledgement of gender as inextricably linked to historical and geographical location, and to the multiple, accumulative, contradictory and hybrid identity markers by which a subject may be positioned. Gynocritical studies of specific traditions of Modernist women's writing (African-American, Chicana, Lesbian), she acknowledges, provide at least partially a mediation of the notion of the universal subject of feminist criticism, but they are still insufficiently flexible to allow for the complexity of overlapping identity discourses. Oppression or privilege are not fixed experiences, she observes, but relative, shifting according to different axes of alterity, across different locations or from different standpoints. As an example, she highlights the diverse relational possibilities when considering the grouping Woolf, Joyce, Lawrence and Jean Rhys, in which a straightforward gynocritical binary division of Joyce and Lawrence as male writers and Woolf and Rhys as women writers evolves into a fluid and multifaceted matrix of power relations when the identity markers of class, sexuality and colonialism is taken into account. Thus, Friedman demonstrates, '[i]n some ways, these writers share common locations; in other ways, their positions are different'. The result is what Friedman describes as a 'relational notion of identity' that refuses both the grand narratives of a male versus female Modernism posited by gynocriticism, and the metanarratives of the masculine/feminine binaries that constitute the symbolic order as defined by gynesis (25).

Friedman calls for the new 'geographics' as the model for contemporary feminist Modernist studies, but it is one in which, as she admits, 'the justification for focusing on women loses its cogency', as gender is always one of a series of circulating identity discourses (23). At the same time she asserts that it remains 'politically imperative that the discourses of gynocriticism and gynesis continue as long as women writers and the issue of the feminine are marginalized or trivialized', indeed observing that within the continued gender politics of academia finding a space for articulating 'an integrative analysis of the multifaceted constituents of identity' might well depend on the continued vitality of these established critical fields (30). What Friedman seeks is a 'more self-consciously locational feminist criticism', one that resists the temptation to position male Modernist writers and male-authored texts as foils for the definition of revisionary female traditions and genealogies of Modernism, and that takes a 'leadership role in the formation of new, more complex geographies of identity and subjectivity, which are being produced in the mobile terrains of the coming millennium' (32).

In a recent essay, 'Periodizing Modernism: Postcolonial Modernities and the Space/Time Borders of Modernist Studies', published in 2006, Friedman answers her own call to arms, pursuing the logic of the 'geographics of positionality' to go 'beyond' postcolonial models of Modernist criticism. 'A full spatialization of modernism changes the map, the canon, and the periodization of modernism dramatically', she argues, allowing for the possibility of 'polycentric modernities and modernisms at different points of time and in different locations' (426). To locate 'modernism' in the first three decades of the twentieth century, Friedman argues, is to assume the hegemony of Western development, to identify Anglo-American and European culture capitals as the 'innovative centres' of Modernist production and other sites as merely their 'imitative peripheries', and to 'close the curtain' on the emergent Modernisms of more recent Modernities. The definition of the arts of late twentieth century post-liberation nations as 'postmodern', according to Friedman, 'is to miss the point entirely. Multiple modernities create multiple modernisms. Multiple modernisms require respatializing and thus reperiodizing modernism' (427). A feminist Modernist studies that cannot defend the legitimacy of a focus on women writers, and a global modernist studies that can 'expand the horizons of time', extending its historical frame to the present day; Friedman's challenge to contemporary Modernist criticism is a radical one, risking the charge of emptying the word 'modernism' of any recognizable meaning (339). It is a charge, however, that she unflinchingly pre-empts, asserting that, far from 'reduc[ing] the concepts of modernity and Modernism to categories that are so inclusive as to be meaningless by theorizing the geohistory of twentieth-century modernism', the new Modernist geographics assures 'that the "periods" of Modernism are multiple and that Modernism is alive and thriving wherever the historical convergence of radical rupture takes place' (339).

11 Mapping the Current Critical Landscape

Andrew Thacker

Locating the Field

In 1976 Malcolm Bradbury and James McFarlane edited a significant and enduring collection of essays, *Modernism: A Guide to European Literature, 1890–1930* (1976). The longevity of this book upon undergraduate reading lists, over 30 years after its initial publication is, of course, a testament to its success as an introduction to the daunting field of modernism. Until Peter Nicholls' *Modernisms* (1995), the Bradbury and McFarlane volume stood as the key introductory text upon the field of modernism, synoptic in its sweep and informed by some of the best existing scholarship of its time. Much of the volume is still stimulating and of relevance today. For example, the section on 'A Geography of Modernism' is an insightful guide to the urban character of modernism. In the 1970s this aspect was understood as part of the international character of modernism as a movement, but today's geographical conception of modernism would be more likely to flesh out any notion of internationalism by also discussing globalisation and postcolonialism, terms not in critical usage 30 years ago.

Bradbury and McFarlane's 'A Geography of Modernism' would also today be replaced by a plural notion of '*Geographies* of Modernism', just as Peter Nicholls' *Modernisms* signalled that the very movement of modernism contained perhaps as many differences as similarities (see Brooker and

Thacker, 2005). One of the strongest tendencies within Anglophone literary studies generally over the last 30 years has been the multiplication of what constitutes the set texts and authors of any historical period. The opening up of the restricted canon of English literature, in terms of gender, sexuality, ethnicity and region, has been one of the striking features of the on-going realignment of literary studies in the UK and beyond. In the case of modernism this revision of the canon can be illustrated by considering the range of authors included in Bradbury and McFarlane. Today one would not be surprised to find the following authors discussed at modernist conferences, or taught on undergraduate syllabi: Djuna Barnes, H.D., Mina Loy, Jean Rhys or the writers of the Harlem Renaissance. None of these, aside from a brief mention of H.D., are indexed in Bradbury and McFarlane. Partly, this might be due to the European focus of the volume, even though one chapter discusses Chicago and New York. However, many of these writers had strong European connections, living in the modernist cities of London, Paris and Vienna, and often writing about them in works such as Barnes' *Nightwood* (1936) or Rhys' *After Leaving Mr Mackenzie* (1930). In another change over the last 30 years, we might note how D.H. Lawrence, discussed fully in Bradbury and McFarlane, is now often marginalised in discussions of modernism.

The introduction of figures such as Barnes, Rhys and H.D. to the modernist canon is due to several factors specific to modernist studies, in addition to the more general reformulation of the English literary canon (for modernism and the canon, see Murray). Not surprisingly, all of these writers are female, and the gender-blindness of Bradbury and McFarlane's volume is all too evident to today's readers. The complex relation between gender, sexuality and modernism is one that has occasioned much critical discussion and will be considered below. Another factor in the emergence of a field of plural modernisms has been the influence of postmodernism. The appearance in the 1980s of works such as Jean-Francois Lyotard's influential *The Postmodern Condition* (English translation, Lyotard, 1984) and Frederic Jameson's classic essay, 'Postmodernism, or the Cultural Logic of Late Capitalism' (1984), seemed to signal that modernism, as a historical period in the arts, was not only over, but that its cultural politics and many of its stylistic attitudes were now considered outdated and reactionary. The latter first appeared in *New Left Review* but was greatly expanded in his book of the same title published in 1991. Modernist authors and texts were said, by certain commentators, to be totalising cultural monoliths, part of a Western 'grand narrative' that smothered diverse kinds of cultural production while demonstrating a politics of snobbery, sexism and anti-semitism, among other things. Certainly, one might find examples of such views among modernist authors but this postmodern accusation is a picture sadly lacking in nuance, as demonstrated in the most recent modernist scholarship. Peter Nicholls, for example, in

Modernisms to be a viewed his task as deliberately intervening against the narrowness of the postmodern dismissal of modernism:

> When I began work on this book, postmodernism was in its heyday. The plural form of my title – Modernisms – thus had something of a polemical intent. . . . My aim in the book was mainly to show that such a modernism, caricatured as it now frequently was, could be seen to constitute only one strand of a highly complex set of cultural developments at the beginning of the century (vii).

The caricatured picture painted by postmodernism has thus led to a revisiting of modernism by critics such as Nicholls and others, resulting in a new awareness of neglected texts and authors, and a fresh insistence upon themes and issues that were central to the modernists themselves. Curiously, we might say that modernism's aging has revivified it – in today's critical landscape it increasingly appears that the usefulness of 'postmodernism' as a critical term has waned.

Shifts in current research interests in modernism become evident if one considers how Bradbury and McFarlane organise their book. Almost half the book is devoted to a consideration of three major literary genres: lyric poetry, the modernist novel and modernist drama. While modernist authors clearly innovated in these three areas – one only has to think of the lasting impact of free verse, stream of consciousness or expressionist drama – in contrast more recent criticism has tended to focus upon how these formal literary experiments were connected to the pervasive social, political and cultural contexts of their day. In other words, many critics now routinely link the cultural and artistic practices of modernism to the previously more sociological categories of *modernity* and *modernization* (See Berman, 1993: 15–36). Hence, recent guides to modernism such as those by David Bradshaw and Tim Armstrong have organised their books by theme or context, rather than by literary genre (Bradshaw, 2003; Armstrong, 2005). Indeed an examination of some of the topics and chapters discussed in these two recent works indicates a massive divergence from the themes considered in Bradbury and McFarlane: gender and sexuality; the body; technology; psychoanalysis and psychology; science; eugenics; publishing history; visual culture and the cinema; spiritualism; race and empire; mass culture and the market and politics (anarchism, suffragism, fascism) are, among many others, now seen as essential in grappling with modernism.

One example, discussed by Tim Armstrong, of this interest in the cultural contexts informing modernist writing is that of the First World War (Armstrong, 2005: 15–22), which focus is also discussed by Trudi Tate, in *Modernism, History and the First World War* (1998). Armstrong's succinct and fascinating account of the impact of the war discusses theorizations of time and modernity (whether the war represented a rupture in the idea of modern times) and Sigmund Freud's psychoanalytic notions of trauma and mourning (how the understanding of shell shock shifted from a physical to a psychological basis), taking in hysteria, rabid animals and melancholia along the way (for Freud see also Paddy, Stinson and Wilson). Armstrong then uses this mixture of theory and history to interrogate short stories by D.H. Lawrence, Wyndham Lewis and Mary Butts. What emerges from this stress upon the various cultural contexts is a much clearer sense of the peculiar impact of the war upon modernist practice than is found in earlier, standard, accounts of the period (see, for example Fussell, 1975). One can still make comments upon the stylistic experiments of modernist writing (Butts's story, 'Speed the Plough' typifies the inconclusive format of many modernist short stories), but a considerably richer understanding of how and why these occur in the text is introduced by locating aesthetic experimentation directly within a range of cultural contexts, rather than simply tracing the innovations of an individual author, or how writers looked to other writers for influence or ideas.

Key Critical Works

To indicate further some of the most significant critical and scholarly work on modernism I want to discuss, in brief, work in three areas that have had a major impact: gender and modernism; high and low culture and cultural institutions (noting that almost inevitably, given the constraints of space, I have had to simplify drastically an incredibly rich set of books that I hope readers will explore in more detail for themselves). Reference to a writer such as Mary Butts indicates how the current field of modernist studies is replete with discussion of many authors not noted in Bradbury and McFarlane. This aspect of the changing canon is discussed further elsewhere in this volume, but it is important to note that the recovery of such authors is determined most of all by the work of critics and scholars in bringing neglected writers back into focus. Questions of gender and sexuality have – as with many other fields of literary study – seen many writers considered afresh, and old texts interrogated in new ways. Three of the major figures in these areas have been Bonnie Kime Scott, Sandra Gilbert and Susan Gubar. Kime Scott's anthology, *The Gender of Modernism* (1990), not only foregrounds the work of many neglected women modernists (for example Djuna Barnes, Nancy Cunard, Rose Macaulay, Charlotte Mew, Jean Rhys and Rebecca West) by reprinting difficult to find extracts from many works, it also raises awareness of how gender was an important topic for many male modernists, such as T.S. Eliot, D.H. Lawrence and James Joyce (for a further discussion of gender see Parsons). Kime Scott's anthology is part of feminist critical work that sought to emphasise 'a gendered reading of modernism' (1), work continued in the massive trilogy of books by Gilbert and Gubar entitled *No Man's Land: The Place of the Woman Writer in the Twentieth Century* (1988; 1989; 1994).[1] It is difficult to summarise the arguments of these three large volumes, which range widely across modernism and later twentieth century writers, but one general point made by Gilbert and Gubar that has had lasting impact is their claim that the modernist period was accompanied by a crisis in the relations between the sexes. They suggest that the emergence of the figure of the New Woman in the 1890s lead to a crisis in masculinity, where many men felt threatened by the emergence of female autonomy: thus modernism was 'a reaction-formation against the rise of literary women' (Gilbert and Gubar, 1988: 156). One literary response, argue Gilbert and Gubar, saw many male authors characterise the cultural styles of modernism in a hard, masculine terminology, such that texts by women writers might not be considered sufficiently 'tough' to be defined as truly modernist. Ezra Pound, for instance, famously said of T.S. Eliot's *The Waste Land* that it ended the idea that poetry was for ladies (for Pound see also Murray, Paddy, Randall, Stinson and Wilson).

The *No Man's Land* trilogy, along with Kime Scott's anthology and works by many other feminist critics in the 1980s and 90s (see, inter alia, Ledger, 1997; Pykett, 1995; Hanscombe and Smyers, 1987; Felski, 1995 and DeKoven, 1991) was thus crucial in the recovery of writers like Butts, Barnes and Rhys, as well as bringing to attention the sexual experimentation among modernist writers, both male and female. Regardless of this limitation the work has been instrumental in uncovering 'other' modernist traditions to that known previously as the 'men of 1914'. If modernist writing is characterised by its experimental qualities it is equally true that many of its practitioners were committed to exploring different forms of sexual and gendered identity such as the real and metaphoric cross-dressing explored by Gilbert and Gubar (Gilbert and Gubar, 1988). One of the strongest current trends in modernist scholarship is the consideration of the complexities of sexual identities articulated in the modernist period by a number of writers, including H.D., Djuna Barnes, Radclyffe Hall, E.M. Forster, Gertrude Stein, Mina Loy and James Joyce. One criticism that has been made of the Gilbert and Gubar version of gender and modernism is that, ultimately, it is rooted in a biographical approach to the field, rather than one that sees gender as a fluid term that marks style and attitude across texts authored by both men and women. Much of the recent work on queer or Sapphic modernisms has sought to avoid this limitation, by utilising theoretical models that emphasise the 'performative' aspects of gendered and sexual identities, often drawing upon the work of Judith Butler (see, for example Doan and Garrity, 2007 and Stevens and Howlett, 2000).

Above it was noted that one reason for the reconfiguration of modernism over the last 20 years was the emergence of postmodernism. One key area in the modernism/postmodernism debate was over the issue of 'high' versus 'low' or popular culture. In his classic, and now much contested account, Andreas Huyssen in *After the Great Divide: Modernism, Mass Culture, Post-modernism* (1986) argues that in the modernist period there existed a 'great divide' between high and low culture, whereby modernists sought to present their work as available only to an elite, educated readership to be distinguished from the audiences for the new mass cultural products in the early twentieth century: the cinema, photography, popular music like jazz or tabloid newspapers. Huyssens's work was indebted to the work of Adorno and Horkheimer on the 'culture industry' in their *Dialectic of Enlightenment*. Huyssens has recently restated his argument in different terms in 'Geographies of Modernism in a Globalizing World' in Brooker and Thacker (2005). The need to keep this divide between high and low helped explain some of the legendary difficulty and obscurity attached to modernist texts – if Joyce's *Ulysses* or Eliot's *Waste Land* could be as easily understood as reading the *Daily Mail* or watching a Charlie Chaplin movie, then in some sense they occupied the same cultural field and to say that one was 'high' culture and hence inherently superior to the other could not easily be defended. With postmodernism the binary divide between high and low was breached, as postmodern novels embraced popular genres like the romance or detective fiction, and postmodernist art embraced the artefacts of popular culture typified, for example in Andy Warhol's famous prints of Marilyn Monroe.

Since the first appearance of Huyssen's work, his argument has received much attention and a number of critiques, perhaps the foremost being that of Michael North in his *Reading 1922* (1999). In this massively influential book, North set out to read as widely as possible in the cultural products of the year 1922, often acknowledged as the key year for the establishment of modernism in the publication of now canonical texts such as *The Waste Land* and *Ulysses*. North's explicit aim was to read materials 'without a priori distinctions and hierarchies' (vi) and the result is a panorama that includes not only major writers of modernist 'high' culture, like Joyce, Eliot, Lawrence, Stein and Hemmingway, but also key thinkers such as philosophers, psychologists and anthropologists like Ludwig Wittgenstein, C.K. Ogden and Bronislaw Malinowski. Allied to these figures North places the work of popular culture from cinema, photography and music, discussing Charlie Chaplin, representations of tourism in the mainstream press, or Howard Carter's excavation of the grave in Egypt of the tomb of King Tutankhamen. The picture of the year drawn by North indicates how high modernists were not screened off from, or uninterested in, modern popular culture. On the contrary, as

North indicates many members of the European avant-garde were strongly influenced and fascinated by American popular culture (206–7). Another indication of this crossing of any 'great divide' is provided by the contemporary critical reaction to Eliot's *The Waste Land* as a poem of what was known as the 'Jazz Age'; one critic referred to Eliot as the 'poet laureate and elegist of the jazz age' (cited North, 146). In this way the formal experimentations of Eliot's poem, with its collage of different styles and abrupt changes of rhythm was seen to reflect, rather than reject, the popular culture it found all around it in 1922. North thus challenges accounts where the rivalry between modernism and postmodernism 'was read back into history . . . as an antipathy between modernism and mass culture, one whose existence has always seemed more a matter of theoretical necessity than of empirical fact' (10). Returning canonical works of modernism to the wider public world in which they emerged shows, suggests North, how the fundamental split between postmodernism and modernism 'has been sustained by a rather limited understanding' of modernism itself (207).

Rather like North's return to the 'Scene of the Modern', Lawrence Rainey's *Institutions of Modernism* (1998), revisits the debate around modernism and mass culture to suggest that the simple opposition between low and high culture, or between texts whose primary aim is to make money like any other form of commodity, and those whose wish to uphold a sense of aesthetic value that resists commodification, does not accurately describe the literary culture of modernism (see Baxter, Murray and Randall). In Rainey's view the 'institutional field of cultural production' in the early twentieth century was 'more variegated and complex than the rigid dichotomy between "high" and "low" allows' (3). Rainey's book examines several canonical modernist writers and texts to see how they can be located in this more complex field of cultural production, whereby modernists often did not reject the institutions of mass culture, such as advertising, patronage and publicity, but instead actively embraced forms of them in order to advance their own careers. Thus, the book explores Ezra Pound's creation of the Imagist movement in poetry as a strategy prompted by the widespread success of Marinetti's Futurist movement. What was significant about Futurism as an avant-garde movement was the way in which Marinetti manipulated the new institutions of mass culture: Futurism was not only discussed by a small coterie of elite artists and writers, instead it was trumpeted across music halls, popular concert halls and mass circulation newspapers. In essence Marinetti presented Futurism as a new cultural product or commodity that needed an aggressive campaign of advertising and marketing – terms not normally associated with the cryptic and courageous experiments of modernism. For Rainey, the impact of Marinetti one upon the Anglo-American avant-garde is profound: he forced 'intellectuals and artists to come to terms with the role of new institutions of mass culture and assess their bearings on the place of art in a cultural marketplace being radically transformed' (38).

The remainder of Rainey's book traces the emergence of some of the new features of this cultural marketplace: the rise of patron-investors (such as John Quinn or Harriet Shaw Weaver); the little magazines such as *The Dial, The Egoist* or *The Little Review*, in which many of the masterpieces of modernism were first published; and the use of limited or deluxe editions of key modernist works, such as Pound's *Hugh Selwyn Mauberley* or Joyce's *Ulysses*, to create commodities whose value increased with their scarcity. *Institutions of Modernism* has been an influential, though controversial, book, part of a wider trend to focus not so much upon the form and content of actual literary texts, but upon, as Rainey terms it, the 'institutions' surrounding such texts. Indeed Rainey notes that his book contains little actual analysis of modernist works (9). This focus upon the cultural institutions of modernism, whether of advertising or publication history, while fascinating for scholars and critics is still regarded as rather puzzling by undergraduates expecting to discover information about the aesthetic qualities of the texts and authors they are reading. This, of course, is no drawback of Rainey's book, or of any other such work, but it does indicate that one future question to be addressed by teachers of modernism is that of how to integrate such work on institutions or material culture into the undergraduate curriculum. Rainey offers strong interpretative opinions, one specifically contentious aspect of *Institutions of Modernism* being the chapter that dismisses the work of H.D. for being a complacent coterie poet (146–68).

Current and Future Trends

The impact of the kind of work found in *Institutions of Modernism* and *Reading 1922* is, I would suggest, ongoing. Here I want to sketch out three lines of inquiry that are occupying a number of current critics and which seem to be set to continue for a number of years: new geographies of modernism; material culture and periodical studies and book history.

I have already noted how Bradbury and McFarlane emphasized the geographical dimensions to modernism many years ago. Recent critical work has sought to expand greatly our understanding of the complex ways in which modernism was located in particular places, how such locations inflected the nature of the modernism encountered there, and how forms of modernism migrated to different locations. Did, for example the American writers such as Stein, Eliot, Pound, Hemmingway and Barnes who were located in Europe for much of their lives produce a different form of modernism from those American writers who stayed at home? Was the American artistic avant-garde of New York Dada itself formed from European visitors such as Marcel Duchamp? How did modernist writers imagine different locations within the cities they inhabited and wrote about? Did they produce metaphorical verisons of the material spaces of cities such as London, Berlin or Paris (see Thacker, 2003)? How was Irish modernism, in writers such as Yeats and Joyce, distinctive because of the colonial situation of Ireland in relation to Britain? (For Yeats: see also Baxter, Paddy, Stinson and Wilson). What happened when modernist styles and attitudes travelled away from the metropolitan capitals (London, Paris, New York) discussed by Bradbury and McFarlane, and were reworked and reimagined in India, China, Japan or the diverse countries of Africa? In what sense can we talk of an African modernism (Woods, 2005) or an Indian modernism (Freedman, 2005; Mitter, 2007)?

The wide-ranging nature of such questions reveal how the work of a comprehensive geography of modernism, inflected by current work in post-colonial studies, has, in a sense, only just begun. The ramifications of such a geographical focus are profound, as Susan Stanford Friedman argues in an important recent article on this topic, entitled 'Periodizing Modernism: Postcolonial Modernities and the Space/Time Borders of Modernist Studies': 'the new geography of modernism needs to locate many centers of modernity across the globe, to focus on the cultural traffic linking them, and to interpret the circuits of reciprocal influence and transformation that take place within highly unequal state relations' (429). Two important consequences of Friedman's argument are that she wishes to abandon 'the ahistorical designation of modernism as a collection of identifiable aesthetic styles' as well as 'the notion of modernism as an aesthetic period' with a single start and end point (432). If we now look for 'multiple modernisms' that can be located across the globe, then we are looking not at a singular modernist epoch, but different regimes of modernism, all engaged in encountering forms of social, economic and political modernity, some of which interconnect with others and some of which operate under a different time schema entirely. Thus, we might argue that an 'Indian modernism' is composed of a number of different elements: indigenous aesthetic and cultural practices that continued throughout the conventional period of Anglo-American modernism; the importation of European modernist styles, often by writers that travelled abroad and then returned (the great Bengali poet, Rabindranath Tagore, met and was admired by many Anglo-American modernists such as Yeats and Pound); and the adoption of complex notions of being 'modern' by writers and artists operating after Anglo-American modernism is said to have finished – the contemporary novelist Amitav Ghosh might thus be said to typify Indian modernism (see Freedman, 2005). Friedman's argument, along with other such work (see Gaonkar, 2001, and the essays in Brooker and Thacker, 2005; Doyle and Winkiel, 2005) offers a profound challenge to many researching and teaching modernism, since it expands greatly the range of material that could come under the umbrella term of 'modernism'; indeed, this might be seen as one of the problems of this kind of spatializing of modernism, that it runs the risk of losing focus entirely and turning all twentieth and twenty-first century litera-ture into some form of modernism.

A geographical or spatial inflexion informs much of the work on material culture that is a second discernable trend in modernist research. Hence work has appeared that examines how cafes and restaurants were important sites of modernist innovation within the public sphere of modernity (McCracken, 2007); or upon the obsessions and anxieties associated with the subways and sewers of great modern cities like Paris or London (Pike, 2005) or, indeed, the modernism of the London Underground itself (Saler, 1999). Much of this work upon the material cutlure of modernism – the 'things' it represented in its works as much as the technological innovations of the period that under-pinned modern life, such as the motor car, X-rays, aeroplanes or typewriters – is interdisciplinary in nature, and relates literature to film, radio, photography and visual culture. Modernism's relationship to technology and modernity is itself very complex, and while certain writers lambast certain of its features – see E.M. Forster on the motor car in *Howards End* (1910) – others, following the celebration of the automobile by Marinetti and the Futurists, critically celebrate the profusion of new material objects in the modern world (see Armstrong, 1998). Joyce's *Ulysses*, for example is stuffed full of the ebb and flow of material life in Dublin 1904 – from the architectural features of the city used by Joyce to interrogate Irish history (such as streets named 'London Bridge Road' or statues of Irish nationalist heroes) to the food and drink consumed by its inhabitants (Leopold Bloom's gorgonzola sandwich and glass of wine for lunch). In one incident Leopold Bloom imagines the provi-sion of that modern invention, the telephone, inside coffins, so that pre-mature burial of those still alive can be averted. Much more work promises to be done on the interaction in the modernist period between the human body and technology, between culture and the material world of modernity. And the theoretical work of Jonathan Crary has been very important in underpinning some of the work on modern forms of subjectivity and visual culture, particularly in *Suspensions of Perception: Attention, Spectacle, and Mod-ern Culture* (1999) focuses on 'attention' demonstrating its centrality to the subjective observer's engagement with alterity ad the objective. His over-arching premise requires 'a rethinking and reconstruction of perception in which art practices were significant but hardly paramount or exclusive com-ponents' (9).

A final trend in current work is upon a related kind of material artefact – that of the books, magazines and manuscripts that comprised literary mod-ernism. In two of the key texts mentioned above, by Michael North and

Lawrence Rainey, very close attention is given to where modernist work was published, and in particular upon the many 'little magazines' which helped foster the experiments of modernism. In 1999 Michael Levenson noted a 'micro-sociology of modernist innovation, within which small groups of artists were able to sustain their resolve . . . to create small flourishing communities' (1999: 6). 'Little magazines' were a key context for such innovation, a medium for artistic self-definition through manifesto, essay and exemplary text and a meeting point for both major and minor contributors to artistic modernism. Such publications were defined as 'little' by virtue of their physical size, low print run, limited life-span, and, in some cases, by their perilous finances, small circulations and minority audiences. Their acknowledged influence in helping establish the movement of modernism across Britain, Ireland, America and Europe, far outweighs their supposedly 'little' status and literally hundreds of such publications are found in the period: *The Little Review, Poetry, transition, Coterie, Poetry and Drama*, and *The English Review* are just a few of the many important titles. Almost all of the major and minor writers of modernism first found their voices in such magazines, and many writers edited or established a periodical. For example, the London based *The Egoist: An Individualist Review*, which ran from 1914 to 1919 was edited for periods by T.S. Eliot and H.D.; Eliot published his most famous critical essay, 'Tradition and the Individual Talent' here; Ezra Pound also served an editorial function for the periodical and ensured that many early Imagist poems and articles were published in its pages; James Joyce had *A Portrait of the Artist as a Young Man* serialised in its pages, along with early extracts from *Ulysses*; and Wyndham Lewis's novel *Tarr* was first published in the magazine. However, between 1916 and 1919 *The Egoist* only ever averaged sales of around 200 and was heavily subsidized by the founding editor Dora Marsden and her supporter, Harriet Shaw Weaver.

Returning the great works of modernism to their original places of publication serves several functions, and is part of what has been called the new periodical studies (Latham & Scholes, 2006) in modernism and elsewhere. We find, for example how literary modernism was often published alongside other kinds of non-literary material, giving a new set of insights into the social and political contexts of modernism. *The Egoist*, for example had been a radical feminist periodical, *The Freewoman*, and then *The New Freewoman* and early work by Joyce and Pound rubs shoulders with articles on prostitution, homosexuality, women's rights and celibacy. Reading modernist literature in relation to these paratexts produces fresh insights into the contemporary landscape in which modernism emerged. The recovery of the original periodical forms of publication also serves to further the process of rediscovering overlooked and forgotten writers in the period, since many such artists never had their work re-published again. Major research work such as the

Modernist Journals Project in the US and the Modernist Magazines Project in the UK are redrawing the landscape of the 'little magazine' in the period and new discoveries are being constantly unearthed in such work and in other critical studies (see Churchill, 2006; McKible, 2002). Two major sources are available online: the Modernist Journals Project at http://dl.lib.brown. edu:8080/exist/mjp/index.xml; and the Modernist Magazines Project at http://www. cts.dmu.ac.uk/exist/mod_mag/index.htm.

Related to the study of modernist periodicals are many other issues surrounding the textual culture of modernism: the archives of modernism; questions of copyright and censorship; the study of the original manuscripts of modernist works; or how the history of the book as a publication format was altered by small presses in the period. Readers are often surprised to learn, for example of how Virginia Woolf published a number of her key novels herself, with the Hogarth Press that she set up with her husband, Leonard Woolf. Such a means of publication gave Woolf a freedom to experiment – as with her early experimental short story, 'The Mark on the Wall' – that she felt would not have been countenanced by mainstream publishers. The arguments that followed Hans Walter Gabler's new edition of *Ulysses* in 1984 and the various different editions that are now available (Gabler's version, the OUP reprint of the original 1922 publication edited by Jeri Johnson, the 1961 Random House edition, etc.) testify to the importance of the material status of the text being studied and the choices and theories made by the editors of these various editions (Mahaffey, 1991). Put bluntly, we are not all reading or teaching the same text of *Ulysses,* and the different editions do give rise to different interpretive decisions and analyses (see Bornstein, 1991). How the manuscript came to rest in its 'final' state as a book opens up yet another range of questions, sometimes considered under the topic of 'genetic criticism' (see Van Hulle, 2004).

As this brief survey of current work indicates there are many major questions still to be answered by critics and scholars working on modernism. As the above discussion of Stanford Friedman suggests one such issue is that of periodisation: extending the geographical scope of the writing we term 'modernist' almost inevitably expands the time frame involved. More debate is required over whether we wish to continue with using the term 'modernist' to describe such works, or whether we wish to make distinguish between when the term is used to identify a particular style or when it is employed to designate a specific historical period. Should we start using the term 'late modernism', as Jameson suggests, for recognisably modernist styles of writing that are published after, say, 1950? Whether the expansion of the scope of the term 'modernism' to refer to texts written throughout the twentieth century, and perhaps beyond, is a help or a hindrance for literary critics is yet to be decided. One thing for certain is that modernism as a field for debate, criticism and study is here to stay. We can look forward to much more exciting research being undertaken under the umbrella term of modernism, and a widening of what is described as modernist. From today's point of view it seems that the future will see more multiple forms of modernism, as debate over 'post-modernism' recedes to the status of historical curiosity, and the forward march of modernist studies continues with gusto.

Glossary

Philip Tew

Avant-garde: Much of modernism, especially in its first phases, can be regarded as an exemplary avant-garde that is a movement at the forefront of change and experimentation, a cultural movement that would popularize radical view ways of viewing life and culture, eclectic, eccentric and yet full of innovative energy. Its artists and intellectuals participated in a complex and varied ways, but in some senses one can trace certain recurrent dispositions in the recognition of the newness, the acceptance of perpetual change and the embracing of cultural dislocation and transformation. For some it was simply an aesthetic and cultural enterprise, for others it was ideological, highly politically charged. There were contradictions, as with suffragettes from the highest classes propounding a set of feminist convictions that might lead to an equalitarian democracy that would surely have appalled at least some of them. Modernist art was often urban and metropolitan, eager to convey the perceptual shock of new technology (aircraft, cinema, radio, telephony) and cultural practices (whitewashed walls and disturbing art, explicit and active sexuality, and a profound sense of the unconscious). The modernist avant-garde in a sense established the very parameters of how the term was to be understood in the future, being anti-traditionalist, its aesthetic economy drawn variously to the exotic, the incongruous, the irrational, the obscure, the scurrilous, the spontaneous and the primitive. Universal absolutes were abandoned, anarchy and nihilism embraced, and many in the avant-garde were drawn to the political extremes: Anarchism, Communism and Fascism.

Carnivalesque: Within literary studies, the term carnivalesque (or carnivalization) is taken from the twentieth century Russian theorist, Mikhail Bakhtin, and his work on the cultural role of carnival in Renaissance Europe. Carnival was originally a Roman Catholic feast, celebrated before the Lenten fast, and was traditionally a period of bodily excess and rule-breaking, when social boundaries could be temporarily and symbolically disrupted. Bakhtin argued that the disruptive and subversive spirit of the carnival was manifest in the work of the sixteenth century French writer, François Rabelais. The carnivalesque enters the literary text in the form of textual disruptions and subversions. Comedy, particularly scatological or grotesque comedy, as well as the mixing of high and low traditions, the sacred and the profane and all manners of excess, vulgarity and irreverence can contribute to the carnivalesque.

Dada or Dadaism: This movement emerged in Zurich during the First World War with a number of refugee artists and writers escaping the conflict, and it came to prominence during 1916 to 1920. Its activities included variously art theory, poetry and graphic design, theatre, art manifestoes and the visual arts. Initially based in neutral Switzerland, its ideology was anti-war and informed by a rejection of the prevailing cultural values. The intention was often to shock through anti-art cultural works, as in 1917 when anticipating the work's rejection Marcel Duchamp submitted to the Society of Independent Artists show the now celebrated *Fountain*, a urinal signed R. Mutt. Dada activities, which tended to be highly politicized and demonstrative prefigured the activities of the Situationists, included public gatherings, demonstrations and publication of art/literary journals. Adherents were passionate about coverage of art, politics and culture and their vehement declarations filled their publications. Some accounts claim that Dada frequent use by Tristan Tzara and Marcel Janco of the words *da, da*, from *yes, yes* in Tzara's native Romanian language; other relate it to in French colloquial child's term for *hobby-horse*. Most involved in Dadaist activities rejected the term.

Deconstruction: In its broadest sense the term Deconstruction describes a method of 'taking apart' statements and descriptions by a process of closely examining the implicit and underlying linguistic and structural aspects of these contributions to narrative and culture. This practice draws heavily upon the work of it leading proponent, Jacques Derrida, and such readings are often largely concerned with revealing contradictions, paradoxes and ambiguities. Meaning and understanding are finally provisional, and the quest for knowledge often reaches an impasse since the deconstructive process lays bare the constructed nature of knowledge and history. Humans create epistemes or systems that essentially sustain or refer to themselves without being natural or dependent upon external features of the world to which they relate. This perception explains the curious simultaneous strident avowals of reading which are nevertheless concerned with perpetual uncertainty that characterizes post-modernism.

Defamiliarization: This term applies specifically to a method of understanding things anew, part of a typically modernist consciousness of change and shifting perspectives. It was used by Russian Formalist Viktor Shklovsky as a term for the process of creatively undermining the familiar, so it suddenly appears unusually reconfigured or uncanny, where routines are seen anew, as in Woolf's *Mrs Dalloway*. In literature defamiliarization often means 'baring the device', which is to highlight the literary process, subverting the mechanics of a text or undermining conventions such as the time sequence in the 'Time Passes' section of Woolf's *To the Lighthouse*. For Shlovsky it represents a central characteristic of aesthetic engagement, described variously as *estrangement, defamiliarization* or *ostranenie* (rendering something strange). It is characteristic of modernist art, but becomes much more explicity and ironically inflected in the postmodern period.

The Enlightenment: This refers to a broad intellectual movement that sought to explain nature and knowledge by a process of rationality or instrumental reason. Usually regarded as associated with the eighteenth century, its proponents believed they had emerged from the 'Dark Ages' and did not limit their attention to the arts, but more broadly so as to include mathematics, astronomy, the mechanical sciences, philosophy and notions of governance. They sought to turn nature to the advantage of human progress. In establishing an overarching system of thought informed by ethics, aesthetics and knowledge generally, its participants variously aspired to expunge superstition and tyranny, introducing in the place of the ignorance which they saw as deriving from both an informed ('enlightened') and reasoning culture. Recently its claims of universality (and its almost uniformly Eurocentric and masculine inflection) have been subject to broad theoretical attack by numerous Twentieth Century thinkers such as Pierre Bourdieu and Michel Foucault. Nevertheless, the concepts of modern democracy with its idea of freedom and participation derive from the Enlightenment movement and its supposedly rational social values. Historically it is marked by the Industrial Revolution, the American and French Revolutions, developments of capitalism and the emergence of socialism, and a fundamental scientific revolution Ernst Cassirer in *The Philosophy of the Enlightenment* (1979) describes Gottfried Leibniz's *Treatise On Wisdom* as conceptually central, effectively setting out the movement's theoretical programme (121–23). Among the numerous other figures are significantly René Descartes, Immanuel Kant and perhaps most especially Sir Isaac Newton who published *Philosophiæ Naturalis Principia Mathematica* (1687) or in English 'the Mathematical Principles of Natural Philosophy' (often *Principia* or *Principia Mathematica* for short).

Epiphany: This term derives from the Greek term indicating 'to manifest' or 'to show' and refers literally to a sudden realization, often a transformative moment when the essence or truth of something is revealed, by adding a last apparently insignificant element that clarifies something larger. In Christianity, it describes the revelation of God in human form in the person of Jesus Christ. Joyce uses epiphany as a literary device in his writing such as in the stories as in the *Dubliners* (1914) and in the novel *Portrait of the Artist as a Young Man* (1916), where fundamental meaning is acquired from a fragment of experience, or a character suddenly revises their view of themselves or their social condition, radically changing their world-view. In the spirit of Dadaism, Marcel Duchamp inverted conventions and expectations by offering a urinal as an exhibited work of art, presenting such an everyday object in a unique fashion so as to induce an epiphany concerning the social practices and expectations of the artwork. One can describe as an epiphany any moment that offers in a flash a larger and holistic understanding of something. It is also used in various traditions to indicate the appearance before a human of a divine figure. American philosopher Edward Pols in *Radical Realism* (1992) drawing on Joyce's fiction put forward the notion that the original emergence of language involved an epiphany, which although sublimated is at the root of all subsequent usages of language.

Epistemology: Traditionally, epistemology (from the Greek *episteme*) or theory of knowledge is the branch of philosophy that considers the nature, scope and systems of knowledge. The emphasis may vary widely. Empiricists conceive of knowledge acquired initially gained through the senses or introspection. Rationalists argue that certain basic beliefs result from rational intuition. Drawing on rationalism and empiricism Kant describes knowledge in terms of the organization of perceptual data based on innate cognitive structures, or 'categories' which including space, time and causality. Pragmatism, which influenced many modernists, considers knowledge in terms of what is perceived to be effective or useful in terms of outcome, maximizing problem-solving, given that no model may ever conceive or include all relevant data. C.S. Peirce abandoned his attempts to ground knowledge in certainty, finding it instead real, but inherently fallible. Constructivism emphasizes the relative, mutative character of knowledge, which is seen as constructed, contingent on convention, human perception and social experience, and therefore arrived at inter-subjectively. Epistemic assumptions can be significant rather than simply theoretical. Einstein's modelled the universe as a closed system where everything – energy, matter, time and position – are interrelated in an orderly fashion. Quantum theory suggested otherwise. It has been argued that Einstein in his later career sought a 'unified field theory' to accord with his theory of General Relativity, where the physics governing the solar system is accommodated by those at the atomic level. Postmodern ideas of knowledge are inflected by a shift from the unitary self as the focus of understanding towards a concept of a 'multiple' view of selfhood or subjectivity, emphasizing a more variegated and complex sense of subjectivities, a multiplicity. Postmodern accounts of epistemology find the 'grand narratives' or meta-narratives that characterized modernity incredulous and obsolete, which suggestions may result in certain consequences when situating knowledge: generalizations or universal claims are effectively negated by the constraints of time and context; science is never value-free nor is it neutral; truth is socially constructed rather than absolute.

Feminism: This refers a range of aesthetic, theoretical and ideological views and commitment generally concerned with the role of women is society, propounding a concept of visibility, involvement and equality. Early involvement is described as first-wave feminism, after around 1960 as second-wave and more recently one might refer to third-wave feminism. Its origins derive from the Enlightenment and specify the work of intellectuals such as Mary Wollstonecraft, who published the immensely influential *A Vindication of the Rights of Women* (1792). Female representation or suffrage, education and property rights were central to early feminists, and modernists were variously insistent that women should participate politically, aesthetically or culturally. Virginia Woolf for instance objected strongly to Victorian ideal of the 'Angel in the House' of domesticity (which figure is said to have been modelled on her conservative mother) as the ideal role for women. In *A Room of One's Own* (1929), Woolf argues for educational opportunities as a conduit for change, particularly as 'women, like men, have other interests besides the perennial interests of domesticity' (125). Among important contemporary critics influenced and informed by their feminist principles are Judith Butler, bell hooks, Sandra Gilbert and Susan Gubar, Luce Irigaray, Julia Kristeva, Toril Moi and Elaine Showalter.

Feminist Criticism: Feminist literary criticism applies feminist politics to the reading of texts, which became prevalent in the 1970s when theorists such as Kate Millett and Elaine Showalter began to examine literary texts from such a perspective. An important early aim of feminist criticism was to expose the prejudicial assumptions made about women in male-authored texts, while later feminists looked instead to female-authored texts, identifying common patterns and themes that, it was argued, were a consequence of women's experiences of male-dominated society. Subsequently, there has been much debate about whether there is such a thing as an *'ecriture feminine'*: an identifiably feminine style of writing. Feminist criticism contains many aspects, and has been productively developed by its association with lesbian, postcolonial and working class criticism.

Fin de siècle: A French term meaning 'end of the century', sometimes referred to as *La Belle Époque*, which signifies a cultural movement of the 1890s (which some see as continuing until the Great War) which for many both contemporaneously and retrospectively marks the end of an era. Traditionally associated with French artists, especially the Symbolists, the term now applies more broadly to a European-wide and American cultural movement in which milieu the early modernist avant-garde emerged. There was both great excitement and apocalyptic pessimism concerning a sense of a changing world. Seen by many as decadent, its zeitgeist was characterized by escapism, extreme aestheticism, fashionable pessimism, sophistication and world-weariness. Part of its artistic vision can be seen in Art Nouveau with its organic, yet eccentric forms and floral motifs derived from the world of vegetative life as found variously in the work of artists, architects and artisans such as Victor Horta, Gustav Klimt, René Lalique, Charles Rennie Mackintosh and Louis Comfort Tiffany. The most famous legacy might be considered the Parisian metro entrances by Hector Guimard that subsequently characterize the landscape of Paris. The *Fin de siècle* is also exemplified in the work of painters and illustrators such as Henri de Toulouse-Lautrec in France, and Aubrey Beardsley in Britain.

Free Indirect Discourse: This narrative technique predates modernism, although it was popularized and used extensively by writers of that period, free indirect discourse, otherwise referred to as *erlebte rede* or *style indirect* is neither direct nor indirect speech, but where the qualities of a third person narration is combined with the kind of close perspective usually associated with a first person account, creating a less conflicted intersection of interior and exterior reflections. The words of a character are enunciated indirectly by a third party in the past tense. In some ways, the technique exhibits characteristics always implicit in the intimacy between authors and the characters they create, a dual voice, or double and split intonation, often contributing to an ironic perspective. Synthesizing or

evoking both speech and thought, free indirect discourse allows rapid transformations, especially from the intimate to the more distant. Typically the narrator will continue using vocabulary and style that indicated the character's
consciousness although apparent within an objective account. This technique is
characteristic of the writing of Jane Austen, as well as James Joyce and Virginia
Woolf. In the latter its use is alongside that of stream of consciousness.

Genre: This is the French word for 'sort' or 'kind', genre describes a set of conventions, usually in writing or art, which mark out a piece of work as belonging to a
particular category. So, for example, a piece of writing will belong to one of the
three main genres – poetry, prose or drama – to the extent to which it shares
their basic conventions. 'Genre fiction' is used to describe novels which share a
quite specific set of conventions to a greater extent than general literary fiction –
for example those associated with crime fiction, the romance, science fiction and
so on. However, both the idea of genre generally and the split between genre
fiction and literary fiction are challenged by those writers commonly described
as postmodern in novels which either defy genre categorization or use a
number of genre conventions usually kept separate.

Historiographic Metafiction: This term originates in the influential work of
Canadian literary theorist, Linda Hutcheon, and relates to metafiction, a
particular mode of self-reflexive self-conscious fiction that developed in parallel
to the postmodern novel from the 1960s alongside postmodernism. Historiographic metafiction is a subset concerned with the nature of historiography
(that is both narrating and theorizing history), and reworks many of the concerns of modernist fiction. Such narratives foreground and reveal the process by
which history is constructed, considering in particular from whose viewpoint
history is being written and what bias this introduces. Such a fictional history
can emphasize the affinity of history to fiction, with modes of characterization
and plotting, a commitment to certain symbols and rhetorical gestures. Historical discourse is thereby deconstructed, and the reader can radically question
the nature of 'truth' in the historical document.

Historiography: This refers to the study and consideration how historical knowledge is established, transmitted and is subject to change. It does not regard
history as fixed, neutral or necessarily truthful, rather examining the writing or
narration of history and the use of historical methods, examining among other
aspects audience, authorship, bias, interpretation, perspective or viewpoint,
sources and style. Central is the concept of historical method, the term for the
techniques and conventions guiding historians in their research of primary,
secondary and tertiary sources, in establishing evidence in order to write history. The process is a kind of evidential cartography that includes issues such as
analogy, archaeological or forensic evidence, archival sources, authenticity and
provenance, best explanation, cross-referencing, eyewitness accounts, oral tradition, reliability, statistics. There will be radical differences between a Marxist or
historical materialist historiography, a feminist one, and the 'metahistory' that
characterizes traditional Nineteenth-Century European accounts that were

attacked by the modernists. Until that point history was considered as akin to biography in being factual, which assumption was the subject of attack by Lytton Strachey in *Eminent Victorians* (1918). In subverting biography as a form, Strachey examines the lives of Cardinal Manning, Florence Nightingale, Thomas Arnold and General Charles George Gordon all famous English individuals in the Victorian Era in terms of an often withering attack upon the pretensions and conceit of that age. Of Gordon he writes 'his fate was mingled with the frenzies of Empire and the doom of peoples. And it was not in peace and rest, but in ruin and horror, that he reached his end (218)'. Theorists such as Walter Benjamin suggest that when history is narrated, any viable *historiography* ought to consider that its shape or construction is inherently complicit with rhetorical structures that determine historical significance and understanding.

Hybridity: This can be used simply a term for mixing, but more recently its point of reference in the cultural and theoretical arenas is to describe the concepts of heterogeneity and plurality, especially with reference both art forms themselves, and the multiplicity inherent in contemporary descriptions of ethnicity, identity, multiculturalism, postcoloniality and spatiality. In terms of modernist aesthetic production it may signify the mixing of styles and modes of representation, where the collage and the palimpsest can be seen as important. It can be applied variously at the level of styles, plot, characterization and other more formal or concrete aspects, such a typefaces and modes of narration.

Intertextuality: A recent term introduced by Julia Kristeva that describes the relation of texts (and of other art objects) to other works of art; it assumes that few if any aesthetic expressions can ignore on a conscious or unconscious level the legacy of the past. On one level it refers to an active, explicit allusion to a prior art object such as James Joyce's *Ulysses*, which contains obvious intertextual references to Homer's *The Odyssey*. Others may be unconscious and therefore be implicit. Also, such an allusional relation may be inflected differently – dependent upon whether it represents an *hommage*, parody or pastiche, for instance – the term and outlined that art is not unique and draws upon established codes and practices, even if to subvert them. The apparently new text (or intertext) relates to a previous one (a pre-text), creating a sequel, if by the same author it is an *autographic sequel*, and by another author an *allographic sequel*. An example of the latter, Jean Rhys's *Wide Sargasso Sea* (1966), radically changes Charlotte Brontë's *Jane Eyre* (1846) moving the essentially untold narrative of Bertha Mason, Rochester's first wife in Brontë's novel, centre-stage. Such modification both interrogate tradition and the role of the individual, creative author, and examples of intertextuality very much depend upon readerly competence to recognize and reinterpret the allusional framework. In postmodernist writing, the relatedness and repetition of texts is palpably and explicitly foregrounded, with overt references to previous works, which can convey a sense of both interrogation and yet stasis. Nothing is original, everything simply a reworked and recycled. Intertextuality is often closely related to parody and pastiche.

Irony: A complex term which is closely associated with postmodernism, although it has a relevance as an aspect of modernist art, especially in terms of challenging cultural and aesthetic conventions and expectations, in the work of such groups as Dadaists who celebrated chance, parody and playfulness, undermining the central role of the artist. In celebrating fragmentariness modern art is differently inflected to its postmodern equivalent in that at least residually the former senses a partial resolution and the latter no longer believes in the possibility of language or symbols. The irony of the modernist is intended to raise consciousness and radicalize by challenging; in the case of postmodern irony the approach is both bleak and full of comic subversion. Irony may involve both self-referential aspects that undermine an object or a statement's validity. More traditionally and rhetorically verbal irony indicates an incongruity between that which is articulated and the actual meaning. In *Irony's Edge: The Theory and Politics of Irony* (1994) Linda Hutcheon considers irony both in terms of 'the space between (and including) the said and unsaid' (12) and the possibility of its meaning being constituted by '*both* the said *and* the unsaid working together to create something new' (63). Despite its reflexivity, the ironic voice assumes a depth of knowledge and understanding that allows complex doubled meanings and their comprehension, and at least implicitly conveys knowledge of the subject of articulation and a commonality with its potential knowing recipient. Underlying this is an aspect that contradicts the apparently explicit intentions of the postmodern ironist in that they explicitly wish to abjure such knowingness, but at least implicitly acknowledge a notion of intellectual transcendence inherent in metafiction for instance when it exhibits a self-conscious use of devices in an ironic and self-reflexive manner. In the postmodern age irony seemed pervasive and suggested no fixity or resolution, allowing perhaps an overall superficiality in many spheres of endeavour, including the aesthetic and ideological, so much so it appeared to permeate the public domain with cynicism on all sides.

Marxism/Marxist: The term can be used to signify an ideology or a political creed based on the works of Karl Marx (1818–1883) who remains a seminal theorist of the modern age. In numerous works he propounds a radical social, economic and political world-view and later followers called this Communism or Marxism. Born in Germany, during studies at the University of Berlin he was influenced by Hegelianism. In 1842 he was editor of influential liberal newspaper, in Cologne, the *Rheinische Zeitung*, and when the authorities closed it he travelled in exile to Paris in 1843 (becoming a communist) to Brussels and later to London. He was supported by his wealthy collaborator, Friedrich Engels (1820–1890), and together they produced the *Communist Manifesto* (1848). Marx's work analysed economic conditions that create class structures, offering a model for their reformulation, which struggle he predicted could overturn of oppression and radicalize social conditions. After visiting Paris and Cologne during 1848 European revolutions, he returned to London to expand his political and economic theories often in the British Museum Library. His work argues that recent human history is shaped by a capitalist ideology and its principles of material production. Among his central observations and terms is that surplus value, which is the essence of the structure and logic of a capitalist mode of production. Man does not control his production, hence he becomes alienated, diverted by commodity fetishism, and the overall economy cannot prevent cycles of growth and collapse with inevitable periodic crises. His ideas have been influential in most spheres both politically and intellectually. Among his major works are: *The Poverty of Philosophy* (1846–1847), *The Eighteenth Brumaire of Louis Napoleon* (1852), *Grundrisse* (1857–1858) and *Capital Vol. 1–III* (1867; 1893; 1894).

Modernism: Even in the preceding period after about 1870, the concept that history and civilization were inherently progressive and such progress was uniformly beneficial was increasing attacked, and in this sense the origins of modernism are predicated on the challenges made by such figures as Henri Bergson, Charles Darwin, Sigmund Freud, Karl Marx and Friedrich Nietzsche, and additionally technological changes that reformulated the zeitgeist. Many thinkers stressed in the modern experience how the division between the real and the apparent collapses, relations becoming spectral or de-realized. With its emphasis on the new Modernism became the overarching label for emergent intellectual movement that flourished from the end of the nineteenth century until the Second World War, producing radical ideas and art-works which self-consciously attempt to reform existing conventions. Many of the early figures committed to a concept of modernist art and culture regarded themselves as 'radicals' or 'Bohemians,' part of the avant-garde. Curiously this included members of the Bloomsbury Group or Set which was made up largely of young intellectuals with families connected to the highest levels of society. By the 1920s this label originating in minority tastes had after the upheaval of the Great War come to define the age. Although critically the term remains much contested in literary studies, it is agreed by many that in terms of the textual genres of prose, poetry or drama much output is largely predicated on challenging traditional methods and the implicit belief that they might adequately represent human experience, and a recurrent theme is the inadequacy of language to express anything essential. In the novel, for example, the result is the abandonment of the established conventions of the nineteenth-century realism. Certain modernist novels – including notably parts of James Joyce's *Ulysses* and Dorothy Richardson's *Pilgrimage* – appear to have no narrator, rather appearing to be fragmented, fractured thoughts, memories and impressions as they flit across the character's mind.

Myth: In origin *myth* or *mythos* refers to a sacred narrative describing the origins of the world and its creatures. The concept of the hierophantic (of the manifestation of the Sacred) can be regarded as central to the mythopoeic, offering an absolute truth of a primordial time before the split into the scared (religion) and the profane (the secular). Myth can also be used more generally to describe the cultural narratives of societies with a ritualistic system of both describing and accounting for reality. Such societies fascinated anthropologists in the modernist period, such as Claude Lévi-Strauss, a major influence upon deconstruction, published four volumes of *Mythologiques* (1969, 1973, 1978 and 1981) which was based on his research which traced a single myth from South America through Central America into the Arctic Circle, positing thereby the fundamental, possibly universal nature of *myth* in human culture. According to the structuralist account although myth seems completely arbitrary it involves both certain contradictory elements and others that resolve such oppositions. The Native American trickster, a raven or a coyote, is unpredictable, able to 'mediate' between life and death. Adopting such symbols is one of many ways in which contemporary literature can incorporate mythic archetypes and patterns. Philosopher Ernst Cassirer enumerates the capacity of a *mythological consciousness* and the *mythopoeic* world to correlate or not distinguish between the metaphysical, magical and reality (materiality), an aspect found in much contemporary fiction with its apparent hybridity of form. Myth remains a complex and difficult term referring to a whole range of ways of understanding, interpreting and narrating a world-view.

Metafiction: This is the term for a fictional narrative that refers explicitly to its own form and artificiality, indicating its artefactual nature. Representational techniques and limitations are highlighted, the relationship between fiction and reality seemingly blurred. Essentially it is characterized by self-consciousness, introspection or an almost narcissistic self-obsession. It is often playful and may incorporate absurd or illogical elements. There may be intertextual references, and parodic renditions of realist conventions or texts. Often the position of the author is both referred to and made the subject of subversion. Examples include John Fowles's *The French Lieutenant's Woman*. However, one must remember that any diminishment of the authorial role remains a narrative poly involving an active fictional illusion. Although regarded as primarily a feature of the postmodern age, aspects appear in the pre-twentieth century texts, the most commonly cited being Laurence Sterne's *Tristram Shandy*. More contemporary metafictional authors would include Martin Amis, Richard Brautigan, Ishmael Reed, Kurt Vonnegut and Jeanette Winterson. Metafiction includes as a subgenre historiographic metafiction.

Metaphysics: This refers to philosophy which explores the principles of reality that transcend scientific or logical explanation, matters concerning the ultimate nature of being and the world. The term combines the Greek 'Meta' meaning 'over' or 'after' and *physiká* translating as 'physics', or the science of the physical world. Editing Aristotle's work about a 100 years after Aristotle's death, Andronicus of Rhodes referred to 14 books as '*Ta meta ta phusika*' or 'the ones after the physical ones' to distinguish them from others concerned with Aristotle's work on a so-called 'first' or original philosophy. The term was interpreted by medieval Latin scholars as 'a science of that beyond the physical', or metaphysics, as signifying a notion of the transcendent, appropriate perhaps since metaphysics seeks an understanding that beyond nature (the physical), exploring underlying essences. As such metaphysicians specifically address such issues as God's existence, the origin or source of creation, what constitutes reality, whether the world exists outside of the mind, and, the objective nature of things and whether they even exist. Metaphysics refers to the essence of things, the fundamental principles of the universe, and addresses the categories of being. Some feminists suggest the deep structures of metaphysics derive from patriarchal principles, a concept of moving from a feminine cave of ignorance to a masculine transcendent realm. Traditionally, some philosophers including Kant have suggested that a true metaphysics is beyond the human mind. More recent schools such as logical positivists and anti-realists claim all metaphysical statements are essentially without meaning. Both deconstructionists and postmodernists insist questions of reference are highly complex and problematic, critiquing traditional metaphysics as reductive since it grounds meaning upon the assumption that the logos (or word) relates to fixed principles or characteristics of reality.

Modernity: This has a different meaning than modernism, since modernity as a term is used to refer to the Modern Age beginning with the Renaissance when conceptually man increasingly regarded himself as the centre of existence, and that rational engagement allows a control of others and nature (hence the colonial expansion from Europe). These notions are further developed during *the Enlightenment*, which regarded the world as describable, rational, empirical and objective, assuming a universal truth that is generally articulated by European males. To be modern is to consciously separate oneself from and diminish the importance of the past, rejecting local cultures and tradition, and otherness in favour of an instrumental rationality. Central was an impulsive sense of the need for order and classification (and both imply inclusion and exclusion). Modernity was conceived in this sense at least implicitly in terms of 'modern spirit', to be found in areas such as scientific progress, rationalist social and economic practices and a secular public sphere. Certain underlying contradictions gesture towards often hidden ambivalence and fragmentariness. Charles Baudelaire explores it ephemeral qualities. Marx prioritizes its logic of class relations, but possesses a Utopian idealism. Its chronologically co-ordinates might be best understood to stretch from the renaissance to a point in the twentieth century.

Parody: Sometimes traditionally referred to as a lampoon, this is used to describe a work that imitates another for the purpose of ridiculing, the making of ironic comment about or directing affectionate humour towards the original, and in contemporary culture is not necessarily dismissive but polemical and allusive of a range cultural practices to convey a more radical or subversive understanding or appreciation by so doing. Contemporary parody mostly uses humorous or satiric imitation. Like pastiche, parody imitates or mimics among other elements, the mannerisms and style of another mode of writing, often reducing the serious to the comic (often by exploiting its bathetic or pompous tendencies). Traditionally, whereas parody mocks the idiosyncrasies of the original, pastiche simply incorporates such previous stylistic idiosyncrasies.

Picaresque Novel: The sub-genre of the novel derives from a Spanish tradition, usually thought of as originating with the anonymous *Lazarillo de Tormes*, published in 1554. Such fiction recounts the wandering adventures of an anti-hero or rogue, and continued its influence in the modernist era in terms of an adaptation of a loose episodic structure for the peregrinations of a central character as with Conrad's *Heart of Darkness* and Woolf's *Orlando*. Cervantes's *Don Quixote* is a famous example of the genre, as is Daniel Defoe's *Moll Flanders* (1722). A modern novel which recounts the fortunes of an everyday character through various humorous episodes can be referred to as picaresque. Although not usually associated with Modernisms, it could be argued to be a significant form of influence on a number of texts, including examples such as Wyndham Lewis's *Tarr* (1918), Djuna Barnes's *Nightwood* (1936) and even Dorothy Rich-ardson's *Pilgrimage* sequence of novels. Moreover, in certain ways aspects of Joyce's *Ulysses* relates to the Picaresque tradition as well as the epic.

Postcolonial Criticism: This very broad term usually refers to the study of the litera-tures of various territories that were once colonized by European imperial nations. Some critics use the term to refer to include the literatures of 'white settler nations' such as Australia, New Zealand and Canada, and to 'Black British' writers: British writers of various ethnic origins. Clearly modernism can be widened to include writers and artists from these constituencies, many of them producing works of art or intellectual statements concerned with the assertion of racial and cultural identity, accounting radically for he processes of history, indigenous traditions and the subversion of Western notions of the colonized 'other'. Postcolonial modernist criticism seeks to explore and analyse the impact of such marginalized cultures and identities.

Postmodernism: The term is increasingly regarded as a cultural phase that began in the 1960s, with a very self-reflexive intellectual and creative culture. Its dynamics originate from an emphasis on the ways in which ideology constructs cultural and social norms ranging from concepts of virtue, goodness and beauty, aesthetics itself more generally, as well as history concepts of ethnicity, gender, nationality and sexuality. It is predicated on a challenge to a world based upon universality and instrumental reason. Postmodernism is a portmanteau term, and has been applied to many different fields being inflected in radically differ-ent ways, describing a variety of artistic and cultural practices. Postmodernism responded to the trauma of the Second World War and addresses the ego-centricity of some of the main modernist assumptions, challenging the 'grand narratives' of Western culture, humanism and progress. It blurs the distinctions set up by aesthetic hierarchies, blending high art with more popular forms. In the novel, postmodernism is less individualistic than modernist texts, both readopting and reforming genre conventions, and tending towards the comic and ironic. Such texts often reject the conventional distinction between fact and fiction. However, in recent years, the usefulness of the term in thinking about contemporary writing has been much challenged. Generally, its artistic produc-tions and writings are characterized by a self-reflexive notions of heterogeneity and playfulness (the ludic). Its favoured modes are irony, kitsch, forms of exag-geration and self-reflexivity so as to challenge traditional boundaries and the modernist assertion of the self (although ironically conceptually and intellectu-ally, postmodernism could be argued that to depend finally upon an intellectual priority of those proficient in comprehending the very incommensurability of the world).

Poststructuralism: This critical method or view emerged in the 1960s, partly from in attempts by French theorists to apply the logic found in the work of the structural linguist Ferdinand de Saussure (1857–1913), emphasizing the arbitrary nature of the relation between the sign and signifier, especially to concepts drawn from Freud, Marx, Nietzsche and others. A key figure was Michel Foucault who describes how if language usage and social norms are products of the systematic aspects of rule-governed systems, it is impossible to obtain an objective, universal view. In essence both collectively and individually as humans we render the apparently objective in particular ways. Those who are deemed mad or insane are the result of an elaborate social and historical configuration that is primarily an ideological formation rather than a rational one. Others poststructuralists include Roland Barthes, Gilles Deleuze, Jacques Lacan and Gayatri Spivak. However, the term remains problematic since there is a great diversity in the work of these theorists, and many reject the label. Derrida's 1966 conference lecture, 'Structure, Sign, and Play in the Human Sciences' highlighted various theoretical limitations to structuralism.

Provincial (and Regional) Novel: In the literary sphere, the *provincial* and *regional novel* represents a tradition of setting fiction outside of the metropolitan centre, exploring the dynamics of a local society, culture and economy, and examples of English provincialism would include the Henry Fielding, the Brontes, Jane Eyre and George Eliot. Although modernist fiction tends to display a metropolitan consciousness, provincially and regionally oriented fictions are found in the work of Elizabeth Bowen, James Hanley, D.H. Lawrence, Rebecca West and of course in a radical sense James Joyce.

Realism: Realism is a complex term, since one must first distinguish between philosophical realism, and literary or narrative realism. The first views life and being (ontology relates to concepts of being and existence) as contiguous with an already present and continuing world, independent of our conceptual schemes, linguistic practices and beliefs. In the arts *realism* refers to the depiction of subjects as they appear without embellishment or explicit mediation, as if the objects were found in the world. In the nineteenth century *literary realism* generally involved depictions (often with descriptive emphases) of contemporary life and manners, very often the ordinary and everyday rather than focusing on stylized or romanticized writing. Literary realism as a cultural movement was formalized in the mid-nineteenth century in France, in writers such as Gustave Flaubert and Guy de Maupassant. Realist writers adopt an elevated, universal knowledge to map out a fictional world where the novel's language aspires to mimesis, the naming and mirroring of the real, and the underlying basis is a world where it is conceived that truth is verifiable scientifically and exists in material objects partly perceived through all five senses. The classic nineteenth century English realist writer is George Eliot, particularly with her provincial novel, *Middlemarch*. Both psychological and social *realism* refocus the fictional viewpoint. Most writing, even much in the experimental tradition, partakes of a world view that invokes at least some levels of philosophical realism.

Satire: Satire is an ancient form of artistic and ideological expression, a literary genre which censures and ridicules human (often individual) vices, abuses, follies or shortcomings by use of exaggeration, burlesque, derision, ridicule irony, sarcasm or other means of intense focus or distortion. Techniques involved are analogy, often unfavourable comparison, double entendre and juxtaposition of divergent and therefore humorous elements or concepts. Traditionally *satire* included the transformation of humans into animals. It is often angry and savage, but is overall intent moral and improving. Jonathan Swift is perhaps the archetypal satirist; more recent examples of satire in the modernist period would include Aldous Huxley's *Brave New World*, Evelyn Waugh's *Scoop* and Woolf's *Orlando*. It is worth noting that many examples of caricature and parody will incorporate satirical elements.

Stream of Consciousness: The term describes a highly impressionistic sense that inflects certain narrative, in which the impression is given of the written equivalent of the character's thought processes, often an erratic jumbled interior monologue responding to random impressions, an intense description of sensory reactions to the world of objects. The term is drawn from the writings of philosopher and psychologist William James, brother of Henry James, who suggests much of our understanding of sensation is immediate and yet indirect, since consciousness is perpetually and rapidly change in ways we barely consciously and rationally fix faced as we are by a stream of thought, feeling, emotion responding to the fullness of the physical. It was introduced to literary studies by May Sinclair. The sense is almost of being adjacent to the person, apprehending their thoughts and experiences with an intense immediacy, full of an almost overwhelming plethora of detail.

Surrealism: Central to this movement which began in the early 1920s was its leader André Breton who explicitly asserted its political and revolutionary agenda. He first studied medicine and psychiatry, treating shell-shocked soldiers in the War in a neurological hospital, adopting a Freudian psychoanalytic approach. Perhaps retrospectively speaking Surrealism's most significant contribution to modernism is perhaps in visual artworks and writings, works known for unexpected juxtapositions, non-sequitur and an element of surprise. Their output included automatic writing experiments where ideas were transcribed spontaneously, often incorporating dream images and symbols, and also work conscious of dialectical methods of synthesis. Surrealism's influence spread from Paris globally, creating a subsequently recognizable style that abandoned the logical sequencing of rationality and everyday experience, preferring rather dream analysis, free association, unconscious linkages that led them to embraced the idiosyncratic. After the first Surrealist Manifesto in 1924, participants produced *La Révolution surréaliste*, an often scandalous and revolutionary journal that survived until 1929, featuring text and art in reproduction, most notably by Giorgio de Chirico, Max Ernst, André Masson and Man Ray.

Taylorism: Frederick Winslow Taylor, whose early seminal work was *The Principles of Scientific Management* (1911), stated his ambitions for industrial production as follows: 'The principal object of management should be to secure the maximum prosperity for the employer, coupled with maximum prosperity for each employé [worker] (9) Rather than employ artisans, Taylor advocated a corporate approach with extreme job differentiation, the use of assembly-line techniques, increased organizational size for economies of a scale, and 'the elimination of all men who refuse to or are unable to adopt the best methods' (49). The outcomes were profound for the modern age, resulting in hierarchical leadership, fixed rather than fluid roles, extremely specialized and divided labour, demand-led economics, and product orientation rather than relations with workforce or customers. One prominent pioneer and advocate was Henry Ford, founder of the eponymous Motor Company in Detroit in 1903. Ford realized rapidly the benefits of these industrial theories, adopting them for Model T production, initiating this new industrial concept of mass production which resulted in systems of mass consumption.

The Uncanny: The concept of the uncanny as used in the literary critical field derives from Sigmund Freud's essay 'The Uncanny' (1919), where he argues that moments experienced by the individual as strange, as intimating the supernatural, are caused by a recurrence of repressed feelings or images evoked by an encounter. The moment of the uncanny suggests or re-invokes the familiar in terms of already experienced desires, emotions and sensations repressed because of traumatic content, therefore rendered as if unfamiliar. For Freud the uncanny is always experienced as both familiar and unfamiliar, both simultaneously *heimlich* and *unheimlich* (homely and strange). Traditionally the uncanny was regarded as indicating the *fearful*, whereas modernism turned towards the ugly, the grotesque in its 'negative' or anti-aesthetics. Freud's work can be used to examine the fearful as a corollary to beauty in this aesthetics of anxiety. Hence the concept has proved useful in denoting that which permeates and breaches boundaries and stable categorizations (such as that between the familiar and the unfamiliar) and which resists safe categorization. The uncanny has been useful to explain the origin and depth of symbols and experience, while useful in readings of text that undermine the stability of all meanings, as it might indicate that all elements are haunted by ghostly opposites, a radical doubling.

Appendix: Teaching, Learning and the Curricula of Modernism

Steven Barfield

Chapter Overview

Introduction

Geographical Variation

Periodisation

Novels and Novelists

Poetry and Poets

Drama and Dramatists

Specialist Modules, Interdisciplinarity and Internationalism

Critical, Secondary Sources

Learning and Teaching Methods

Comparing Curriculum Structure and Assessment in North
   American and Britain

Conclusion

Sources for Further Research

This chapter is available online at
www.continuumbooks.com/resources/9780826488435

Notes on Contributors

Nicola Allen teaches modules on British fiction at Birmingham City University and Northampton University. She has published (among other things) a monograph entitled *Marginality in the Contemporary British Novel* (2008) and has co-written a chapter in Cynthia Kuhn and Lance Rubin's collection *Reading Chuck Palahniuk: Monsters, Mayhem, and Metafiction* (2009).

Steve Barfield is a Senior Lecturer in English at the University of Westminster. His major research interests are in the work of Samuel Beckett (especially the intersections of psychoanalysis, philosophy and performance theory with his work), as well as contemporary British drama and theatre, fantasy/children's literature and postcolonial literature. Among his publications are 'Beckett and Heidegger: A Critical Survey' in Richard Lane (ed.), *Beckett and Philosophy*, Palgrave, 2002 and 'Philosophy, Psychoanalysis and Parody: Exceedingly Beckett' (with Philip Tew) and 'The Resources of Unrepresentability: A Lacanian Glimpse of Beckett's Three Dialogues' both in *Samuel Beckett Today/Aujourd'hui*.

Jeannette Baxter is a Senior Lecturer in English and Writing at Anglia Ruskin University, Cambridge, specialising in twentieth century and contemporary fiction. She is the author of *J.G. Ballard's Surrealist Imagination: Spectacular Authorship* (Ashgate, 2008), and the editor of *Contemporary Critical Perspectives: J.G. Ballard* (Continuum, 2008). Recent publications include articles and book chapters on Postmodernism, Angela Carter, Ian McEwan, J.G. Ballard and Kazuo Ishiguro.

Gary Day is a Principal Lecturer in English at De Montfort University. He is the author of *Re-reading Leavis: Culture and Literary Criticism* (1996); *Class* (2001) and *Literary Criticism: A New History* (2008). He is co-editor, with Bridget Keegan, of *The Eighteenth Century Handbook* and regularly contributes satirical pieces to *The Higher*.

Alex Murray is a Lecturer in English literature at the University of Exeter. He is the author of *Recalling London: Literature and History in the work of Iain Sinclair and Peter Ackroyd* (2007) and co-editor of *The Work of Giorgio Agamben: Law Literature, Life* (2008). He is currently writing a monograph on Agamben, as well as a study of late Victorian decadence and national identity.

David Ian Paddy is Associate Professor of English language and literature at Whittier College, a liberal arts college near Los Angeles. He teaches courses in modern and contemporary British literature, drama, creative writing, science fiction and Celtic literature. His primary research area is contemporary Welsh fiction. He has written on Angela Carter, Jackie Kay, Jeff Noon, Niall Griffiths and is currently writing a monograph on J.G. Ballard.

Dr Deborah L. Parsons is a Senior Lecturer in nineteenth and twentieth century English literature at the University of Birmingham. She is the author of *Streetwalking the Metropolis* (2000), *Djuna Barnes* (2003) and *Theorists of the Modernist Novel: Joyce, Richardson, Woolf* (2007). She is currently a Harry Ransom Mellon Fellow, and is writing a monograph critically reappraising the work of Edith, Osbert and Sacheverell Sitwell.

Bryony Randall is Lecturer in English literature at the University of Glasgow. She is the author of *Modernism, Daily Time and Everyday Life* (2007), and has also published on Imagist poetry, Gertrude Stein, lifewriting and the protomodernist writer George Egerton. She is co-editing a collection of essays entitled *Woolf in Context*.

Emmett Stinson is a PhD Candidate at the University of Melbourne. His thesis is entitled 'Avant-Garde Satires of the Avant-Garde: Wyndham Lewis, William Gaddis and Gilbert Sorrentino'. He has received The Melbourne Age Short Story Award and a Lannan Poetry fellowship. He serves as fiction editor of *Wet Ink: The Magazine of New Writing*.

Philip Tew is Professor of Contemporary English literature at Brunel University, London, a fellow of the Royal Society of Arts, and a member of the Royal Society of Literature. His monographs include *B.S. Johnson: A Critical Reading* (Manchester UP, 2001), *Jim Crace* (Manchester UP, 2006) and *The Contemporary British Novel* (Continuum, 2004, rev. ed. 2007). The latter work was translated and published in Serbia by Svetovi Press. He has published numerous essays and chapters in a variety of fields including contemporary British fiction, theory and meta-realism and American literature. He is joint commissioning and general editor for Palgrave's New British Fiction series and Continuum's Literature series. Tew is Director of both the UK Network for Modern Fiction Studies and the Brunel Centre for Contemporary Writing, and also editor of *Symbiosis: A Journal of Anglo-American Literary Relations*.

Andrew Thacker is Professor of English and Director of the Centre for Textual Studies at De Montfort University, Leicester. He is the author of *Moving Through Modernity: Space and Geography in Modernism* and co-editor of *Geographies of Modernism*. His current research is a large project upon Modernist magazines.

Leigh Wilson is a Senior Lecturer in English literature at the University of Westminster. She works on modernism and on contemporary fiction and is the author of *Modernism* (Continuum, 2007).

Notes

Chapter 8

1   The same year that Woolf said human character changed and the same year that Robert Tressell finished *The Ragged Trousered Philanthropists (1914)*, a devastating analysis of the causes of poverty. It is instructive to remember that this novel is rarely discussed in relation to Modernism, despite being more influential than perhaps any other novel of the period, in political if not literary terms, and despite containing many Modernist techniques that all serve as means to an end rather than as ends in themselves.

Chapter 10

1   For feminist readings of Joyce's fiction as appropriating and valorizing a 'feminine' discourse and linguistic style, see Vicky Mahaffey, *Reauthorizing Joyce* (Cambridge: Cambridge UP, 1988); Suzette Henke, *James Joyce and the Politics of Desire* (London: Routledge, 1990) and Karen Lawrence 'Joyce and Feminism' in Derek Attridge (ed.), *The Cambridge Companion to James Joyce* (Cambridge: Cambridge UP, 1990).

Chapter 11

1   See also: Kime Scott (1995) *Refiguring Modernism, two volumes.*

Annotated Bibliography

Note: where a first edition is not used, if the year of original publication is included it will be appended in additional parenthesis thus [1996].

Achebe, C. (1988), 'An image of Africa: racism in Conrad's Heart of Darkness' in R. Kimbrough (ed.), *Joseph Conrad, Heart of Darkness*. New York: Norton, pp. 251–62.

Adorno, T., Benjamin, W., Bloch, E., Brecht, B. and Lukács, G. (1990), *Aesthetics and Politics* Afterword by Frederic Jameson. London: Verso, 1990.

Albright, D. (2006), *Quantum Poetics: Yeats, Pound, Eliot, and the Science of Modernism*. Cambridge: Cambridge University Press.

Albright considers the work of modernist poets such as Yeats, Eliot and Pound, in the light of quantum poetics' search for scientific metaphors within the language of poetry. Albright's work thus follows thematically and conceptually the modernist taste for redefining the theoretical impulses of poetry along scientific lines of enquiry; and in doing so Albright details and explores the use of physics in the work of Yeats, Eliot and Pound. Albright's conclusion is that the poetry of these three figures challenges the long-held belief that science and poetry are separate and instead suggests that the two disciplines should be redefined as parts of the same 'quest'.

Anon. (1915), 'Preface', in *Some Imagist Poets: An Anthology*. London: Constable, pp. v–viii.

Armes, R. (1978), *A Critical History of the British Cinema*. London: Secker & Warburg.

Armstrong, T. (2005), *Modernism: A Cultural History*. Cambridge: Polity.

Armstrong's focus in this history of modernism is the broader cultural, social, academic, historical and political trends that formed and informed the period surrounding the genesis and development of modernism; as such this text defines the term 'modernism' in its widest setting. In order to achieve this 'opening out' of the term Armstrong refers to some lesser discussed figures such as Mary Butts, Muriel Rukeyser and Sterling Brown alongside his re-analysis of canonical figures such as Pound, Eliot and Woolf.

—— (1998), *Modernism, Technology and the Body: A Cultural Study*. Cambridge: Cambridge University Press.

Artaud, A. (1958), *The Theatre and its Double*. New York: Grove Press.

Artaud draws a parallel between the theatre's double and Jung's 'shadow' and suggests that the irrational aspects of theatre are a valid way resisting complacency in theatrical production. Artaud identifies language itself as one of the major cultural perpetrators of this neutralising complacency.

Ashcroft, B., Gareth, G. and Helen, T. (eds) (1989), *The Empire Writes Back: Theory and Practice in Post-Colonial Literatures*. London: Routledge.

An accessible survey of the central problems and issues in post-colonial scholarship.

Attridge, D. and Marjorie, H. (eds) (2000), *Semicolonial Joyce*. Cambridge: Cambridge University Press.

Avery, T. and Bratlinger, P. (2003), 'Reading and modernism: mind hungers' common and uncommon' in D. Bradshaw (ed.) *A Concise Companion to Modernism*. Oxford: Blackwell, pp. 243–61.

Ayers, D. (2004), *Modernism: A Short Introduction*. London: Blackwell.

Ayers' text aims to demonstrate the thematic concerns that link the work of the canonical and the less well-known writers that have been called or called themselves modernist. Ayers' focus is literary and although he does discuss the influence of German Marxism and French deconstruction upon the movement, Ayers focus is on English and American modernism; particularly the work of T.S. Eliot, Virginia Woolf, D.H. Lawrence, Wallace Stevens, H.D., Nancy Cunard, Wyndham Lewis and Mina Loy.

Baker, H.A. (1987), *Modernism and the Harlem Renaissance*. London and Chicago: Chicago University Press.

Banfield, A. (2007), 'Remembrance and tense past', in M. Shiach (ed.), *The Cambridge Companion to the Modernist Novel*. Cambridge: Cambridge University Press: pp. 48–64.

Braybon, G. (1981), *Women Workers in the First World War*. London: Croom Helm.

Braybon, G. and Summerfield, P. (1987), *Out of the Cage: Women's Experience in Two World Wars*. London: Pandora.

Baudelaire, C. (1998), 'The painter of modern life', in V. Kolocotroni, J. Goldman and O. Taxidou (eds), *Modernism: An Anthology of Sources and Documents*. Chicago: University of Chicago Press, pp. 102–8.

Bauman, Z. (1991), *Modernity and Ambivalence*. Ithaca, New York: Cornell University Press.

Beckett, S. (2006a), 'Dante ... Bruno . Vico .. Joyce', in S. Beckett (ed.), *The Grove Centenary Edition: Volume IV: Poems, short fiction, criticism*. New York: Grove Press, pp. 495–510.

—— (2006b), *Molloy*, in *Samuel Beckett: The Grove Centenary Edition: Volume II: The Novels*. New York: Grove Press, pp. 3–170.

—— (1983), *Worstward Ho*. London: J. Calder.

Bell, C. (1914), *Art*. London: Chatto and Windus.

—— (1993), 'The artistic problem', in S.P. Rosenbaum (ed.), *A Bloomsbury Group Reader*. Oxford: Blackwell, pp. 102–6.

Bell, M. (2006), *Literature, Modernism and Myth: Belief and Responsibility in the Twentieth Century*. Cambridge: Cambridge University Press.

Bell explores the flexible relationship between modernist thinkers and the modernist pre-occupation with myth to conclude that writers such as Pound and Joyce use mythic allusions within their work to such different ends that it is impossible to totalise the relationship between the two. Bell highlights the link between contemporary discussions concerning the role and responsibilities of literature in a liberal age and the use of myth as a non-totalizing element in the work of modernist authors such as Joyce.

—— (2003), 'Nietzscheanism: The Superman and the all-too-human' in D. Bradshaw (ed.), *A Concise Companion to Modernism*. Oxford: Blackwell, pp. 56–74.

Benjamin, W. (1973) [1955], 'The work of Art in the Age of Mechanical Reproduction', in *Illuminations*. Ed. Hannah Arendt. Trans. Harry Zohn. London: Collins/Fontana: pp. 219–53.

Benstock, S. (1986), *Women of the Left Bank: Paris, 1900–1940*. London: Virago.

Bergonzi, B. (1986), *The Myth of Modernism and Twentieth-Century Literature*. Brighton: Harvester.

Bergson, H. (1988) [1912], *Matter and Memory*. New York: Zone Books.

Bergson's study, *Matter and Memory*, introduced the current selectionist theories of memory, and considers how the findings of biological science can be integrated with a theory of consciousness.

Berman, M. (1983), *All That is Solid Melts Into Air: The Experience of Modernity*. London: Verso.

Berman's text essentially seeks to explain and analyse the links between modernity and modernism. Berman takes an anti-Foucaldian approach to historicising the modern era and to this end subdivides modernity into three phases: '. . . In the first phase, which goes roughly from the start of the sixteenth century to the end of the eighteenth, people are just beginning to experience modern life; they hardly know what has hit them. (. . .) Our second phase begins with the great revolutionary wave of the 1790's. With the French Revolution and its reverberations, a great modern public abruptly and dramatically comes to life. (. . .) In the twentieth century, our third and final phase, the process of modernization expands to take in virtually the whole world, and the developing world culture of modernism achieves spectacular triumphs in art and thought' (16–17).

Bhabha, H.K. (1994), *The Location of Culture*. London: Routledge.

Blum, C.S. (1996), *The Other Modernism: F.T Marinetti's Futurist Fiction of Power*, California: University of California Press.

Blum's text provides a feminist psychoanalytic account of the fiction of F.T. Marinetti, paying particular attention to textual practices in the writer's fiction and political publications.

Boone, J.A. (1998), *Libidinal Currents: Sexuality and the Shaping of Modernism*. Chicago: University of Chicago Press.

Boone draws links between emerging theories of sexuality, particularly Freud's theory of the libidinal instinct and Foucault's theory of sexual discourse and the textual innovations of modernist writers such as Kate Chopin, Virginia Woolf, William Faulkner and Doris Lessing. Boones suggests that these texts are better understood within the context of contemporary theories concerning sexuality; and this text maps the links between modernist literary works and their Freudian and/or Foucauldian context.

Bornstein, G. (ed.) (1991), *Representing Modernist Texts: Editing as Interpretation*. Ann Arbor: University of Michigan Press.

Bradbury, M. and McFarlane, J. (eds) (1976), *Modernism: A Guide to European Literature, 1890–1930*. Harmondsworth: Penguin.

The guide examines the work of figures such as Apollinaire, Brecht, Joyce, Kafka, Strindberg and Yeats; amongst others. Bradbury and MacFarlane take a biographical approach to the study of modernism and focus on the lives and the artistic tensions between its key exponents.

Bradshaw, D. (2002), *A Concise Companion to Modernism*. London: Blackwell.

Bradshaw's text focuses on the cultural and social backdrop to the development of modernism; included in the ten chapters are discussions of the role of eminent theories including eugenics, primitivism, Freudianism, and Nietzscheanism in shaping the cultural landscape out of which modernism arose and evolved. The text focuses on modernism in the visual arts, music and architecture, film and philosophy as well as literary modernism, and as such regards modernism as a cultural phenomenon not simply a literary one.

Breton, A. (1969) [1924], 'Manifesto of surrealism: (1924).' in T.R. Seaver and H.R. Lane (eds), *Manifestoes of Surrealism*. Ann Arbor: University of Michigan Press, pp. 1–47.

Briusov, V. (2001), 'Against naturalism in the theater', in B. Cardullo and R. Knopf (eds), *Theater of the Avant-garde 1890–1950: a Critical Anthology*. New Haven: Yale University Press: pp. 72–6.

Broe, M.L. and Ingram, A. (eds) (1989), *Women's Writing in Exile*. Chapel Hill: University of North Carolina Press.

Brooker, P. (1992), *Modernism/Postmodernism*. London: Longman.

Modernism/Postmodernism provides readers with abridged versions of influential critical essays that have shaped the contemporary development between

Modernism and Postmodernism. Brooker provides an introduction and comprehensive notes for each of the sections of *Modernism/Postmodernism*. As such this text would provide a valuable introduction to the issues surrounding modernism's survival in the twentieth century. Brooker's inclusion of essays that explore Third World, Black and Feminist perspectives also make it a suitably comprehensive guide.

—— and A. Thacker (eds) (2005), *Geographies of Modernism: Literatures, Cultures, Spaces*. London: Routledge.

Brown, R.D. and Gupta, S. (2004), *Aestheticism and Modernism: Debating Twentieth-Century Literature 1900–1960*. London: Routledge.

Burger, P. (1984), *Theory of the Avant-Garde*. Minneapolis: University of Minnesota Press.

Butler, C. (1994), *Early Modernism: Literature, Music, and Painting in Europe 1900–1916*. Oxford: Oxford University Press.

Butler moves away from what he regards as an overly literary approach to the study of modernism and instead he draws together examples from the literary, music and visual arts world to make his case for the emergence of the modernist self. Butler analyses changing concepts of personal identity and suggest that these changes are manifested across the arts at the start of the twentieth century.

Butler, J. (1990), *Gender Trouble: Feminism and the Subversion of Identity*. London: Routledge.

Carey, J. (1992), *The Intellectuals and the Masses: Pride and Prejudice Among the Literary Intelligentsia, 1880–1939*. London: Faber and Faber.

Cassirer, E. (1979), *The Philosophy of the Enlightenment*. Princeton, NJ: Princeton University Press.

Churchill, S.W. (2006), *The Little Magazine 'Others' and the Renovation of Modern American Poetry*. Aldershot: Ashgate.

Clark, T.J. (2001), *Farewell to an Idea: Episodes from a History of Modernism*. New Haven: Yale University Press.

Clarke's book concerns the social nature of form; he employs a series of 'limit-cases', spanning from David's Death of Marat, 1793, to Pollock's Number 1, 1948 in order to substantiate his argument that it is possible to bring together modernist theory and a social history (or theory) of art.

Clarke, S. (1991), *Sentimental Modernism: Women Writers and the Revolution of the Word*. Indiana: Indiana University Press.

Cole, S. (2007), *Modernism, Male Friendship, and the First World War*. Cambridge: Cambridge University Press.

Conrad, J. (1988) [1902], R. Kimborough (ed.), *The Heart of Darkness*. New York and London: Norton.
—— (1967), 'Preface to the nigger of the narcissus.' in W.F. Wright (ed.), *Joseph Conrad On Fiction*, Lincoln U.S.A: University of Nebraska Press, pp. 160–64.

Conrad, P. (1999), *Modern Times, Modern Places*. New York: Alfred A. Knopf.

Cooper, J.X. (2004), *Modernism and the Culture of Market Society*. Cambridge: Cambridge University Press.

Crary, J. (1999), *Suspensions of Perception: Attention, Spectacle and Modern Culture*. Massachusetts: MIT Press.

Culingford, E. (1981), *Yeats, Ireland and Fascism*. London: Macmillan.

Daly, N. (2004), *Literature, Technology, and Modernity, 1860–2000*. Cambridge: Cambridge University Press.

Danius, S. (2002), *The Senses of Modernism*. Ithaca: Cornell University Press.

DeKoven, M. (1999), 'Modernism and gender' in M. Levenson (ed.), *The Cambridge Companion to Modernism*. Cambridge: Cambridge University Press, pp. 174–93.
—— (1991), *Rich and Strange: Gender, History, Modernism*. Princeton, NJ: Princeton University Press.

DeKoven discusses water imagery as a symbol in texts from the African-American and feminist canons alongside better known modernist texts to reveal 'the gender-inflected ambivalence of modernist writers'. Dekoven argues that while they argued for change male modernists also feared the loss of power that this change to the hegemony would bring about.

Doan, L.L. and Garrity, J. (eds) (2007), *Sapphic Modernities: Sexuality, Women, and English Culture*. Basingstoke: Palgrave Macmillan.

Dowson, J. (2002), *Women, Modernism and British Poetry, 1910–1939: Resisting Femininity*. London: Ashgate.

Doyle, L. and Winkiel, L. (eds) (2005), *Geomodernisms: Race, Modernism, Modernity*. Bloomington: Indiana University Press.

Eagleton, T. (1983), *Literary Theory: An Introduction*. Oxford: Blackwell.

Eliot, T.S. (1975) [1921], 'The metaphysical poets' in Frank Kermode (ed), *Selected Prose of T.S. Eliot*. London: Faber and Faber, pp. 59–67.
—— (1975) [1919], 'Tradition and the individual talent' in Frank Kermode (ed), *Selected Prose of T.S. Eliot*. London: Faber and Faber, pp. 37–44.
—— (2002) [1922], 'The Waste Land', in T.S. Eliot (ed) *Selected Poems*. London: Faber and Faber, pp. 39–64.
—— (1975) [1919], 'Ulysses, Order, and Myth' in F. Kermode (ed), *Selected Prose of T.S. Eliot*. London: Faber and Faber, pp. 175–78.

Elliott, B. and Jo-Ann, W. (1994), *Women Artists and Writers: Modernist (im)positionings*. London: Routledge.

Ellmann, R. (1959), *James Joyce*. Oxford: Oxford University Press.
—— and Fiedelson, C. (1965), *The Modern Tradition: Backgrounds of Modern Literature*. New York: Oxford University Press.

Emig, R. (1995), *Modernism in Poetry: Motivations, Structures and Limits*. London: Longman.

Esty, J. (2003), *A Shrinking Island: Modernism and National Culture in England*, Princeton: Princeton University Press.

Eucken, R. (1912), *Main Currents of Modern Thought: A Study of the Spiritual and Intellectual Movements of the Present Day*, Trans. M. Booth. London and Leipsic: T. Fisher Unwin.

Eysteinsson, A. (1990), *The Concept of Modernism*. Ithaca: Cornell University Press.

Faulkner, P. (1986), *A Modernist Reader: Modernism in England 1910–1930*. London: Batsford.
—— (1990), *Modernism*. London: Routledge.

Felski, R. (1995), *The Gender of Modernity*. Cambridge, MA: Harvard University Press.

Fordham, J. (2002), *James Hanley: Modernism and the Working Class*. Cardiff: University of Wales Press.

Forster, E.M. (1927), *Aspects of the Novel*. London: Arnold.

Foucault, M. (2000), 'What is enlightenment?' in *The Essential Works of Foucault 1954–1984, Volume 1 Ethics, Subjectivity and Truth*. Hugh, Rabinow (ed.). Trans. R. Hurley et al. London: Penguin: pp. 303–19.

Frazer, J.G. (1963), *The Golden Bough: A Study in Magic and Religion*. New York: Macmillan.

Freedman, A. (2003), *Death, Men, and Modernism: Trauma and Narrative in British Fiction from Hardy to Woolf*. New York and London: Routledge.
—— (2005), 'On the Ganges side of modernism: Raghubir Singh, Amitav Ghosh, and the Postcolonial Modern', in L. Doyle and L. Winkiel (eds), *Geomodernisms: Race, Modernism, Modernity*. Bloomington: Indiana University Press.

Friedman, S.S. (1996), ' "Beyond" gynocriticism and gynesis: the geographics of identity and the future of feminist criticism', *Tulsa Studies in Women's Literature*. Volume 15, Issue 1, pp. 13–40.
—— (1999), 'Gender, spatiality and geopolitics in the New Modernist Studies', *New Modernisms 1*, Pennsylvania State University.
—— (2006), 'Periodizing modernism: postcolonial modernities and the space/time borders of modernist studies', *Modernism/Modernity*. Volume 13, Issue 3, pp. 425–43.

Fritzsche, P. (1996), *Reading Berlin 1900*. Cambridge: Harvard University Press.

Frosh, S. (2002), 'Psychoanalysis in Britain: the rituals of deconstruction' in D. Bradshaw (ed.), *A Concise Companion to Modernism*. London: Blackwell, pp. 116–37.

Fussell, P. (1975), *The Great War and Modern Memory*. Oxford: Oxford University Press.

Gaonkar, D.P. (2001), *Alternative Modernities*. Durham, NC: Duke University Press.

Garratt, C. (2004), *Introducing Modernism*, London: Icon.

This text is a compact and illustrated introduction to the thinkers behind modernism; which outlines the major contributions to the field made by figures such as Picasso, Joyce and Schoenberg; and situates the movement of modernism against and within the backdrop of the political, social, artistic and academic trends of the late nineteenth and the early twentieth century.

Gikande, S. (2006), 'Preface: modernism in the world', *MODERNISM/modernity*. Volume 13, Issue 3, pp. 419–24.

Gilbert, S.M. and Gubar, S. (1988, 1989, 1994), *No Man's Land: The Place of the Woman Writer in the Twentieth Century. 3 vols.* New Haven and London: Yale University Press.
—— (1985), 'Sexual linguistics: gender, language, sexuality', *New Literary History*. pp. 515–43.

Gilles, M.A. (2003), 'Bergsonism: "Time out of mind." ' D. Bradshaw (ed.), *A Concise Companion to Modernism*. Oxford: Blackwell, pp. 95–115.

Gilman, C.P. (1911), *The Man-Made World, or Our Androcentric Culture*. London and Leipsic: T. Fisher Unwin.

Goldman, J. (2003), *Modernism, 1910–1945: Image to Apocalypse*. London: Palgrave Macmillan.
—— (2001), *The Feminist Aesthetics of Virginia Woolf: Modernism, Post-Impressionism, and the Politics of the Visual*. Cambridge: Cambridge University Press.

Gonne, M. (1940), 'Yeats and Ireland', in S. Gwyn (ed.) *Scattering Branches: Tributes to the Memory of W.B. Yeats*. London: Macmillan, pp. 22–33.

Griffin, R. (2007), *Modernism and Fascism: The Sense of a New Beginning Under Mussolini and Hitler*. London: Palgrave Macmillan.

Griffin traces the links between Western modernity and the regimes of Mussolini and Hitler. Griffin suggests that the Modernist quest for transcendence and purpose in life is born out of the same context that witnessed the rise of fascism in Europe. Griffin uses the literature of the modernist era as evidence of this context and thus provides an historical, cultural reading of the links between fascism and modernism.

Hanscombe, G. and Smyers, V. (1987), *Writing for their Lives: The Modernist Woman 1910–1940*, London: Virago.

Harwood, J. (1995), *Eliot to Derrida: The Poverty of Interpretation*. Basingstoke: Macmillan.

Heath, S. (1989), 'Male feminism', in A. Jardine and P. Smith (ed.), *Men in Feminism*. London: Routledge.

Henke, S. (1990), *James Joyce and the Politics of Desire*. London: Routledge.

Hewitt, A. (1993), *Fascist Modernism: Aesthetics, Politics and the Avant-Garde*. Stanford, CA: Stanford University Press.

Hobsbawm, E. (1994), *The Age of Extremes: The Short Twentieth Century, 1914–1991*. London: Michael Joseph.

Huble, T. (1996), *Whose India?: The Independence Struggle in British and Indian Fiction and History*. Leicester: Leicester University Press.

Hutcheon, L. (1994), *Irony's Edge: The Theory and Politics of Irony*. London and New York: Routledge.

Huyssen, A. (1986), *After the Great Divide: Modernism, Mass Culture, Postmodernism*. Bloomington: Indiana University Press.

Isherwood, C. (1984) [1946], *Prater Violet*. London: Methuen.

Jacobs, K. (2001), *The Eye's Mind: Literary Modernism and Visual Culture*. Cornell: Cornell University Press.

Jaffe, A. (2005), *Modernism and the Culture of Celebrity*. Cambridge: Cambridge University Press.

Jameson, F. (2000), M. Hardt and K. Weeks (eds), *The Jameson Reader*. Oxford: Blackwell.
—— (1991), *Postmodernism, or, the Cultral Logic of Late Capitalism*. Durham: Duke University Press.
—— (2002), *Singular Modernity*, London: Verso.

Jardine, A. (1982), 'Gynesis', *Diacritics*. Volume 12, Issue 2, pp. 54–65.
—— (1985), *Gynesis: Configurations of Woman and Modernity*. Ithaca: Cornell University Press.

Jarrell, R. (1986) [1942], 'The End of the Line', in R. Jarrell (ed.) *Kipling, Auden & Co.: Essays and Reviews 1935–1964*. Manchester: Carcanet, pp. 76–83.

Jensen, M. (2007), 'Tradition and revelation: moments of being in Virginia Woolf's major novels', in M. Shiach (ed.), *The Cambridge Companion to the Modernist Novel*. Cambridge: Cambridge University Press, pp. 112–25.

Joyce, J. (2000), in J. Johnson (ed.), *A Portrait of the Artist as a Young Man*. Oxford: Oxford University Press.
—— (1992) [1922], *Ulysses*. Harmondsworth: Penguin.

Kafka, F. (2000), *Metamorphosis and other stories*. Trans. and ed. M. Pasley. London: Penguin.

Kaplan, S.J. (1975), *Feminist Consciousness in the Modern British Novel*. Urbana: University of Illinois Press.

Keating, P. (1991), *The Haunted Study: A Social History of the English Novel 1875–1914*. London: Fontana Press.

Kenner, H. (1971), *The Pound Era*. Berkeley and Los Angeles: University of California Press.

Kern, S. (2003), *The Culture of Time and Space, 1880–1918* (2nd edn). Cambridge, Massachusetts and London: Harvard University Press.

Kiberd, D. (1995), *Inventing Ireland: The Literature of the Modern Nation*. Massachusetts: Harvard University Press.

Knapp, J.F. (1988), *Literary Modernism and the Transformation of Work*. Evanston: Northwestern University Press.

Kolocotroni, V., Goldman, J. and Taxidou, O. (1999), *Modernism: An Anthology of Sources and Documents*. Chicago: University of Chicago Press.

Kolocotroni, Goldman and Taxidou have sourced 150 essays, articles, manifestos and other writings of the scientific, political and aesthetic avant-garde between 1840 and 1950. Including works by Gustave Flaubert, Ezra Pound and James Joyce, Charles Darwin, W.E.B. Du Bois and Adolf Hitler. The anthology also includes manifestos from the futurists, cubists, Dadaists, surrealists and anarchists.

Lamos, C. (1998), *Deviant Modernism: Sexual and Textual Errancy in T.S. Eliot, James Joyce, and Marcel Proust*. Cambridge: Cambridge University Press.

Latham, S. and Scholes, R. (2006), 'The rise of periodical studies,' *PMLA*, Volume March 121, Issue 2, pp. 517–31.

Lawrence, D.H. (2002) [1925], 'The novel and the feelings', *Study of Thomas Hardy and Other Essays* in The Cambridge Edition of the Works of D.H. Lawrence. B. Steele (ed.), Cambridge: Cambridge University Press, pp. 193–98.
—— (1995) [1915], in *The Rainbow*. M. Kinkead-Weekes (ed.), London and New York: Penguin.
—— (1978), 'Surgery for the novel – or a bomb', in *Phoenix: The Posthumous Papers of D.H. Lawrence, 1936*. E.D. McDonald (ed.), New York: Viking Press, pp. 517–20.
—— (1978), 'Why the novel matters', in *Phoenix: The Posthumous Papers of D.H. Lawrence, 1936*. E.D. McDonald (ed.), London: Penguin: 533–38.

Lawrence, K. (1990), *'Joyce and feminism'* in *The Cambridge Companion to James Joyce*. D. Attridge (ed.), Cambridge: Cambridge University Press.

Ledger, S. (1997), *The New Woman: Fiction and Feminism at the Fin de Siècle*, Manchester: Manchester University Press.

Lefebvre, H. (2006), *Critique of Everyday Life: From Modernity to Modernism (Towards a Metaphilosophy of Daily Life)*, Vol 3. Trans. G. Elliott. London: Verso.

Levenson, M. (1986), *A Genealogy of Modernism: A Study of English Literary Doctrine 1908–1922*, Cambridge: Cambridge University Press.
—— (1999), *The Cambridge Companion to Modernism*. Cambridge: Cambridge University Press.

The Cambridge Companion to Modernism is comprised of ten essays that cover the work of Joyce, Woolf, Stein, Picasso, Chaplin, H.D. and Freud amongst others. The text covers the wider category of modernism but has an emphasis on literary modernism. The companion constitutes a scholarly engagement with the themes and key texts of modernism.

Lewis, P. (2007), *The Cambridge Introduction to Modernism*. Cambridge: Cambridge Univesity Press.

Lewis, W. (ed.) (1915), *BLAST: Review of the Great English Vortex*, Santa Barbara, CA: Black Sparrow Press.

Longenbach, J. (1994), ' "Mature poets steal": Eliot's allusive practice' in A. David Moody, *The Cambridge Companion to T.S. Eliot*. Cambridge: Cambridge University Press, pp. 176–88.
—— (1999), 'Modern Poetry (1999)', M. Levenson (ed.), *The Cambridge Companion to Modernism*. Cambridge: Cambridge University Press, pp. 100–29.
—— (1991), *Stone Cottage: Pound, Yeats and Modernism*. Oxford: Oxford University Press.

Loos, A. (1998), 'Ornament and Crime'. V. Kolocotroni, J. Goldman and O. Taxidou V. (eds), *Modernism: An Anthology of Sources and Documents*, Chicago: University of Chicago Press, pp. 77–81.

Loy, M. (2001), 'Feminist Manifesto', in M.A. Caws (ed), *Manifesto: A Century of Isms*. Lincoln: University of Nebraska Press, pp. 611–13.

Lucas, J. (1986), *Modern English Poetry from Hardy to Hughes*, London: Batsford.

Lukács, G. (2006), *The Meaning of Contemporary Realism*, London: Merlin.

Lyall, S. (2006), *Hugh MacDiarmid's Poetry and Politics of Place: Imagining a Scottish Republic*, Edinburgh: Edinburgh University Press.

Lyotard, J-F. (1984), *The Postmodern Condition: A Report on Knowledge*, Manchester: Manchester University Press.

MacCarthy, D. (1932), *Criticism*. London and New York: Putnam.

MacClancy, J. (2003), 'Anthropology: "The latest form of evening entertainment"', in D. Bradshaw (ed.), *A Concise Companion to Modernism*. Oxford: Blackwell, pp. 75–94.

Mahaffey, V. (1988), *Reauthorizing Joyce*. Cambridge: Cambridge University Press.
—— (1991), 'Intential error: the paradox of editing Joyce's Ulysses', in G. Bornstein (ed.), *Representing Modernist Texts: Editing as Interpretation*. Ann Arbor: University of Michigan Press, pp. 171–91.

Mallarmé, S. (1956), '*Crisis in Poetry*', in *Mallarmé: Selected Prose Poems, Essays & Letters*. Trans. and Introd. B. Cook, Baltimore: Johns Hopkins University Press.

Marinetti, F.T. (1972) [1909], *The Founding and Manifesto of Futurism*. in R.W. Flint (ed.), *Marinetti: Selected Writings*. Trans. R.W. Flint and A.A. Coppotelli. London: Secker and Warburg, 39–44.

Marwick, A. (1991), *The Deluge: British Society and the First World War* (2nd edn). London: Macmillan.

Marx, J. (2005), *The Modernist Novel and the Decline of Empire*. Cambridge: Cambridge University Press.

Marx, K. (1978), 'The German ideology', in R.C. Tucker (ed.), *The Marx-Engels Reader* (2nd edn). New York: W.W. Norton and Company, pp. 146–200.

—— and Engels, F. (1978), 'Manifesto of the Communist Party', in R.C. Tucker (ed.), *The Marx-Engels Reader* (2nd ed.) New York: W.W. Norton and Company, pp. 469–500.

—— (1973), *Selected Works*. London: Lawrence and Wishart.

McCracken, S. (2007), *Masculinities, Modernist Fiction and the Urban Public Sphere*, Manchester: Manchester University Press.

McGann, J.J. (1993), *Black Riders: The Visible Language of Modernism*, Princeton: Princeton University Press.

McKible, A. (2002), *The Space and Place of Modernism: The Russian Revolution, Little Magazines, and New York*. New York and London: Routledge.

Menand, L. (2007), *Discovering Modernism: T.S. Eliot and His Context*, Oxford: Oxford University Press.

Meyer, S. (2000), *The Experimental Arabic Novel: Postcolonial Literary Modernism in the Levant*. Albany: State University of New York Press.

Miller, A.J. (2008), *Modernism and the Crisis of Sovereignty*. London: Routledge.

Miller, C. (2005), *Cultures of Modernism: Marianne Moore, Mina Loy, and Else Lasker-Schuler*, Michigan: University of Michigan Press.

Mitchell, J. (1985), 'Introduction I', in J. Mitchell and J. Rose (eds), *Feminine Sexuality: Jacques Lacan and the école freudienne*. New York: W.W. Norton, pp. 1–26.

Mitter, P. (2007), *The Triumph of Modernism: India's Artists and the Avant-Garde 1922–1947*. London: Reaktion.

Moi, T. (1985), *Sexual/Textual Politics: Feminist Literary Theory*. London: Methuen.

Murry, J.M. (1930), *The Problem of Style*. Oxford: Oxford University Press.

Nicholls, P. (1995), *Modernisms: A Literary Guide*. London: Palgrave Macmillan.

Nicholson, V. (2002), *Among the Bohemians: Experiments in Living 1900–1939*. London: Penguin.

Nietzsche, F. (1968), *The Will to Power*. Trans. W. Kauffmann and H.J. Hollingdale. New York: Vintage.

Nordau, M. (1998), 'Degeneration', in V. Kolocotroni, J. Goldman and O. Taxidou (eds), *Modernism: An Anthology of Sources and Documents*. Chicago: University of Chicago Press, pp. 22–7.

Norris, M. (1974), *The Decentered Universe of 'Finnegans Wake': A Structuralist Analysis*. Baltimore: Johns Hopkins University Press.

North, M. (1999), *Reading 1922: A Return to the Scene of the Modern*, Oxford: Oxford University Press.

Orage, A.R. [Alfred] (1935), 'The art of reading', in H. Read and D. Saurat (eds), *A.R. Orage: Selected Essays and Critical Writings*. London: Stanley Nott, pp. 3–122.

Ouditt, S. (1994), *Fighting Forces, Writing Women: Identity and Ideology in the First World War*. London: Routledge.

Owen, A. (2004), *The Place of Enchantment: British Occultism and the Culture of the Modern*. Chicago and London: University of Chicago Press.

Panek, R. (2005), *The Invisible Century: Einstein, Freud and the Search for Hidden Universes*. London: Fourth Estate.

Parsons, D. (2006), *Theorists of the Modernist Novel: James Joyce, Dorothy Richardson and Virginia Woolf*. London: Routledge.

Pater, W. (1986) [1873], *The Renaissance: Studies in Art and Poetry*. Introd. A. Phillips. Oxford and New York: Oxford University Press.

Perloff, M. (2001), *21st-century Modernism: The New Poetics*, Oxford: Blackwell.

Pethica, J.L. (2000), *Yeats's Poetry, Drama and Prose*. New York: Norton.

Pike, D.L. (2005), *Subterranean Cities: The World Beneath Paris and London, 1800–1945*. Ithaca: Cornell University Press.

Pinkney, T. (1990), *D.H. Lawrence and Modernism*. Iowa: University of Iowa Press.

Pippin, R.B. (1999), *Modernism as a Philosophical Problem: On the Dissatisfactions of European High Culture*. Oxford: Blackwell.

Potter, R. (2006), *Modernism and Democracy: Literary Culture 1900–1930*. Oxford: Oxford University Press.

Pound, E. (1954) [1911], 'A retrospect', in *Literary Essays of Ezra Pound*. Introd. T.S. Eliot. London and Boston: Faber and Faber, pp. 3–14.

Pugh, M. (2002a), *The March of the Women: A Revisionist Analysis of the Campaign for Women's Suffrage, 1866–1914*, Oxford: Oxford University Press.

—— (2002b), *The Making of Modern British Politics, 1867–1945* (3rd edn). Oxford: Blackwell.

Pykett, L. (1995), *Engendering Fictions: The English Novel in the Early Twentieth Century*. London: Edward Arnold.

Radford, J. (1980), *'Introduction' to The Life and Death of Harriett Frean*. London: Virago.

Rainey, L. (1999), 'The Cultural Economy of Modernism' in M. Levenson (ed), *The Cambridge Companion to Modernism*. Cambridge: Cambridge University Press, pp. 33–69.
—— (1998), *Institutions of Modernism: Literary Elites and Public Cultures*. New Haven and London: Yale University Press.
—— (2005), *Modernism: An Anthology*. Oxford: Blackwell.

A comprehensive anthology of Anglo-American modernist fiction; incorporating James Joyce, Gertrude Stein, Virginia Woolf, T.S. Eliot, Ezra Pound, Wallace Stevens, Marianne Moore and Samuel Beckett. The anthology includes extensive notes and bibliographical material.

Raitt, S. (2000), *May Sinclair: A Modern Victorian*. Oxford: Clarendon.

Reed, C. (2004), *Bloomsbury Rooms: Modernism, Subculture, and Domesticity*. New Haven and London: Yale University Press.

Rigby, N. and Booth, H.J. (2000), *Modernism and Empire*. Manchester: Manchester University Press.

Rigby suggests that although modernism sought to question literary and social customs, its conservative and reactionary tendencies, in effect, schematized the colonial project.

Rosenbaum, S.P. (ed.) (1993), *A Bloomsbury Group Reader*. Oxford: Blackwell.

Rothenstein, W. (1940), 'Yeats as a Painter Saw Him', in S. Gwyn (ed.) *Scattering Branches: Tributes to the Memory of W.B. Yeats*. London: Macmillan, pp. 35–55.

Saler, M.T. (1999), *The Avant-Garde in Interwar England: Medieval Modernism and the London Underground*. Oxford: Oxford University Press.

Sarvan, C.P. (1988) [1963], 'Racism and the *Heart of Darkness*' reprinted in R. Kimborough (ed.) *Joseph Conrad: Heart of Darkness*. London: Norton, pp. 280–85.

Sass, L. (1992), *Madness and Modernism: Insanity in the Light of Modern Art, Literature and Thought*. New York: Basic Books.

Schorske, C.E. (1981), *Fin-de-Siècle Vienna: Politics and Culture*. New York: Vintage.

Scott, B.K. (1990), *The Gender of Modernism*. Bloomington: Indiana University Press.
—— (2007), *Gender in Modernism: New Geographies, Complex Intersections*. Illinois: University of Illinois Press.
—— (1987), *James Joyce: Feminist Readings*. London: Harvester.
—— (1984), *Joyce and Feminism*. Bloomington: Indiana University Press.
—— (1995), *Refiguring Modernism: Volume One, The Women of 1928*. Bloomington: Indiana University Press.
—— (1995), *Refiguring Modernism: Volume Two, Postmodern Feminist Readings of Woolf, West and Barnes*. Bloomington: Indiana University Press.

Sedgwick, E.K. (1990), *Epistemology of the Closet*. Berkeley: University of California Press.

Shaw, G.B. (1994) [1904], Preface to *John Bull's Other Island*. London: Penguin.

Shiach, M. (2004), *Modernism, Labour and Selfhood in British Literature and Culture*. Cambridge: Cambridge University Press.

Shklovsky, V. (1965), 'Art as Technique', *Russian Formalist Criticism: Four Essays*. Trans. L.T. Lemon and M.J. Reis (eds). Lincoln: University of Nebraska Press, pp. 3–24.

Showalter, E. (ed.) (1993), *Daughters of Decadence: Women Writers of the Fin-de-Siècle*. London: Virago.

—— (1987), *The Female Malady: Women, Madness and English Culture 1830–1980*. London: Virago.

Showalter's text charts the cultural attitudes towards, and advances in diagnosis and treatment of psychiatric and neurasthenic conditions that occurred simultaneously with the cultural and aesthetic movements associated with modernism. Showalter's text provides an insight into how changes in scientific understanding of the human mind occurred concurrently with the modernist interaction with such issues.

—— (1977), *A Literature of Their Own*. London: Virago.

—— (1998), 'Twenty Years On: *A Literature of Their Own* Revisited', *Novel*. Volume 31, Index 3, pp. 399–413.

—— (1985), 'Towards a feminist poetics', in E. Showalter (ed.) *The New Feminist Criticism: Essays on Women, Literature, and Theory*. London: Virago, pp. 125–43.

Simmel, G. (1950), in (ed.) K.H. Wolff, *The Sociology of Georg Simmel*. New York: The Free Press.

Singh, F.B. (1988) [1963], 'The Colonialistic Bias of *Heart of Darkness*' reprinted in R. Kimborough (ed.) Joseph Conrad, *Heart of Darkness*. London: Norton, pp. 268–88.

Smith, A. (1998), *Nationalism and Modernism*. London: Routledge.

Smith examines the relationship between modernism and nationalism, and suggests that the modernist outlook forms a natural predecessor to the current cultural emphasis on nationalism and ethnicity.

Steele, R. and Addison, J. (1988), in Angus Ross (ed.), *Selections from the Tatler and the Spectator*. Harmondsworth: Penguin.

Stein, G. (2005) [1926], 'Composition as Explanation', in L. Rainey (ed.), *Modernism: An Anthology*. Malden, MA: Blackwell, pp. 407–11.

Stevens, H. and Howlett, C. (eds) (2000), *Modernist Sexualities*. Manchester: Manchester University Press.

Strachey, L. (1918), *Eminent Victorians*. London: Chatto & Windus.

Strindberg, A. (1994), *Plays One: The Father, Miss Julie and The Ghost Sonata*. Trans. M. Meyer. London: Methuen.

Strychacz, T. (1993), *Modernism, Mass Culture and Professionalism*. Cambridge: Cambridge University Press.

Stubbs, P. (1979), *Women and Fiction: Feminism and the Novel 1890–1920*. Sussex: Harvester.

Surette, L. (1993), *The Birth of Modernism: Ezra Pound, T.S. Eliot, W.B. Yeats and the Occult*. Montreal and Kingston: McGill-Queen's University Press.

Symons, A. (1899), *The Symbolist Movement in Literature*. London: William Heinemann.

Tambling, J. (1993), 'Essay' in S. Reid (ed.), *Mrs Dalloway and To the Lighthouse*. Basingstoke: Palgrave Macmillan, pp. 57–70.

Tarnas, R. (1991), *The Passion of the Western Mind: Understanding the Ideas That Have Shaped Our World View*. New York: Harmony Books.

Tarnas takes an historical approach to understanding the mindset of modern man. Beginning with an examination of the ancient Greeks Tarnas in his text charts the development of the central ideas from Aristotle to the present that he believes have contributed to the 'modern outlook', arguing the modern mind is founded largely on Cartesian-Kantian philosophical assumptions abolishing the intuitive in favour of the systematic.

Tate, T. (1998), *Modernism, History and the First World War*. Manchester: Manchester University Press.

Taylor, F.W. (1911), *The Principles of Scientific Management*. New York: Harper Row. Online version available at http://www.gutenberg.org/etext/6435.

Thacker, A. (2003), *Moving Through Modernity: Space and Geography in Modernism*. Manchester: Manchester University Press.

Thormahlen, M. (2003), *Rethinking Modernism*. London: Palgrave Macmillan.

Thormahlen believes that the term 'modernism' was fixed by the 1970s, but that the common usage of the term at this time was too exclusive, believing this to be an unsatifactory situation. Thormahlen re-visits staple individual texts and authors in order to challenge traditional versions and definitions of modernism and to proffer a more open definition of the term.

Touraine, A. (1995), *Critique of Modernity*. Trans. David Macey. Oxford: Blackwell.

Trotter, D. (2001), *Paranoid Modernism: Literary Experiment, Psychosis, and the Professionalisation of English Society*. Oxford: Oxford University Press.

Tucker, R.C. (1978), *The Marx-Engels Reader* (2nd edn). New York: Norton.

Tzara, T. (1977) [1918], *Dada Manifesto: 1918*. in Tristan Tzara *Seven Dada Manifestos and Lampisteries*. Trans. Barbara Wright. London: John Calder, pp. 3–13.

Van Hulle, D. (2004), *Textual Awareness: A Genetic Study of Late Manuscripts by Joyce, Proust, and Mann*. Ann Arbor: University of Michigan Press.

Whitworth, M.H. (2003), 'Physics: "A Strange Footprint" ' in D. Bradshaw (ed.), *A Concise Companion to Modernism*, Malden, MA: Blackwell: pp. 200–20.

Wilde, O. (1974), 'The Preface', in I. Murray (ed.) *The Picture of Dorian Gray*. London and New York: Oxford University Press, pp. xxxiii–xxxiv.

Williams, R. (2007), *Politics of Modernism*. London: Verso.

Williams charts the relationship between revolutionary socialist politics and the artistic movement of modernism. Williams foregrounds the cultural (rather than purely aesthetic) implications and expressions of modernism and seeks to assess the consequences of modernism outside of the critical tropes of postmodernism.

Wilson, E. (1948), *Axel's Castle: A Study in the Imaginative Literature of 1870–1930*. New York: Charles Scribner's Sons.

Winter, J.M. (1998), *Sites of Memory, Sites of Mourning: The Great War in European Cultural Memory* (2nd edn). Cambridge: Cambridge University Press.

Winter, J.M. (2003), *The Great War and the British People* (2nd edn). London: Palgrave.

Wollaeger, M.A. (2006), *Modernism, Media, and Propaganda: British Narrative from 1900 to 1945*. Princeton: Princeton University Press.

Wollaeger's text provides a history of the relationship between modernism and propaganda in Britain during the first half of the twentieth century, and suggests that, rather than being separate cultural developments, the two are connected and that British modernism is better understood in the context of the history of modern propaganda.

Woods, T. (2005), 'Memory, geography, identity: African writing and modernity'. in P. Brooker and A. Thacker (eds), *Geographies of Modernism*. Abingdon: Routledge.

Woolf, V. (1988) [1924], 'Character in fiction' in A. McNeillie (ed.), *The Essays of Virginia Woolf*, Volume 3, London: Hogarth, pp. 420–38.
—— (1979) [1977], in A. Oliver Bell (ed.), *The Diary of Virginia Woolf Volume 1: 1915–1919*. Hardmondsworth: Penguin.
—— (1981) [1978], in A.O. Bell (ed.), *The Diary of Virginia Woolf Volume 2: 1920–1924*. Hardmondsworth: Penguin.
—— (1994) [1925], 'Modern fiction', A. McNeillie (ed.), *The Essays of Virginia Woolf*, Volume IV, London: Hogarth, pp. 157–65.
—— (1924), 'Mr Bennett and Mrs Brown.' *Collected Essays*, Volume 1, London: Hogarth Press.
—— (1981) [1925], *Mrs Dalloway*. New York and London: Harcourt.
—— (1929), *A Room of One's Own*. Hogarth Press, London.
—— (1964) [1927], *To the Lighthouse*. London: Penguin.
—— (1931), *The Waves*. New York: Harcourt.

Wordsworth, W. and Coleridge, S.T. (2005) [1798], *The Lyrical Ballads*, London: Routledge.

Wrigley, C. (2003), 'The impact of the first world war', in C. Wrigley (ed.) *A Companion to Early Twentieth-Century Britain*. Malden, MA and Oxford: The Historical Association and Blackwell, pp. 502–16.

Yeats, W.B. (1990), *Collected Poems*. A. Martin (ed.), London: Arena.
—— (2000), 'The Irish literary theatre', *Yeats's Poetry, Drama, and Prose*. in J.L. Pethica (ed.), New York: W.W. Norton, pp. 267–69.
—— (1954), in *Letters of W.B. Yeats*. A. Wade (ed.), London: Rupert Hart-Davis.

Useful Websites

Title: Some Cultural Forces Driving Literary Modernism
Author and Date Last Updated: Professor John Lye (1996)
Address: www.brocku.ca/english/courses/2F55/forces.html
Note: Lists some of the cultural forces driving literary modernism, this is a decent introduction but is by no means an exhaustive list.

Title: Literary Modernism, 1915–1945
Author and Date Last Updated: Dr. Michael O'Conner (2005)
Address: www.millikin.edu/aci/crow/basics/modernism.html
Note: Links literary modernism with the modernist movement that occurred in the visual arts.

Title: Overview of Literary Modernism
Author and Date Last Updated: Dr Del Gizzo (2004)
Address: http://www9.georgetown.edu/faculty/sd224/Classes/handouts/LiteraryModernsim.htm
Note: A brief overview of some of the tactics of literary modernism; it is not an exhaustive list.

Title: *Journal of Aesthetic Education*, Vol. 21, No. 4 (Winter, 1987), 162–63
Author and Date Last Updated: Various
Address: http://links.jstor.org/sici?sici=0021-8510(198724)21%3A4%3C162%3AAGOMAS%3E2.0.CO%3B2-H
Note: Athens password required for access.

Title: Online Literary Criticism Collection
Author and Date Last Updated: The Internet Public Library (2008)
Address: http://www.ipl.org/div/litcrit/bin/litcrit.out.pl?au=joy-47
Note: Provides links to online versions of primary texts and secondary material. Please note that articles may not be full text versions in all cases.

Title: Project Gutenberg
Author and Date Last Updated: Various (2008)
Address: http://www.gutenberg.org/wiki/Main_Page

Note: provides free e-texts of out of copyright works (a useful source for early primary texts).

Title: Modernism Links
Author and Date Last Updated: Prof. Nancy Knowles (2002)
Address: http://www2.eou.edu/~nknowles/winter2002/engl322links.html
Note: provides links to useful websites that detail the main themes and concerns of modernism and provides specific lists for key writers.

Title: *International Review of Modernism*
Author and Date Last Updated: Prof. Leonard Orr (editor)
Address: http://www.modernism.wsu.edu/
Note: 'A peer-reviewed electronic journal that publishes critical and historical essays, book reviews and extended review-essays on new scholarly and critical books on modernist literature and culture situated in historical and national contexts'.

Title: *The First Moderns* (EOU electronic book)
Author and Date Last Updated: William R. Everdell [1997] (2002)
Address: http://www.netlibrary.com/Details.aspx
Note: An e-book that details the beginnings and early history of Modernism.

Title: 'Chapter 7: Early Twentieth-Century-Modernism: A Brief Introduction.'
PAL: Perspectives in American Literature: A Research and Reference Guide.
Author and Date Last Updated: Paul P. Reuben (2008)
Address: http://web.csustan.edu/english/reuben/pal/chap7/7intro.html
Note: A useful site for those new to modernism. The site provides an outline of modernism, with a focus on American literary modernism, and a list of useful study questions.

Title: 'Schematic differences between modernism and postmodernism' from Ihab Hassan
Author and Date Last Updated: Barbara Norgard (2003)
Address: http://www.class.uh.edu/english/ta/perkins/m_p_list.htm
Note: A useful site, although perhaps slightly outdated approach to the differences between modernism and postmodernism.

Title: 'Modernism' *Guide to Literary Terms*
Author and Date Last Updated: Jack Lynch (2002)
Address: http://andromeda.rutgers.edu/~jlynch/Terms/modernism.html
Note: A very short and concise definition, useful as a reference tool but does not provide much insight. Note: This is an e-version of the paper text, Lynch, Jack (2002). *Guide to Literary Terms*. New Brunswick. NJ: Rutgers UP.

Title: *Modern Fiction Studies*
Author and Date Last Updated: John N. Duvall (editor) and Robert P. Marzec, (Associate Editor) (2008)

Address: http://www.cla.purdue.edu/academic/engl/mfs/
Note: A peer-reviewed electronic version of the paper journal that publishes critical and historical essays, book reviews and extended review-essays; published for the Purdue English Department by the Johns Hopkins UP. Please Note: subscription to Project Muse is required to read entire journal online.

Title: *Modernism Forum*
Author and Date Last Updated: Various (2008)
Address: http://classicalpoetryforums.com/forumdisplay.php?f=13
Note: An American forum for the discussion of modernist poetry. Posts are of varied quality, but a good source for debate. The forum contains a lot of dialogue concerning key texts, particularly Eliot's 'Prufrock'.

Title: The Modernist Studies Association
Author and Date Last Updated: Melba Cuddy-Keane (2008)
Address: http://msa.press.jhu.edu/index.html
Note: This is the official website of The Modernist Studies Association, an association that aims to promote the study of modernism in its cultural and literary settings. This website contains information on forthcoming conferences and is an 'Allied Organization' of the Modern Language Association.

Index